PROMISES
FULFILLED

PROMISES FULFILLED

Christianity, Islam, and the Bahá'í Faith

Nabil I. Hanna

Bahá'í
PUBLISHING

Wilmette, Illinois

Bahá'í Publishing
415 Linden Avenue, Wilmette, Illinois 60091-2844

13   12   11   10   4   3   2   1

Library of Congress Cataloging-in-Publication Data

Hanna, Nabil I.
  Promises fulfilled : Christianity, Islam, and the Baha'i Faith / Nabil I. Hanna.
     p. cm.
  Includes bibliographical references.
  ISBN 978-1-931847-77-3 (acid-free paper) 1. Bahai Faith—Apologetic works. 2.
Bahai Faith—Relations—Christianity. 3. Christianity and other religions—Bahai
Faith. 4. Bahai Faith—Relations—Islam. 5. Islam—Relations—Bahai Faith. I.
Title.
  BP368.H36 2010
  297.9'32—dc22
                                    2010020876

Cover design by Robert A. Reddy
Book design by Patrick Falso

Acknowledgments

To my loving parents, Olga and Iskandar Hanna

and

to my dear wife, Dora Jean

Author's Note

Selections from the Holy Bible are from the King James Version and the Revised Standard Version of the Old and New Testaments. Selections from the Holy Qur'án are from J. M. Rodwell's translation and N. J. Dawood's translation.

The Bahá'í writings are taken from a number of sources. They include writings from Bahá'u'lláh (Glory of God), the Promised Manifestation of God for this age; those of His Forerunner, the Báb (Gate); and the writings and talks of 'Abdu'l-Bahá (the son of Bahá'u'lláh), who in accordance to the Will and Testament of Bahá'u'lláh became the Center of the Covenant of the Bahá'í Faith after the passing of Bahá'u'lláh. Also included are extracts from the writings of Shoghi Effendi, who was appointed by 'Abdu'l-Bahá as the Guardian of the Bahá'í Faith. Extracts from the writings of various Bahá'í authors are also included.

Extracts and outline of topics are from *Bible Proofs: A Fireside Aid for Teaching Christians*, compiled by Nabil I. Hanna, 1988.

Contents

Contents

Preface

The purpose of this book is to enable the reader to construe the meanings of selected verses from the Bible and Qur'án, which clearly indicate the fact that Bahá'u'lláh (meaning *the Glory of God* or *the Glory of the Lord*) is the Promised One of all religions Who ushered in the Promised Day of God. Bahá'ís believe that He is the Lord of Hosts, the Spirit of Truth, the Comforter, the King of Glory, the Son of Man Who shall come in the Glory of the Father, Jehovah, the Great Announcement, the Summoner, the Mahdí, the Qá'im, the Qayyúm—the One alluded to in all the Holy Books and awaited by the majority of the peoples of the world. The verses in this book are drawn from the sacred writings, and they demonstrate the oneness of God—the divine and unknowable essence—the oneness of His Messengers (or Manifestations of God), and the basic oneness of His religion and its evolution throughout the ages.

The chapters of this book deal with the significant topics that often arise when discussions turn to Christian and Islamic topics on the central Bahá'í claim that Bahá'u'lláh fulfills the promises and prophecies of the followers of all religions regarding the Promised One. These discussions inevitably give rise to questions concerning the Word of God, the Day of Resurrection and Judgment, salvation, the meaning of life and death, miracles, parables, the seal of the Prophets, and other topics.

The brief introduction to biblical and Qur'ánic verses at the beginning of each chapter is not intended to explain in detail the meanings of the verses but rather to introduce the topic and accentuate the theme. The selections from the Bahá'í sacred writings added after the biblical and Qur'ánic verses provide further elaboration on the meanings of said verses. These sacred texts, whether from the Bible, the Qur'án, or the Bahá'í scriptures, can be used in study classes, interfaith gatherings, or in similar discussions and can serve as an easy reference for religious studies. These texts also give the reader an opportunity to meditate upon and compare biblical, Qur'ánic, and Bahá'í teachings on a given topic.

One should not be drawn into futile arguments over the different translations and interpretations of the Bible and the Qur'án endorsed by various sects but rather should become acquainted with the intrinsic spiritual meanings of the scriptures.

It is only by the grace of God we have been privileged to live in this new age, ushering in the Promised Day of God foretold by all the Prophets and Messengers, the day when "His Will" shall be done on earth as it is in heaven. Bahá'u'lláh says, "Great indeed is this Day! The allusions made to it in all the sacred Scriptures as the Day of God attest its greatness. The soul of every Prophet of God, of every Divine Messenger, hath thirsted for this wondrous Day. All the divers kindreds of the earth have, likewise, yearned to attain it" (*Gleanings from the Writings of Bahá'u'lláh*, no. 7.2).

— PART 1 —

HE WHO WAS PROMISED

1

The Promised One

The holy scriptures foretell the coming of the Promised Day and allude to it in many passages. In essence, the verses concerning this glorious, Promised Day of God state that there will come a day when the Kingdom of God will be established and His will shall be done on earth as it is in heaven. Evil will be destroyed, the righteous will rule, the wolf and the lamb shall feed together, there will be no more war, there will be an end to sorrow and suffering, and the earth shall shine with the light of her Lord. All this will gradually be established after the coming of the Promised One foretold in the holy scriptures. The Bible describes that day by saying, "And I John saw the holy city, New Jerusalem, coming down from God out of heaven, prepared as a bride adorned for her husband. And I heard a great voice out of heaven saying, Behold, the tabernacle of God is with men, and He will dwell with them, and they shall be His people, and God himself shall be with them, and be their God."*

Bahá'u'lláh explains what is meant by the "holy city, New Jerusalem, coming down from God out of heaven" by saying: *That city is none other than the Word of God revealed in every age and dispensation. In the days of Moses it*

---
* Revelation 21:1–3.

was the Pentateuch; in the days of Jesus the Gospel; in the days of Muḥammad the Messenger of God the Qur'án; in this day the Bayán; and in the dispensation of Him Whom God will make manifest His own Book—the Book unto which all the Books of former Dispensations must needs be referred, the Book which standeth amongst them all transcendent and supreme. In these cities spiritual sustenance is bountifully provided, and incorruptible delights have been ordained. The food they bestow is the bread of heaven, and the Spirit they impart is God's imperishable blessing."*

The verses in this chapter demonstrate that it is not Christ Himself in the body who will come again, but rather the Spirit, and that He will come with a new name. Some of the designations presented in the Bible concerning the Promised One are the Glory of the Lord, the Spirit of Truth, the Lord of Hosts, the Comforter, the King of Glory, the Day of Jehovah, and the Son of Man who shall come in the glory of the Father. Some of the designations given in the Qur'án concerning the Promised One are the Mahdí, the Qá'im, the Summoner, and the Great Announcement.

This great and joyous Promised Day, the Day of God foretold by all the Prophets and Messengers, has been ushered in—it was proclaimed by the Báb in 1844, and inaugurated by Bahá'u'lláh in 1863. Bahá'u'lláh, which literally means "The Glory of God" or "The Glory of the Lord" is the Promised One foretold by all previous religions. The Báb refers to Bahá'u'lláh as Him Whom God shall make manifest and describes Him by saying, *"He Whom God shall make manifest is indeed the Primal Veil of God. Above this Veil ye can find nothing other than God, while beneath it ye can discern all things emanating from God . . . If ye seek God, it behooveth you to seek Him Whom God shall make manifest . . ."*†

---

* Bahá'u'lláh, The Book of Certitude, ¶219.
† The Báb, *Selections from the Writings of the Báb,* no. 5:2:2–3.

Bahá'u'lláh Himself depicts this great Day by saying, *"This is the Day whereon the unseen world crieth out, 'Great is thy blessedness, O earth, for thou hast been made the footstool of thy God, and been chosen as the seat of His mighty throne.'"**

'Abdu'l-Bahá describes this great Promised Day by saying, *"Praise be to God! This is a day wherein the lights and splendors have awakened progress throughout the East and the West. Many holy souls in former times longed to witness this century, lamenting night and day, yearning to be upon the earth in this cycle; but our presence and privilege is the beneficent gift of the Lord."*†

* Bahá'u'lláh, quoted in Shoghi Effendi, *The Advent of Divine Justice*, p. 66.
† 'Abdu'l-Bahá, *The Promulgation of Universal Peace*, p. 334.

Selected verses from the Holy Bible concerning the coming of the Promised One:

John 16:12–13 – I have yet many things to say unto you, but ye cannot bear them now. Howbeit when he, the Spirit of truth, is come, he will guide you into all truth: for he shall not speak of himself; but whatsoever he shall hear, that shall he speak: and he will show you things to come.

John 14:16–17 – And I will pray the Father, and he shall give you another Comforter, that he may abide with you for ever; Even the Spirit of truth; whom the world cannot receive, because it seeth him not, neither knoweth him: but ye know him; for he dwelleth with you, and shall be in you.

Revelation 3:11–12 – Behold, I come quickly: hold that fast which thou hast, that no man take thy crown. Him that overcometh will I make a pillar in the temple of my God, and he shall go no more out: and I will write upon him the name of my God, and the name of the city of my God, which is new Jerusalem, which cometh down out of heaven from my God: and I will write upon him my new name.

Revelation 21:1–3 – And I John saw the holy city, New Jerusalem, coming down from God out of heaven, prepared as a bride adorned for her husband. And I heard a great voice out of heaven saying, Behold, the tabernacle of God is with men, and He will dwell with them, and they shall be His people, and God himself shall be with them, and be their God.

John 14:26 – But the Comforter, which is the Holy Ghost, whom the Father will send in my name, he shall teach you all things, and bring all things to your remembrance, whatsoever I have said unto you.

John 15:26 – But when the Comforter is come, whom I will send unto you from the Father, even the Spirit of truth, which proceedeth from the Father, he shall testify of me.

John 16:7 – Nevertheless I tell you the truth; It is expedient for you that I go away: for if I go not away, the Comforter will not come unto you; but if I depart, I will send him unto you.

John 14:30 – Hereafter I will not talk much with you: for the prince of this world cometh, and hath nothing in me.

Matthew 16:27 – For the Son of man shall come in the glory of his Father with his angels; and then he shall reward every man according to his works.

Psalms 24:7–10 – Lift up your heads, O ye gates; and be ye lift up, ye everlasting doors; and the King of glory shall come in.

Who is this King of glory? The LORD strong and mighty, the LORD mighty in battle.

Lift up your heads, O ye gates; even lift them up, ye everlasting doors; and the King of glory shall come in.

Who is this King of glory? The LORD of hosts, he is the King of glory.

Isaiah 11:1–9 – And there shall come forth a rod out of the stem of Jesse, and a Branch shall grow out of his roots:

And the spirit of the Lord shall rest upon him, the spirit of wisdom and understanding, the spirit of counsel and might, the spirit of knowledge and of the fear of the Lord;

And shall make him of quick understanding in the fear of the Lord: and he shall not judge after the sight of his eyes, neither reprove after the hearing of his ears:

But with righteousness shall he judge the poor, and reprove with equity for the meek of the earth: and he shall smite the earth with the rod of his mouth, and with the breath of his lips shall he slay the wicked.

And righteousness shall be the girdle of his loins, and faithfulness the girdle of his reins.

The wolf also shall dwell with the lamb, and the leopard shall lie down with the kid; and the calf and the young lion and the fatling together; and a little child shall lead them.

And the cow and the bear shall feed; their young ones shall lie down together: and the lion shall eat straw like the ox.

And the sucking child shall play on the hole of the asp, and the weaned child shall put his hand on the cockatrice's den.

They shall not hurt nor destroy in all my holy mountain: for the earth shall be full of the knowledge of the Lord, as the waters cover the sea.

Habakkuk 2:14 – For the earth shall be filled with the knowledge of the glory of the Lord, as the waters cover the sea.

John 11:40 – Jesus saith unto her, Said I not unto thee, that, if thou wouldest believe, thou shouldest see *the glory of God?*

Luke 12:37 – Blessed are those servants, whom the lord when he cometh shall find watching.

Selected verses from the Holy Qur'án and Hadíth concerning the coming of the Promised One:

Sura 46:30 – Al-Ahqáf – O our people! Obey the Summoner of God, and believe in him, that He may forgive your sins, and rescue you from an afflictive punishment.

Sura 3:7 – Ál-'Imrán – O our Lord! For the day of whose coming there is not a doubt, thou wilt surely gather mankind together. Verily, God will not fail the promise.

Sura 19:34 – Maryam – And the peace of God was on me the day I was born, and will be the day I shall die, and the day I shall be raised to life.

Sura 13:38–39 – Al-Ra'd – To each age its Book. What He pleaseth will God abrogate or confirm: for with Him is the source of revelation.

Sura 50:40 – Qáf – And listen for the day whereon the crier shall cry from a place near to every one alike.

Sura 55:1–4 – Al-Rahmán –
The God of Mercy
Hath taught the Koran,
Hath created man,
Hath taught him articulate speech [the Bayán].

Sura 39:68–69 – Al-Zumar – And there shall be a blast on the trumpet, and all who are in the Heavens and all who are in the Earth shall expire, save those whom God shall vouchsafe to live. Then shall there be another blast on it, and lo! they shall gaze around them:

And the earth shall shine with the light of her Lord.

Sura 79:6–8 & 13 – Al-Názi'át – One day, the disturbing trumpet-blast shall disturb it,
Which the second blast shall follow:
Men's hearts on that day shall quake:—
Verily, it will be but a single blast.

Sura 83:6 – Al-Mutaffifín – The day when mankind shall stand before the Lord of the worlds.

Sura 14:5 – Ibráhím – Of old did we send Moses with our signs: and said to him, "Bring forth thy people from the darkness into the light, and remind them of the days of God."

Sura 7:33 – Al-A'ráf – O children of Adam! There shall come to you Apostles from among yourselves, rehearsing my signs to you; and whoso shall fear God and do good works, no fear shall be upon them, neither shall they be put to grief.

Sura 78:1–4 – Al-Naba' – Of what ask they of one another?
Of the great News.
The theme of their disputes.
Nay! They shall certainly know its truth!

Sura 23:45–46 – Al-Mu'minún – Neither too soon, nor too late, shall a people reach its appointed time. Then sent we our apostles one after another.

Sura 30:29 – Al-Rúm – Set thou thy face then, as a true convert, towards the Faith which God hath made, and for which He hath made man. No change is there in the creation of God. This is the right Faith, but the greater part of men know it not.

Sura 98:1–2 – Al-Bayyina – The unbelievers among the people of the Book, and the Polytheists, did not waver, until the clear evidence had come to them; A messenger from God, reciting to them the pure pages wherein are true Scriptures!

Sura 89:22–23 – Al-Fajr – But when the earth shall be crushed with crushing, crushing,

And thy Lord shall come and the angels rank on rank.

Abu-'Abdi'lláh, quoted in Bahá'u'lláh, The Book of Certitude, ¶269 – Abu-'Abdi'llah, questioned concerning the character of the Mahdí, answered saying: "He will perform that which Muḥammad, the Messenger of God, hath performed, and will demolish whatever hath been before Him even as the Messenger of God hath demolished the ways of those that preceded Him."

Káfí, Tablet of Fátimih, quoted in Bahá'u'lláh, The Book of Certitude, ¶273 – . . . concerning the character of the Qá'im: "He shall manifest the perfection of Moses, the splendor of Jesus, and the patience of Job. His chosen ones shall be abased in His day. Their heads shall be offered as presents even as the heads of the Turks and the Daylamites. They shall be slain and burnt. Fear shall seize them; dismay and alarm shall strike terror into their hearts. The earth shall be dyed with their blood. Their womenfolk shall bewail and lament. These indeed are my friends!"

Biḥár, quoted in Bahá'u'lláh, The Book of Certitude, ¶282 – "In our Qá'ím there shall be four signs from four Prophets, Moses, Jesus, Joseph, and Muḥammad. The sign from Moses is fear and expectation; from Jesus, that which was spoken of Him; from Joseph, imprisonment and dissimulation; from Muḥammad, the revelation of a Book similar to the Qur'án."

Ṣádiq, quoted in Bahá'u'lláh, The Book of Certitude, ¶281 – Mufaḍḍal asked Ṣádiq saying: "What of the sign of His manifestation, O my master?" He made reply: "In the year sixty, His Cause shall be made manifest, and His Name shall be proclaimed."

Sura 7:50–51 – Al-A'ráf – And now have we brought them the Book: with knowledge have we explained it; a guidance and a mercy to them that believe.

What have they to wait for now but its interpretation? When its interpretation shall come, they who aforetime were oblivious of it shall say, "The Prophets of our Lord did indeed bring the truth . . ."

Selected verses from the Bahá'í sacred texts
concerning the coming of the Promised One:

Magnified be Thy name, O my God, for that Thou hast manifested the
Day which is the King of Days, the Day which Thou didst announce unto
Thy chosen Ones and Thy Prophets in Thy most excellent Tablets, the Day
whereon Thou didst shed the splendor of the glory of all Thy names upon
all created things. Great is his blessedness whosoever hath set himself towards
Thee, and entered Thy presence, and caught the accents of Thy voice.

Bahá'u'lláh, Bahá'í Prayers, p. 194.

O kings of the earth! He Who is the sovereign Lord of all is come. The Kingdom is God's, the omnipotent Protector, the Self-Subsisting. Worship none
but God, and, with radiant hearts, lift up your faces unto your lord, the Lord
of all names. This is a Revelation to which whatever ye possess can never be
compared, could ye but know it.

Bahá'u'lláh, The Kitáb-i-Aqdas, ¶78.

"Followers of the Gospel," Bahá'u'lláh addressing the whole of Christendom
exclaims, *"behold the gates of heaven are flung open. He that had ascended unto
it is now come. Give ear to His voice calling aloud over land and sea, announcing
to all mankind the advent of this Revelation—a Revelation through the agency
of which the Tongue of Grandeur is now proclaiming: 'Lo, the sacred Pledge
hath been fulfilled, for He, the Promised One, is come!'" "The voice of the Son
of Man is calling aloud from the sacred vale: 'Here am I, here am I, O God my
God!' . . . whilst from the Burning Bush breaketh forth the cry: 'Lo, the Desire
of the world is made manifest in His transcendent glory!' The Father hath come.
That which ye were promised in the Kingdom of God is fulfilled. This is the
Word which the Son veiled when He said to those around Him that at that time*

they could not bear it . . . Verily the Spirit of Truth is come to guide you unto all truth . . . He is the One Who glorified the Son and exalted His Cause . . ." "The Comforter Whose advent all the scriptures have promised is now come that He may reveal unto you all knowledge and wisdom. Seek Him over the entire surface of the earth, haply ye may find Him."

Bahá'u'lláh, quoted in Shoghi Effendi,
The World Order of Bahá'u'lláh, pp. 104–5.

Say: O peoples of the earth! By the righteousness of God! Whatever ye have been promised in the Books of your Lord, the Ruler of the Day of Return, hath appeared and been made manifest. Beware lest the changes and chances of the world hold you back from Him Who is the Sovereign Truth.

Bahá'u'lláh, *Tablets of Bahá'u'lláh,* p. 231.

He, verily, hath again come down from heaven, even as He came down from it the first time. Beware lest ye dispute that which He proclaimeth, even as the people before you disputed His utterances. Thus instructeth you the True One, could ye but perceive it.

Bahá'u'lláh, *Tablets of Bahá'u'lláh,* p. 11.

This is the One Who hath been glorified by Muḥammad, the Apostle of God, and before Him by the Spirit [Jesus] and yet before Him by the One Who discoursed with God [Moses]. This is the Point of the Bayán calling aloud before the Throne, saying: "By the righteousness of God, ye have been created to glorify this Most Great Announcement, this Perfect Way which lay hid within the souls of the Prophets, which was treasured in the hearts of the chosen ones of God and was written down by the glorious Pen of your Lord, the Possessor of Names."

Bahá'u'lláh, *Tablets of Bahá'u'lláh,* p. 103.

O thou who art waiting, tarry no longer, for He is come. Behold His Tabernacle and His Glory dwelling therein. It is the Ancient Glory, with a new Manifestation.

Bahá'u'lláh, quoted in Esslemont, *Bahá'u'lláh and the New Era*, p. 29.

In Thy holy Books, in Thy Scriptures and Thy Scrolls Thou hast promised all the peoples of the world that Thou Thyself shalt appear and shalt remove the veils of glory from Thy face, even as Thou didst announce in Thy words unto Thy Friend through Whom the Day-Star of Revelation shone brightly above the horizon of Hijaz, and the dawning light of divine Truth shed its radiance among all men, proclaiming: "The Day when mankind shall stand before the Lord of the worlds." And before Muḥammad Thou didst impart this glad-tiding unto Him Who conversed with Thee, saying: "Bring forth thy people from the darkness into the light and remind them of the days of God." Moreover Thou didst proclaim this truth unto the Spirit and unto Thy Prophets and Thy Messengers, whether of the remote or more recent past.

Bahá'u'lláh, *Tablets of Bahá'u'lláh*, pp. 113–14.

Say: O concourse of the rulers and of the learned and the wise! The Promised Day is come and the Lord of Hosts hath appeared. Rejoice ye with great joy by reason of this supreme felicity. Aid Him then through the power of wisdom and utterance. Thus biddeth you the One Who hath ever proclaimed, "Verily, no God is there but Me, the All-Knowing, the All-Wise."

Bahá'u'lláh, *Tablets of Bahá'u'lláh*, pp. 239–40.

"For this is the Day which the one true God, glorified be He, hath announced in all His Books, unto His Prophets and His Messengers." "This is a Revelation, under which, if a man shed for its sake one drop of blood, myriads of oceans will be his recompense." "A fleeting moment, in this Day, excelleth centuries of a bygone

age. . . . Neither sun nor moon hath witnessed a day such as this Day." "This is the Day whereon the unseen world crieth out, 'Great is thy blessedness, O earth, for thou hast been made the footstool of thy God, and been chosen as the seat of His mighty throne.'" "The world of being shineth, in this Day, with the resplendency of this Divine Revelation. All created things extol its saving grace, and sing its praises. The universe is wrapt in an ecstasy of joy and gladness. The Scriptures of past Dispensations celebrate the great Jubilee that must needs greet this most great Day of God. Well is it with him that hath lived to see this Day, and hath recognized its station."

Bahá'u'lláh, quoted in Shoghi Effendi, *The Advent of Divine Justice*, p. 78.

O kings of Christendom! Heard ye not the saying of Jesus, the Spirit of God, . . . He saith: "When He, the Spirit of Truth, is come, He will guide you into all truth." And yet behold how, when He did bring the truth, ye refused to turn your faces towards Him, and persisted in disporting yourselves with your pastimes and fancies. Ye welcomed Him not, neither did ye seek His Presence, that ye might hear the verses of God from His own mouth, and partake of the manifold wisdom of the Almighty, the All-Glorious, the All-Wise.

Bahá'u'lláh, "Súriy-i-Mulúk," *The Summons of the Lord of Hosts*, ¶15.

"The Father hath come. That which ye were promised in the Kingdom of God is fulfilled. This is the Word which the Son veiled when He said to those around Him that at that time they could not bear it . . . Verily the Spirit of Truth is come to guide you unto all truth . . . He is the One Who glorified the Son and exalted His Cause . . ." "The Comforter Whose advent all the scriptures have promised is now come that He may reveal unto you all knowledge and wisdom. Seek Him over the entire surface of the earth, haply ye may find Him."

Bahá'u'lláh, quoted in Shoghi Effendi, *The World Order of Bahá'u'lláh*,

pp. 104–5.

They that have hearts to understand, they that have quaffed the Wine of love, who have not for one moment gratified their selfish desires, will behold, resplendent as the sun in its noon-tide glory, those tokens, testimonies, and evidences that attest the truth of this wondrous Revelation, this transcendent and divine Faith.

Bahá'u'lláh, The Book of Certitude, ¶280.

In the past the divines were perplexed over this question, a question which He Who is the Sovereign Truth hath, during the early years of His life, Himself heard them ask repeatedly: "What is that Word which the Qá'im will pronounce whereby the leaders of religion are put to flight?" Say, that Word is now made manifest and ye have fled ere ye heard it uttered, although ye perceive it not. And that blessed, that hidden, that concealed and treasured Word is this: "'HE' hath now appeared in the raiment of 'I.' He Who was hidden from mortal eyes exclaimeth: Lo! I am the All-Manifest." This is the Word which hath caused the limbs of disbelievers to quake. Glorified be God! All the heavenly Scriptures of the past attest to the greatness of this Day, the greatness of this Manifestation, the greatness of His signs, the greatness of His Word, the greatness of His constancy, the greatness of His pre-eminent station. Yet despite all this the people have remained heedless and are shut out as by a veil. Indeed all the Prophets have yearned to attain this Day. David saith: "Who will bring me into the Strong City?" [Psalms 59:9; 108:10.] By Strong City is meant 'Akká. Its fortifications are very strong and this Wronged One is imprisoned within its walls. Likewise it is revealed in the Qur'án: "Bring forth thy people from the darkness into the light and announce to them the days of God." [Qur'án 14:5]

Bahá'u'lláh, *Tablets of Bahá'u'lláh*,
pp. 258–59.

Call out to Zion, O Carmel, and announce the joyful tidings: He that was hidden from mortal eyes is come! His all-conquering sovereignty is manifest; His all-encompassing splendour is revealed. Beware lest thou hesitate or halt. Hasten forth and circumambulate the City of God that hath descended from heaven, the celestial Kaaba round which have circled in adoration the favoured of God, the pure in heart, and the company of the most exalted angels. Oh, how I long to announce unto every spot on the surface of the earth, and to carry to each one of its cities, the glad-tidings of this Revelation—a Revelation to which the heart of Sinai hath been attracted, and in whose name the Burning Bush is calling: "Unto God, the Lord of Lords, belong the kingdoms of earth and heaven."

Bahá'u'lláh, Tablets of Bahá'u'lláh, pp. 4–5.

O concourse of patriarchs! He Whom ye were promised in the Tablets is come. Fear God, and follow not the vain imaginings of the superstitious. Lay aside the things ye possess, and take fast hold of the Tablet of God by His sovereign power. Better is this for you than all your possessions. Unto this testifieth every understanding heart, and every man of insight. Pride ye yourselves on My Name and yet shut yourselves out as by a veil from Me? This indeed is a strange thing!

Bahá'u'lláh, quoted in Shoghi Effendi, The Promised Day is Come, ¶252.

O concourse of bishops! Ye are the stars of the heaven of My knowledge. My mercy desireth not that ye should fall upon the earth. My justice, however, declareth: "This is that which the Son hath decreed." And whatsoever hath proceeded out of His blameless, His truth-speaking, trustworthy mouth, can never be altered. The bells, verily, peal out My Name, and lament over Me, but My spirit rejoiceth with evident gladness.

Bahá'u'lláh, Tablets of Bahá'u'lláh, p. 13.

O concourse of priests! Leave the bells, and come forth, then, from your churches. It behoveth you, in this day, to proclaim aloud the Most Great Name among the nations. Prefer ye to be silent, whilst every stone and every tree shouteth aloud: "The Lord is come in His great glory!"? Well is it with the man who hasteneth unto Him. Verily, he is numbered among them whose names will be eternally recorded and who will be mentioned by the Concourse on High. Thus hath it been decreed by the Spirit in this wondrous Tablet. He that summoneth men in My name is verily, of Me, and he will show forth that which is beyond the power of all that are on earth. Follow ye the Way of the Lord and walk not in the footsteps of them that are sunk in heedlessness. Well is it with the slumberer who is stirred by the Breeze of God and ariseth from amongst the dead, directing his steps towards the Way of the Lord. Verily, such a man is regarded in the sight of God, the True One, as a jewel amongst men and is reckoned with the blissful.

Say: In the East the light of His Revelation hath broken; in the West have appeared the signs of His dominion. Ponder this in your hearts, O people, and be not of those who have turned a deaf ear to the admonitions of Him Who is the Almighty, the All-Praised. Let the Breeze of God awaken you. Verily, it hath wafted over the world. Well is it with him that hath discovered the fragrance thereof and been accounted among the well-assured.

Bahá'u'lláh, *Tablets of Bahá'u'lláh*, p. 13.

Announce thou unto the priests: Lo! He Who is the Ruler is come. Step out from behind the veil in the name of thy Lord, He Who layeth low the necks of all men. Proclaim then unto all mankind the glad-tidings of this mighty, this glorious Revelation. Verily, He Who is the Spirit of Truth is come to guide you unto all truth. He speaketh not as prompted by His own self, but as bidden by Him Who is the All-Knowing, the All-Wise.

Bahá'u'lláh, *Tablets of Bahá'u'lláh*, p. 12.

O concourse of divines! This is the day whereon nothing amongst all things, nor any name amongst all names, can profit you save through this Name which God hath made the Manifestation of His Cause and the Dayspring of His Most Excellent Titles unto all who are in the kingdom of creation. Blessed is that man that hath recognized the fragrance of the All-Merciful and been numbered with the steadfast. Your sciences shall not profit you in this day, nor your arts, nor your treasures, nor your glory. Cast them all behind your backs, and set your faces towards the Most Sublime Word through which the Scriptures and the Books and this lucid Tablet have been distinctly set forth. Cast away, O concourse of divines, the things ye have composed with the pens of your idle fancies and vain imaginings. By God! The Day-Star of Knowledge hath shone forth above the horizon of certitude.

Bahá'u'lláh, *Tablets of Bahá'u'lláh*, p. 211.

By Him Who is the Great Announcement! The All-Merciful is come invested with undoubted sovereignty. The Balance hath been appointed, and all them that dwell on earth have been gathered together. The Trumpet hath been blown, and lo, all eyes have stared up with terror, and the hearts of all who are in the heavens and on the earth have trembled, except them whom the breath of the verses of God hath quickened, and who have detached themselves from all things.

Bahá'u'lláh, *Gleanings from the Writings of Bahá'u'lláh*, no. 17.1.

The Revelation which, from time immemorial, hath been acclaimed as the Purpose and Promise of all the Prophets of God, and the most cherished Desire of His Messengers, hath now, by virtue of the pervasive Will of the Almighty and at His irresistible bidding, been revealed unto men. The advent of such a Revelation hath been heralded in all the sacred Scriptures.

Bahá'u'lláh, *Gleanings from the Writings of Bahá'u'lláh*, no. 3.1.

The time foreordained unto the peoples and kindreds of the earth is now come. The promises of God, as recorded in the holy Scriptures, have all been fulfilled. Out of Zion hath gone forth the Law of God, and Jerusalem, and the hills and the land thereof, are filled with the glory of His Revelation. Happy is the man that pondereth in his heart that which hath been revealed in the Books of God, the Help in Peril, the Self-Subsisting.

Bahá'u'lláh, *Gleanings from the Writings of Bahá'u'lláh*,

no. 10.1.

This is the Day whereon the true servants of God partake of the life-giving waters of reunion, the Day whereon those that are nigh unto Him are able to drink of the soft-flowing river of immortality, and they who believe in His unity, the wine of His Presence, through their recognition of Him Who is the Highest and Last End of all, in Whom the Tongue of Majesty and Glory voiceth the call: "The Kingdom is Mine. I, Myself, am, of Mine own right, its Ruler."

Bahá'u'lláh, *Gleanings from the Writings of Bahá'u'lláh*,

no. 14.15.

He *[The Báb]* hath previously made known unto you that which would be uttered by this Dayspring of Divine wisdom. He said, and He speaketh the truth: "He *[Bahá'u'lláh]* is the One Who will under all conditions proclaim: 'Verily, there is none other God besides Me, the One, the Incomparable, the Omniscient, the All-Informed.'" This is a station which God hath assigned exclusively to this sublime, this unique and wondrous Revelation. This is a token of His bounteous favor, if ye be of them who comprehend, and a sign of His irresistible decree. This is His Most Great Name, His Most Exalted Word, and the Dayspring of His Most Excellent Titles, if ye could understand. Nay more, through Him every Fountainhead, every Dawning-place

24

of Divine guidance is made manifest. Reflect, O people, on that which hath been sent down in truth; ponder thereon, and be not of the transgressors.

Bahá'u'lláh, The Kitáb-i-Aqdas, ¶143.

He saith: "Say to them that are of a fearful heart: be strong, fear not, behold your God." This blessed verse is a proof of the greatness of the Revelation, and of the greatness of the Cause, inasmuch as the blast of the trumpet must needs spread confusion throughout the world, and fear and trembling amongst all men.

Bahá'u'lláh, Epistle to the Son of the Wolf, p. 147.

Great indeed is this Day! The allusions made to it in all the sacred Scriptures as the Day of God attest its greatness. The soul of every Prophet of God, of every Divine Messenger, hath thirsted for this wondrous Day. All the divers kindreds of the earth have, likewise, yearned to attain it.

Bahá'u'lláh, *Gleanings from the Writings of Bahá'u'lláh*, no. 7.2.

He, the Revealer of the unseen Beauty, addressing one day His disciples, referred unto His passing, and, kindling in their hearts the fire of bereavement, said unto them: "I go away and come again unto you." And in another place He said: "I go and another will come, Who will tell you all that I have not told you, and will fulfill all that I have said." Both these sayings have but one meaning, were ye to ponder upon the Manifestations of the Unity of God with Divine insight.

Bahá'u'lláh, *Gleanings from the Writings of Bahá'u'lláh*, no. 13.5.

I swear by the righteousness of God! Verily this is the Primal Point, arrayed in His new attire and manifested in His glorious Name. He at present beholdeth everything from this Horizon. Indeed He is supreme over all things. Amongst the Concourse on High He is known as the Most Great Announcement and in the Realms of Eternity as the Ancient Beauty, and before the Throne by this Name [The Most Great Name] which hath caused the footsteps of them that are endued with understanding to slip.

Say, I swear by God! In this Revelation even before a single verse was sent down from the realm of holiness and sublimity, the supreme testimony of God had been fulfilled for all the inmates of heaven and the dwellers on earth; moreover, We have revealed the equivalent of whatsoever was sent down in the Dispensation of the Bayán. Fear ye God and suffer not your deeds to be rendered vain and be not of them that are sunk in heedlessness. Open your eyes that ye may behold the Ancient Beauty from this shining and luminous station.

Say, God is my witness! The Promised One Himself hath come down from heaven, seated upon the crimson cloud with the hosts of revelation on His right, and the angels of inspiration on His left, and the Decree hath been fulfilled at the behest of God, the Omnipotent, the Almighty.

Bahá'u'lláh, *Tablets of Bahá'u'lláh*, p. 182.

By the righteousness of God! But for the anthem of praise voiced by Him Who heralded the divine Revelation, this Wronged One would never have breathed a word which might have struck terror into the hearts of the ignorant and caused them to perish. Dwelling on the glorification of Him Whom God shall make manifest—exalted be His Manifestation—the Báb in the beginning of the Bayán saith: "He is the One Who shall proclaim under all conditions, 'Verily, verily, I am God, no God is there but Me, the Lord of all created things. In truth all others except Me are My creatures. O, My creatures! Me alone do ye worship.'" Likewise in another instance He, magnifying the Name of Him Who shall be made manifest, saith: "I would be the first to adore Him." Now it behoveth one to reflect upon the significance of the "Adorer" and the "Adored One," that perchance the people of the earth may partake of a dewdrop from the ocean of divine knowledge and may be enabled to perceive the greatness of this Revelation. Verily, He hath appeared and hath unloosed His tongue to proclaim the Truth. Well is it with him who doth acknowledge and recognize the truth, and woe betide the froward and the wayward.

Bahá'u'lláh, *Tablets of Bahá'u'lláh*, p. 53.

Say, He Whom God shall make manifest is indeed the Primal Veil of God. Above this Veil ye can find nothing other than God, while beneath it ye can discern all things emanating from God. He is the Unseen, the Inaccessible, the Most Exalted, the Best Beloved.

If ye seek God, it behooveth you to seek Him Whom God shall make manifest . . .

The Báb, *Selections from the Writings of the Báb*,

no. 5:2:2–3.

He Who hath revealed the Qur'án unto Muḥammad, the Apostle of God, or-daining in the Faith of Islam that which was pleasing unto Him, hath likewise revealed the Bayán, in the manner ye have been promised, unto Him Who is your Qá'im, your Guide, your Mahdí, your Lord, Him Whom ye acclaim as the manifestation of God's most excellent titles. Verily the equivalent of that which God revealed unto Muḥammad during twenty-three years, hath been revealed unto Me within the space of two days and two nights. However, as ordained by God, no distinction is to be drawn between the two. He, in truth, hath power over all things.

The Báb, *Selections from the Writings of the Báb*, no. 5:10:2.

This is the glorious time of which the Lord Jesus Christ spoke when He told us to pray "Thy Kingdom come, Thy Will be done on earth as it is in Heaven."

'Abdu'l-Bahá, *Paris Talks*, no. 28.21.

Thou didst ask as to chapter 14, verse 30 of the Gospel of John, where the Lord Christ saith, "Hereafter I will not talk much with you: for the Prince of this world cometh, and hath nothing in Me." The Prince of this world is the Blessed Beauty; and "hath nothing in Me" signifieth: after Me all will draw grace from Me, but He is independent of Me, and will draw no grace from Me. That is, He is rich beyond any grace of Mine.

'Abdu'l-Bahá, *Selections from the Writings of 'Abdu'l-Bahá*,

no. 145.3.

In the day of the manifestation of the Lord of Hosts, and at the epoch of the divine cycle of the Omnipotent which is promised and mentioned in all the books and writings of the Prophets—in that day of God, the Spiritual and Divine Kingdom will be established, and the world will be renewed; a new spirit will be breathed into the body of creation; the season of the divine spring will come; the clouds of mercy will rain; the sun of reality will shine; the life-giving breeze will blow; the world of humanity will wear a new garment; the surface of the earth will be a sublime paradise; mankind will be educated; wars, disputes, quarrels and malignity will disappear; and truthfulness, righteousness, peace and the worship of God will appear; union, love and brotherhood will surround the world; and God will rule for evermore—meaning that the Spiritual and Everlasting Kingdom will be established. Such is the day of God.

'Abdu'l-Bahá, *Some Answered Questions*, pp. 56–57.

"I testify before God," proclaims Bahá'u'lláh, *"to the greatness, the inconceivable greatness of this Revelation. Again and again have We in most of Our Tablets borne witness to this truth, that mankind may be roused from its heedlessness." "In this most mighty Revelation,"* He unequivocally announces, *"all the Dispensations of the past have attained their highest, their final consummation." "That which hath been made manifest in this preeminent, this most exalted Revelation, stands unparalleled in the annals of the past, nor will future ages witness its like." "He it is,"* referring to Himself He further proclaims, *"Who in the Old Testament hath been named Jehovah, Who in the Gospel hath been designated as the Spirit of Truth, and in the Qur'án acclaimed as the Great Announcement." "But for Him no Divine Messenger would have been invested with the robe of prophethood, nor would any of the sacred scriptures have been revealed. To this bear witness all created things."*

Shoghi Effendi, *The World Order of Baha'u'llah*, pp. 103–4.

To Him Jesus Christ had referred as the *"Prince of this world,"* as the *"Comforter"* Who will *"reprove the world of sin, and of righteousness, and of judgment,"* as the *"Spirit of Truth"* Who *"will guide you into all truth,"* Who *"shall not speak of Himself, but whatsoever He shall hear, that shall He speak,"* as the *"Lord of the Vineyard,"* and as the *"Son of Man"* Who *"shall come in the glory of His Father" "in the clouds of heaven with power and great glory,"* with *"all the holy angels"* about Him, and *"all nations"* gathered before His throne. To Him the Author of the Apocalypse had alluded as the *"Glory of God,"* as *"Alpha and Omega," "the Beginning and the End," "the First and the Last."* Identifying His Revelation with the *"third woe,"* he, moreover, had extolled His Law as *"a new heaven and a new earth,"* as the *"Tabernacle of God,"* as the *"Holy City,"* as the *"New Jerusalem, coming down from God out of heaven, prepared as a bride adorned for her husband."* To His Day Jesus Christ Himself had referred as *"the regeneration when the Son of Man shall sit in the throne of His glory."* To the hour of His advent St. Paul had alluded as the hour of the *"last trump,"* the *"trump of God,"* whilst St. Peter had spoken of it as the *"Day of God, wherein the heavens being on fire shall be dissolved, and the elements shall melt with fervent heat."* His Day, he, furthermore, had described as *"the times of refreshing,"* *"the times of restitution of all things, which God hath spoken by the mouth of all His holy Prophets since the world began."*

Shoghi Effendi, *God Passes By*, pp. 95–96.

To Him Isaiah, the greatest of the Jewish prophets, had alluded as the *"Glory of the Lord,"* the *"Everlasting Father,"* the *"Prince of Peace,"* the *"Wonderful,"* the *"Counsellor,"* the *"Rod come forth out of the stem of Jesse"* and the *"Branch grown out of His roots,"* Who *"shall be established upon the throne of David,"* Who *"will come with strong hand,"* Who *"shall judge among the nations,"* Who *"shall smite the earth with the rod of His mouth, and with the breath of His lips slay the wicked,"* and Who *"shall assemble the outcasts of Israel, and gather together the dispersed of Judah from the four corners of the earth."* Of Him David had sung in his Psalms, acclaiming Him as the *"Lord of Hosts"* and the *"King of Glory."* To Him Haggai had referred as the *"Desire of all nations,"* and Zechariah as the *"Branch"* Who *"shall grow up out of His place,"* and *"shall build the Temple of the Lord."* Zechariah had extolled Him as the *"Lord"* Who *"shall be king over all the earth,"* while to His day Joel and Zephaniah had both referred as the *"day of Jehovah,"* the latter describing it as *"a day of wrath, a day of trouble and distress, a day of wasteness and desolation, a day of darkness and gloominess, a day of clouds and thick darkness, a day of the trumpet and alarm against the fenced cities, and against the high towers."* His Day Ezekiel and Daniel had moreover, both acclaimed as the *"day of the Lord,"* and Malachi described as *"the great and dreadful day of the Lord"* when *"the Sun of Righteousness"* will *"arise, with healing in His wings,"* whilst Daniel had pronounced His advent as signalizing the end of the *"abomination that maketh desolate."*

Shoghi Effendi, *God Passes By*, pp. 94–95.

His mission is to proclaim that the ages of the infancy and of the childhood of the human race are past, that the convulsions associated with the present stage of its adolescence are slowly and painfully preparing it to attain the stage of manhood, and are heralding the approach of that Age of Ages when swords will be beaten into plowshares, when the Kingdom promised by Jesus Christ will have been established, and the peace of the planet definitely and permanently ensured.

Shoghi Effendi, *The Promised Day is Come*, ¶ii.

A humiliation less spectacular yet historically more significant awaited Pope Pius IX. It was to him who regarded himself as the Vicar of Christ that Bahá'u'lláh wrote that *"the Word which the Son [Jesus] concealed is made manifest,"* that *"it hath been sent down in the form of the human temple,"* that the Word was Himself, and He Himself the Father. It was to him who styling himself *"the servant of the servants of God"* that the Promised One of all ages, unveiling His station in its plenitude, announced that *"He Who is the Lord of Lords is come overshadowed with clouds."* It was he, who, claiming to be the successor of St. Peter, was reminded by Bahá'u'lláh that *"this is the day whereon the Rock [Peter] crieth out and shouteth . . . saying: 'Lo, the Father is come, and that which ye were promised in the Kingdom is fulfilled.'"* It was he, the wearer of the triple crown, who later became the first prisoner of the Vatican, who was commanded by the Divine Prisoner of 'Akká to *"leave his palaces unto such as desire them,"* to *"sell all the embellished ornaments"* he possessed, and to *"expend them in the path of God,"* and to *"abandon his kingdom unto the kings,"* and emerge from his habitation with his face *"set towards the Kingdom."*

Shoghi Effendi, The Promised Day is Come, ¶127.

"He around Whom the Point of the Bayán (Báb) hath revolved is come" is Bahá'u'lláh's confirmatory testimony to the inconceivable greatness and preeminent character of His own Revelation. *"If all who are in heaven and on earth,"* He moreover affirms, *"be invested in this day with the powers and attributes destined for the Letters of the Bayán, whose station is ten thousand times more glorious than that of the Letters of the Qur'ánic Dispensation, and if they one and all should, swift as the twinkling of an eye, hesitate to recognize My Revelation, they shall be accounted, in the sight of God, of those that have gone astray, and regarded as 'Letters of Negation.'"* *"Powerful is He, the King of Divine might,"* He, alluding to Himself in the Kitáb-i-Íqán, asserts, *"to extinguish with one letter of His wondrous words, the breath of life in the whole of the Bayán and the people thereof, and with one letter bestow upon them a new and everlasting life, and cause them to arise and speed out of the sepulchers of their vain and selfish desires."* *"This,"* He furthermore declares, *"is the king of days,"* the *"Day of God Himself,"* the *"Day which shall never be followed by night,"* the *"Springtime which autumn will never overtake,"* *"the eye to past ages and centuries,"* for which *"the soul of every Prophet of God, of every Divine Messenger, hath thirsted,"* for which *"all the divers kindreds of the earth have yearned,"* through which *"God hath proved the hearts of the entire company of His Messengers and Prophets, and beyond them those that stand guard over His sacred and inviolable Sanctuary, the inmates of the Celestial Pavilion and dwellers of the Tabernacle of Glory."* *"In this most mighty Revelation,"* He moreover, states, *"all the Dispensations of the past have attained their highest, their final consummation."* And again: *"None among the Manifestations of old, except to a prescribed degree, hath ever completely apprehended the nature of this Revela-*

32

tion." Referring to His own station He declares: *"But for Him no Divine Messenger would have been invested with the Robe of Prophethood, nor would any of the sacred Scriptures have been revealed."*

Shoghi Effendi, *God Passes By*,

pp. 98–99.

He was formally designated Bahá'u'lláh, an appellation specifically recorded in the Persian Bayán, signifying at once the glory, the light and the splendor of God, and was styled the "Lord of Lords," the "Most Great Name," the "Ancient Beauty," the "Pen of the Most High," the "Hidden Name," the "Preserved Treasure," "He Whom God will make manifest," the "Most Great Light," the "All-Highest Horizon," the "Most Great Ocean," the "Supreme Heaven," the "Pre-Existent Root," the "Self-Subsistent," the "Day-Star of the Universe," the "Great Announcement," the "Speaker on Sinai," the "Sifter of Men," the "Wronged One of the World," the "Desire of the Nations," the "Lord of the Covenant," the "Tree beyond which there is no passing." He derived His descent, on the one hand, from Abraham (the Father of the Faithful) through his wife Katurah, and on the other from Zoroaster, as well as from Yazdigird, the last king of the Sásáníyán dynasty. He was moreover a descendant of Jesse, and belonged, through His father, Mírzá 'Abbás, better known as Mírzá Buzurg—a nobleman closely associated with the ministerial circles of the Court of Fath-'Alí Sháh—to one of the most ancient and renowned families of Mázindarán.

Shoghi Effendi, *God Passes By*,

p. 94.

To Him Muḥammad, the Apostle of God, had alluded in His Book as the *"Great Announcement,"* and declared His Day to be the Day whereon *"God"* will *"come down"* *"overshadowed with clouds,"* the Day whereon *"thy Lord shall come and the angels rank on rank,"* and *"The Spirit shall arise and the angels shall be ranged in order."*

Shoghi Effendi, God Passes By, p. 96.

One of the traditions of <u>Sh</u>í'áh Islám states that when the Promised One appears He will utter one word which will cause people to flee Him. Bahá'u'lláh has explained in a Tablet that this word is the changing of 'He' into 'I'; instead of saying 'He is God', the Manifestation of God in this day will say 'I am God', and people bereft of understanding and insight will turn away from him.

Adíb Taherzadeh, The Revelation of Bahá'u'lláh, Vol. I, p. 46.

2

The Signs of His Coming

The holy scriptures give us many signs to watch for that signal the advent of the Promised One. In both the Bible and the Qur'án, some signs can be taken literally, and others figuratively. These signs include changes in both heaven and earth; the sun being darkened and the moon not giving its light; the stars falling from heaven; natural disasters, earthquakes, famines and diseases taking place in the world; the spreading of decadence, immorality, arrogance, injustice, and wickedness among man; preaching the Gospel throughout the world; the restoration of the fortunes of Israel and the return of the Israelites to the Holy Land; the spread of sciences and knowledge throughout the world; religion becoming an empty word on the tongues of many people; grievous calamities befalling nations at the hands of their rulers; women forsaking their suckling babes, casting the burden in their womb; and men forsaking their brothers, mothers, fathers, wives, and children.

Although the existence of some of these signs is obvious, others must be regarded from a spiritual perspective, similar to the signs that were mentioned in the Old Testament that would herald the first coming of Christ. The Jews were expecting these signs to occur literally when Christ came. However, was the sun darkened? Did the moon cease to shine or turn into blood?

Even if these signs were to take place literally this time—for instance, "the sun will be dark at its rising and the moon will not shed its light," "the stars will be falling from heaven, and the powers in the heavens will be shaken"— then how would it be possible to "see the Son of man coming in clouds with great power and glory"?* Would anyone be alive without the heat of the sun and light to see the Son of man coming in clouds? Would life on the planet continue to exist if even only one star were to come close enough to "fall" to the earth? As we know, many stars are thousands or millions of times larger than our planet, and no star could even approach the earth without the whole world being destroyed.

Furthermore, the scriptures also say, "The kingdom of God is not coming with signs to be observed; nor will they say, 'Lo, here it is!' or 'There!' for behold, the kingdom of God is in the midst of you."† How could some verses say that the sun will be darkened and the stars will fall from heaven while other verses say that the kingdom of God is not coming with signs to be observed? The verse also says, "for behold, the kingdom of God is in the midst of you." Even more amazing, the holy scriptures say in yet another verse, "But the day of the Lord will come as a thief in the night."‡ The thief will be in the house, and the owner will be unaware of His presence.

It is obvious that these signs have an intrinsic spiritual meaning, that during this Day the Promised One will be in our "midst" precisely as was the case in previous Dispensations, and that the majority of the people will not be aware of His presence. It would be the greatest of Days, yet the people will be occupied with their own affairs and unaware of this great Day. During this

---

* Mark 13:25–26.
† Luke 17:21.
‡ 2nd Peter 3:10.

time, the sun will continue to rise and set day after day, and the moon and the stars will continue to shine in their constellations.

The Bahá'í sacred writings teach us that the signs foretold in the holy scriptures are allegorical. In one of the explanations of the words *sun* and *moon*, Bahá'u'lláh says, *"That the term 'sun' hath been applied to the leaders of religion is due to their lofty position, their fame, and renown. Such are the universally recognized divines of every age, who speak with authority, and whose fame is securely established. If they be in the likeness of the Sun of Truth, they will surely be accounted as the most exalted of all luminaries; otherwise, they are to be recognized as the focal centers of hellish fire. Even as He saith: 'Verily, the sun and the moon are both condemned to the torment of infernal fire.'"** Bahá'u'lláh's portrayal of the leaders of religion as "the most exalted of all luminaries" due to their lofty position also explains the Qur'ánic verse stating that "the sun and moon are both condemned to the torment of infernal fire." If by "sun" the Qur'án meant the physical "sun" that rises and sets every day and is the source of life and light to all created things, why would it be condemned to the torment of infernal fire? The "sun" itself is an inferno, so condemning it to the torment of infernal fire makes no sense, unless as explained by Bahá'u'lláh, it refers to the religious leaders who could be "the most exalted of all luminaries" or "the focal centers of hellish fire." Therefore, one can conclude that the verses in the sacred scriptures stating "the sun shall be darkened and the moon shall not give her light . . ." refer to when religious leaders no longer reflect the light of the Sun of Truth. Bahá'u'lláh explains this further by saying: *". . . by these terms is intended the divines of the former Dispensation, who live in the days of the subsequent Revelations, and who hold the reins of religion in their grasp. If these divines be illumined by the light of*

---

* Bahá'u'lláh, The Book of Certitude, ¶36.

*the latter Revelation they will be acceptable unto God, and will shine with a light everlasting. Otherwise, they will be declared as darkened, even though to outward seeming they be leaders of men. . . ."**

Bahá'u'lláh tells us that all the promises of the sacred scriptures have come to pass, and He writes, ". . . *whatsoever was promised in the sacred Scriptures hath been fulfilled. This is the Day of great rejoicing. It behoveth everyone to hasten towards the court of His nearness with exceeding joy, gladness, exultation and delight and to deliver himself from the fire of remoteness."*†

However, the tribulations encompassing the world today did not end with the coming of the Promised One; on the contrary, they have been and are continuing to increase day by day. This is because of man's refusal to accept the new Revelation from God and his persistence in practicing dated laws incompatible to the present day World Order revealed by Bahá'u'lláh. The majority of mankind, as in previous Dispensations, has not recognized the signs of the Promised Day and continue in their waywardness. The present tribulations will continue and intensify until mankind turns humbly and submissively toward God. Bahá'u'lláh writes, *"The world is in travail, and its agitation waxeth day by day. Its face is turned towards waywardness and unbelief. Such shall be its plight, that to disclose it now would not be meet and seemly. Its perversity will long continue. And when the appointed hour is come, there shall suddenly appear that which shall cause the limbs of mankind to quake. Then, and only then, will the Divine Standard be unfurled, and the Nightingale of Paradise warble its melody."*‡ 'Abdu'l-Bahá has written, *"Know thou that hardship and privation shall increase day by day, and the people shall thereby be*

---

* Ibid., ¶34.
† Bahá'u'lláh, *Tablets of Bahá'u'lláh*, pp. 78–79.
‡ Bahá'u'lláh, *Gleanings from the Writings of Bahá'u'lláh*, no. 61.1.

afflicted. The doors of joy and happiness shall be closed on all sides, and terrible wars shall occur. Frustration and despair shall encompass the people until they are forced to turn to the One True God."

---

* 'Abdu'l-Bahá, in a Tablet to Isabella D. Brittingham, quoted in J. E. Esslemont, *Bahá'u'lláh and the New Era*, p. 272.

Some of the verses from the Holy Bible concerning the signs of His coming:

Mark 13:25–26 – And the stars of heaven shall fall, and the powers that are in heaven shall be shaken. And then shall they see the Son of man coming in the clouds with great power and glory.

Isaiah 13:9–16 – Behold, the day of the Lord cometh, cruel both with wrath and fierce anger, to lay the land desolate: and he shall destroy the sinners thereof out of it.

For the stars of heaven and the constellations thereof shall not give their light: the sun shall be darkened in his going forth, and the moon shall not cause her light to shine.

And I will punish the world for their evil, and the wicked for their iniquity; and I will cause the arrogancy of the proud to cease, and will lay low the haughtiness of the terrible.

I will make man more precious than fine gold; even a man than the golden wedge of Ophír.

Therefore, I will shake the heavens, and the earth shall remove out of her place, in the wrath of the Lord of hosts, and in the day of his fierce anger.

Joel 2:10 & 31 – The earth shall quake before them; the heavens shall tremble: the sun and the moon shall be dark, and the stars shall withdraw their shining.

The sun shall be turned into darkness, and the moon into blood, before the great and terrible day of the Lord come.

Joel 3:15–16 – The sun and the moon shall be darkened, and the stars shall withdraw their shining.

The Lord also shall roar out of Zion, and utter his voice from Jerusalem; and the heavens and the earth shall shake: but the Lord will be the hope of his people, and the strength of the children of Israel.

Zephaniah 1:14–15 – The great day of the Lord is near, it is near, and hasteth greatly, even the voice of the day of the Lord: the mighty man shall cry there bitterly.

That day is a day of wrath, a day of trouble and distress, a day of wasteness and desolation, a day of darkness and gloominess, a day of clouds and thick darkness.

1 Chronicles 17:9 – Also I will ordain a place for my people Israel, and will plant them, and they shall dwell in their place, and shall be moved no more; neither shall the children of wickedness waste them any more, as at the beginning,

Jeremiah 31:27–28 – Behold, the days come, saith the Lord, that I will sow the house of Israel and the house of Judah with the seed of man, and with the seed of beast.

And it shall come to pass, that like as I have watched over them, to pluck up, and to break down, and to throw down, and to destroy, and to afflict; so will I watch over them, to build, and to plant, saith the Lord.

Amos 9:14–15 – I will restore the fortunes of my people Israel; they shall rebuild deserted cities and live in them, they shall plant vineyards and drink their wine, make gardens and eat the fruit.

Once more I will plant them on their own soil, and they shall never again be uprooted from the soil I have given them. It is the word of the Lord your God.

Romans 11:26–27 – And so all Israel shall be saved: as it is written, There shall come out of Zion the Deliverer, and shall turn away ungodliness from Jacob: For this is my covenant unto them, when I shall take away their sins.

Nahum 2:3–4 – The chariots flash like flame . . . rage in the streets, they rush to and fro through the squares; they gleam like torches, they dart like lightning.

Daniel 12:1 – And at that time shall Michael stand up, the great prince which standeth for the children of thy people: and there shall be a time of trouble, such as never was since there was a nation even to that same time: and at that time thy people shall be delivered, every one that shall be found written in the book.

1 Timothy 4:1–3 – Now the Spirit speaketh expressly, that in the latter times some shall depart from the faith, giving heed to seducing spirits, and doctrines of devils; Speaking lies in hypocrisy; having their conscience seared with a hot iron;

Forbidding to marry, and commanding to abstain from meats, which God hath created to be received with thanksgiving of them which believe and know the truth.

2 Timothy 3:1–5 – This know also, that in the last days perilous times shall come. For men shall be lovers of their own selves, covetous, boasters, proud, blasphemers, disobedient to parents, unthankful, unholy, Without natural affection, trucebreakers, false accusers, incontinent, fierce, despisers of those that are good, Traitors, heady, highminded, lovers of pleasures more than lovers of God; Having a form of godliness, but denying the power thereof: from such turn away.

Mark 13:7–10 – And when ye shall hear of wars and rumours of wars, be ye not troubled: for such things must needs be; but the end shall not be yet. For nation shall rise against nation, and kingdom against kingdom: and there shall be earthquakes in divers places, and there shall be famines and troubles: these are the beginnings of sorrows.

But take heed to yourselves: for they shall deliver you up to councils; and in the synagogues ye shall be beaten: and ye shall be brought before rulers and kings for my sake, for a testimony against them.

And the gospel must first be published among all nations.

Matthew 24:29–31 – Immediately after the tribulation of those days shall the sun be darkened, and the moon shall not give her light, and the stars shall fall from heaven, and the powers of the heavens shall be shaken:

And then shall appear the sign of the Son of man in heaven: and then shall all the tribes of the earth mourn, and they shall see the Son of man coming in the clouds of heaven with power and great glory.

And he shall send his angels with a great sound of a trumpet, and they shall gather together his elect from the four winds, from one end of heaven to the other.

Luke 17:20–21 – Being asked by the Pharisees when the kingdom of God was coming, he answered them, "The kingdom of God is not coming with signs to be observed; nor will they say, 'Lo, here it is!' or 'There!' for behold, the kingdom of God is in the midst of you."

Luke 21:25 – And there will be signs in sun and moon and stars, and upon the earth distress of nations in perplexity at the roaring of the sea and the waves, men fainting with fear and with foreboding of what is coming on the world; for the powers of the heavens will be shaken.

Matthew 24:14 – And this gospel of the kingdom shall be preached in all the world for a witness unto all nations; and then shall the end come.

Matthew 24:21–22 – For then shall be great tribulation, such as was not since the beginning of the world to this time, no, nor ever shall be. And except those days should be shortened, there should no flesh be saved: but for the elect's sake those days shall be shortened.

2nd Epistle, Peter 2:1–3 – But there were false prophets also among the people, even as there shall be false teachers among you, who privily shall bring in damnable heresies, even denying the Lord that bought them, and bring upon themselves swift destruction, And many shall follow their pernicious ways; by reason of whom the way of truth shall be evil spoken of, And through covetousness shall they with feigned words make merchandise of you . . .

2nd Epistle, Peter 3:3–4 – . . . there shall come in the last days scoffers, walking after their own lusts, and saying, Where is the promise of His coming?

2nd Epistle, Peter 3:10 – But the day of the Lord will come as a thief in the night; . . .

Some of the verses from the Holy Qur'án and Hadíth concerning the signs of His coming:

Sura 22:1–2 – Al-Haj – O Men of Mecca, fear your Lord. Verily, the earthquake of the last Hour will be a tremendous thing!

On the day when ye shall behold it, every suckling woman shall forsake her sucking babe; and every woman that hath a burden in her womb shall cast her burden; and thou shalt see men drunken, yet they are not drunken: but it is the mighty chastisement of God!

Sura 27:90 – Al-Namlah – And thou shalt see the mountains, which thou thinkest so firm, pass away with the passing of a cloud! 'Tis the work of God, who ordereth all things! of all that ye do is He well aware.

Sura 17:4 – Al-Isrá' – And we solemnly declared to the children of Israel in the Book, 'Twice surely will ye enact crimes in the earth, and with great loftiness of pride will ye surely be uplifted.'

Sura 29:25 – Al-'Ankabút – But on the day of resurrection some of you shall deny the others, and some of you shall curse the others; and your abode shall be the fire, and ye shall have none to help.

Sura 75:7–19 – The Resurrection – But when the eye shall be dazzled, And when the moon shall be darkened, And the sun and the moon shall be together. On that day man shall cry, 'Where is there a place to flee to?' But in vain,—there is no refuge—With thy Lord on that day shall be the sole asylum. On that day shall man be told of all that he hath done first and last;

Yea, a man shall be the eye witness against himself: And even if he put forth his plea. . . . (Move not thy tongue in haste to follow and master this revelation: For we will see to the collecting and the recital of it; But when we have recited it, then follow thou the recital, And, verily, afterwards it shall be ours to make it clear to thee.)

Sura 80:34–38 – 'Abasa – But when the stunning trumpet blast shall arrive, on that day shall a man fly from his brother, and his mother and his father, and his wife and his children; for every man of them on that day his own concerns shall be enough.

Sura 81:1–20 – Al-Takwir – But When the sun shall be Folded Up, And when the stars shall fall, And when the mountains shall be set in motion, And when the she-camels shall be abandoned, And when the wild beasts shall be gathered together, And when the seas shall boil, And when the souls shall be paired with their bodies, And when the female child that had been buried alive shall be asked For what crime she was put to death, And when the leaves of the Book shall be unrolled, And when the Heavens shall be stripped away, And when Hell shall be made to blaze, And when Paradise shall be brought near, Every soul shall know what it hath produced. It needs not that I swear by the stars of retrograde motions, Which move swiftly and hide themselves away, And by the night when it cometh darkening on, And by the dawn when it brighteneth, That this is the word of an illustrious Messenger, Endued with power, having influence with the Lord of the Throne.

Sura 83:6–15 – Al-Mutaffifin – The day when mankind shall stand before the Lord of the worlds.

Yes! the register of the wicked is in Sidjin.

And who shall make thee understand what Sidjin is?

It is a book distinctly written.

Woe, on that day, to those who treated our signs as lies,

Who treated the day of judgment as a lie!

None treat it as a lie, save the transgressor, the criminal,

Who, when our signs are rehearsed to him, saith, "Tales of the Ancients!"

Yes; but their own works have got the mastery over their hearts.

Yes; they shall be shut out as by a veil from their Lord on that day;

'Aválim, quoted in Bahá'u'lláh, The Book of Certitude, ¶270 – "A Youth from Baní-Hás̲h̲im shall be made manifest, Who will reveal a new Book and promulgate a new law . . ."Most of His enemies will be the divines."

Ṣádiq, quoted in Bahá'u'lláh, The Book of Certitude, ¶270 – "There shall appear a Youth from Baní-Hás̲h̲im, Who will bid the people plight fealty unto Him. His Book will be a new Book, unto which He shall summon the people to pledge their faith. Stern is His Revelation unto the Arab. If ye hear about Him, hasten unto Him."

Hadíth, quoted in Shoghi Effendi, *The World Order of Bahá'u'lláh, p. 179 –* "In the latter days a grievous calamity shall befall My people at the hands of their ruler, a calamity such as no man ever heard to surpass it. So fierce will it be that none can find a shelter. God will then send down One of My descendants, One sprung from My family, Who will fill the earth with equity and justice, even as it hath been filled with injustice and tyranny."

Sura 17:16 – Al-Isrá' – We never punish until we had first sent an apostle.

Some of the passages from the Bahá'í sacred texts explaining the signs of the coming of the Promised One:

And now, concerning His words—"The sun shall be darkened, and the moon shall not give her light, and the stars shall fall from heaven." By the terms "sun" and "moon," mentioned in the writings of the Prophets of God, is not meant solely the sun and moon of the visible universe. Nay rather, manifold are the meanings they have intended for these terms. In every instance they have attached to them a particular significance. Thus, by the "sun" in one sense is meant those Suns of Truth Who rise from the dayspring of ancient glory, and fill the world with a liberal effusion of grace from on high. These Suns of Truth are the universal Manifestations of God. . . . Thus it is that through the rise of these Luminaries of God the world is made new, the waters of everlasting life stream forth, the billows of loving-kindness surge, the clouds of grace are gathered, and the breeze of bounty bloweth upon all created things. It is the warmth that these Luminaries of God generate, and the undying fires they kindle, which cause the light of the love of God to burn fiercely in the heart of humanity. It is through the abundant grace of these Symbols of Detachment that the Spirit of life everlasting is breathed into the bodies of the dead. Assuredly the visible sun is but a sign of the splendor of that Daystar of Truth, that Sun Which can never have a peer, a likeness, or rival.

Bahá'u'lláh, The Book of Certitude, ¶31.

The term "suns" hath many a time been applied in the writings of the "immaculate Souls" unto the Prophets of God, those luminous Emblems of Detachment. Among those writings are the following words recorded in the "Prayer of Nudbih":* "Whither are gone the resplendent Suns? Whereunto

---

* "Lamentation" attributed to the Twelfth Imám.

have departed those shining Moons and sparkling Stars?" Thus, it hath become evident that the terms "sun," "moon," and "stars" primarily signify the Prophets of God, the saints, and their companions, those Luminaries, the light of Whose knowledge hath shed illumination upon the worlds of the visible and the invisible.

In another sense, by these terms is intended the divines of the former Dispensation, who live in the days of the subsequent Revelations, and who hold the reins of religion in their grasp. If these divines be illumined by the light of the latter Revelation they will be acceptable unto God, and will shine with a light everlasting. Otherwise, they will be declared as darkened, even though to outward seeming they be leaders of men. . . .

Bahá'u'lláh, The Book of Certitude, ¶33.

As to the words—"Immediately after the oppression of those days"—they refer to the time when men shall become oppressed and afflicted, the time when the lingering traces of the Sun of Truth and the fruit of the Tree of knowledge and wisdom will have vanished from the midst of men, when the reins of mankind will have fallen into the grasp of the foolish and ignorant, when the portals of divine unity and understanding—the essential and highest purpose in creation—will have been closed, when certain knowledge will have given way to idle fancy, and corruption will have usurped the station of righteousness. Such a condition as this is witnessed in this day when the reins of every community have fallen into the grasp of foolish leaders, who lead after their own whims and desire. On their tongue the mention of God hath become an empty name; in their midst His holy Word a dead letter.

Bahá'u'lláh, The Book of Certitude, ¶28.

In like manner, strive thou to comprehend from these lucid, these powerful, conclusive, and unequivocal statements the meaning of the "cleaving of the heaven"—one of the signs that must needs herald the coming of the last Hour, the Day of Resurrection. As He hath said: "When the heaven shall be cloven asunder." By "heaven" is meant the heaven of divine Revelation, which is elevated with every Manifestation, and rent asunder with every subsequent one. By "cloven asunder" is meant that the former Dispensation is superseded and annulled. I swear by God! That his heaven being cloven asunder is, to the discerning, an act mightier than the cleaving of the skies!

Bahá'u'lláh, The Book of Certitude, ¶46.

That the term "sun" hath been applied to the leaders of religion is due to their lofty position, their fame, and renown. Such are the universally recognized divines of every age, who speak with authority, and whose fame is securely established. If they be in the likeness of the Sun of Truth, they will surely be accounted as the most exalted of all luminaries; otherwise, they are to be recognized as the focal centers of hellish fire. Even as He saith: "Verily, the sun and the moon are both condemned to the torment of infernal fire."*

. . . by the words "the sun shall be darkened, and the moon shall not give her light, and the stars shall fall from heaven" is intended the waywardness of the divines, and the annulment of laws firmly established by divine Revelation, all of which, in symbolic language, have been foreshadowed by the Manifestation of God. None except the righteous shall partake of this cup, none but the godly can share therein.

Bahá'u'lláh, The Book of Certitude, ¶36, ¶41.

And now, concerning His words: "And He shall send His angels. . . ." By "angels" is meant those who, reinforced by the power of the spirit, have con-

---

* Qur'án 55:5.

sumed, with the fire of the love of God, all human traits and limitations, and have clothed themselves with the attributes of the most exalted Beings and of the Cherubim.

Bahá'u'lláh, The Book of Certitude, ¶86.

And now, with reference to His words: "And then shall all the tribes of the earth mourn, and they shall see the Son of man coming in the clouds of heaven with power and great glory." These words signify that in those days men will lament the loss of the Sun of the divine beauty, of the Moon of knowledge, and of the Stars of divine wisdom. Thereupon, they will behold the countenance of the promised One, the adored Beauty, descending from heaven and riding upon the clouds. By this is meant that the divine Beauty will be made manifest from the heaven of the will of God, and will appear in the form of the human temple. The term "heaven" denoteth loftiness and exaltation, inasmuch as it is the seat of the revelation of those Manifestations of Holiness, the Daysprings of ancient glory. These ancient Beings, though delivered from the womb of their mother, have in reality descended from the heaven of the will of God. Though they be dwelling on this earth, yet their true habitations are the retreats of glory in the realms above. Whilst walking amongst mortals, they soar in the heaven of the divine presence.

Bahá'u'lláh, The Book of Certitude, ¶74.

Among them are those who have said: "Have the verses been sent down?" Say: "Yea, by Him Who is the Lord of the heavens!" "Hath the Hour come?" "Nay, more; it hath passed, by Him Who is the Revealer of clear tokens! Verily, the Inevitable is come, and He, the True One, hath appeared with proof and testimony. The Plain is disclosed, and mankind is sore vexed and fearful. Earthquakes have broken loose, and the tribes have lamented, for fear of God, the Lord of Strength, the All-Compelling." Say: "The stunning trumpet blast hath been loudly raised, and the Day is God's, the One, the Unconstrained." "Hath the Catastrophe come to pass?" Say: "Yea, by the Lord of Lords!" "Is the resurrection come?" "Nay, more; He Who is the Self-Subsisting hath appeared with the Kingdom of His signs." "Seest thou men laid low?" "Yea, by my Lord, the Exalted, the Most High!" "Have the tree stumps been uprooted?" "Yea, more; the mountains have been scattered in dust; by Him the Lord of attributes!" They say: "Where is Paradise, and where is Hell?" Say: "The one is reunion with Me; the other thine own self, O thou who dost associate a partner with God and doubtest." They say: "We see not the Balance." Say: "Surely, by my Lord, the God of Mercy! None can see it except such as are endued with insight." "Have the stars fallen?" Say: "Yea, when He Who is the Self-Subsisting dwelt in the Land of Mystery (Adrianople). Take heed, ye who are endued with discernment!" All the signs appeared when We drew forth the Hand of Power from the bosom of majesty and might. Verily, the Crier hath cried out, when the promised time came and they that have recognized the splendors of Sinai have swooned away in the wilderness of hesitation, before the awful majesty of thy Lord, the Lord of creation. The trumpet asketh: "Hath the Bugle been sounded?" Say: "Yea, by the King of Revelation!, when He mounted the throne of His Name, the All-Merciful." Darkness hath been chased away by the dawning-light of mercy of thy Lord, the Source of all light. The breeze of the All-Merciful hath wafted, and the souls have been quickened in the tombs of their bodies. Thus hath the decree been fulfilled by God, the Mighty, the Beneficent.

Bahá'u'lláh, *Tablets of Bahá'u'lláh,* pp. 117–18.

Say: The heavens have been folded together, and the earth is held within His grasp, and the corrupt doers have been held by their forelock, and still they understand not. They drink of the tainted water, and know it not. Say: The shout hath been raised, and the people have come forth from their graves, and arising, are gazing around them. Some have made haste to attain the court of the God of Mercy, others have fallen down on their faces in the fire of Hell, while still others are lost in bewilderment. The verses of God have been revealed, and yet they have turned away from them. His proof hath been manifested, and yet they are unaware of it. And when they behold the face of the All-Merciful, their own faces are saddened, while they are disporting themselves. They hasten forward to Hell Fire, and mistake it for light. Far from God be what they fondly imagine! Say: Whether ye rejoice or whether ye burst for fury, the heavens are cleft asunder, and God hath come down, invested with radiant sovereignty. All created things are heard exclaiming: "The Kingdom is God's, the Almighty, the All-Knowing, the All-Wise."

Bahá'u'lláh, *Gleanings from the Writings of Bahá'u'lláh*, no. 17.4.

In the same way, Israel, scattered all over the world, was not reassembled in the Holy Land in the Christian cycle; but in the beginning of the cycle of Bahá'u'lláh this divine promise, as is clearly stated in all the Books of the Prophets, has begun to be manifest. You can see that from all the parts of the world tribes of Jews are coming to the Holy Land; they live in villages and lands which they make their own, and day by day they are increasing to such an extent that all Palestine will become their home.

'Abdu'l-Bahá, *Some Answered Questions*, pp. 65–66.

The Book of Isaiah announces that the Messiah will conquer the East and the West, and all nations of the world will come under His shadow, that His Kingdom will be established, that He will come from an unknown place, that the sinners will be judged, and that justice will prevail to such a degree that the wolf and the lamb, the leopard and the kid, the sucking child and the asp, shall all gather at one spring, and in one meadow, and one dwelling. The first coming was also under these conditions, though outwardly none of them came to pass. Therefore, the Jews rejected Christ. . . .

The second coming of Christ also will be in like manner: the signs and conditions which have been spoken of all have meanings, and are not to be taken literally. Among other things it is said that the stars will fall upon the earth. The stars are endless and innumerable, and modern mathematicians have established and proved scientifically that the globe of the sun is estimated to be about one million and a half times greater than the earth, and each of the fixed stars to be a thousand times larger than the sun. If these stars were to fall upon the surface of the earth, how could they find place there? It would be as though a thousand million of Himalaya mountains were to fall upon a grain of mustard seed. According to reason and science this thing is quite impossible. What is even more strange is that Christ said: "Perhaps I shall come when you are yet asleep, for the coming of the Son of man is like the coming of a thief."* Perhaps the thief will be in the house, and the owner will not know it.

'Abdu'l-Bahá, *Some Answered Questions*, pp. 111–12.

This age is indeed as a hundred other ages: should ye gather the yield of a hundred ages, and set that against the accumulated product of our times, the yield of this one era will prove greater than that of a hundred gone before. Take ye, for an example, the sum total of all the books that were ever written in ages past, and compare that with the books and treatises that our era hath produced: these books, written in our day alone, far and away exceed the total number of volumes that have been written down the ages. See how

---

* Thessalonians, 5:2; 2 Peter, 3:10.

powerful is the influence exerted by the Daystar of the world upon the inner essence of all created things!

But alas, a thousand times alas! The eyes see it not, the ears are deaf, and the hearts and minds are oblivious of this supreme bestowal. Strive ye then, with all your hearts and souls, to awaken those who slumber, to cause the blind to see, and the dead to rise.

'Abdu'l-Bahá, *Selections from the Writings of 'Abdu'l-Bahá*, no. 73.6–7.

3

He Comes in the Clouds

The holy scriptures tell us that the Promised One will come to earth "in the clouds," "on the clouds," "with the clouds," "overshadowed with clouds"— "and every eye shall see him." Even if we take these verses literally, it would be clear that if anyone descended from heaven in the clouds, those very clouds would hide Him from sight, and the people on the earth—even those who are right below those very clouds, let alone the rest of the world—would not see Him. Furthermore, what is more amazing, the scriptures say that His coming on or in the clouds will happen after "the sun shall be darkened, and the moon shall not give her light, and the stars of heaven shall fall, and the powers that are in heaven shall be shaken. *And then shall they see* the Son of man coming in the clouds with great power and glory."*

It is obvious that the verses in the sacred scriptures have their own terminology and their own intrinsic meanings. The Bahá'í sacred texts explain the meaning of the "clouds" as barriers that prevent humanity from recognizing the true Manifestation of God. They are clouds of prejudice, pride and idle fancy, tradition and manmade dogma, rituals, and customs and preconceived

---

* Mark 13:24–26.

59

notions current among people. Even the seemingly ordinary and simple appearance of a Manifestation of God in a physical body, with all of its limitations, can hinder the soul from recognizing the true Manifestation of God.

The coming of the Promised One is often overshadowed in the minds of the majority of the people on earth and, as in previous Dispensations, mankind does not recognize the new Manifestation of God.

Some of the verses in the Holy Bible concerning the coming of the Promised One overshadowed by clouds:

Daniel 7:13–14 – I saw in the night visions, and, behold, one like the Son of man came with the clouds of heaven, and came to the Ancient of days, and they brought him near before him.

And there was given him dominion, and glory, and a kingdom, that all people, nations, and languages, should serve him: his dominion is an everlasting dominion, which shall not pass away, and his kingdom that which shall not be destroyed.

Matthew 16:27 – For the Son of man shall come in the glory of his Father with his angels; and then he shall reward every man according to his works.

Matthew 24:30 – And then will appear the sign of the Son of man in heaven, and then all the tribes of the earth will mourn, and they will see the Son of man coming on the clouds of heaven with power and great glory.

Matthew 26:64 – Jesus saith unto him, Thou hast said: nevertheless I say unto you, Hereafter shall ye see the Son of man sitting on the right hand of power, and coming in the clouds of heaven.

Mark 14:61–62 – Again the high priest asked him, "Are you the Christ, the Son of the Blessed?" And Jesus said, "I am; and you will see the Son of man seated at the right hand of Power, and coming with the clouds of heaven."

Mark 13:24–27 – But in those days, after that tribulation, the sun shall be darkened, and the moon shall not give her light, And the stars of heaven shall fall, and the powers that are in heaven shall be shaken.

And then shall they see the Son of man coming in the clouds with great power and glory.

And then shall he send his angels, and shall gather together his elect from the four winds, from the uttermost part of the earth to the uttermost part of heaven.

Luke 21:27 – And then they will see the Son of man coming in a cloud with power and great glory.

Revelation 1:7 – Behold, he cometh with clouds; and every eye shall see him. . . .

Some of the verses in the Holy Qur'án concerning the coming of the Promised One overshadowed by clouds:

Sura 2:206 – Al-Baqarah – What can such expect but that God should come down to them overshadowed with clouds, and the angels also, and their doom be sealed?

Sura 25:27 – Al-Furqán – On that day shall the heaven with its clouds be cleft, and the angels shall be sent down, descending.

Sura 44:9–13 – Al-Dukhán – But mark them on the day when the Heaven shall give out a palpable smoke, which shall enshroud mankind: this will be an afflictive torment.

They will cry, "Our Lord! Relieve us from this torment: see! We are believers."

But how did warning avail them, when an undoubted apostle had come to them; and they turned their backs on him, and said, "Taught by others, possessed?"

Sura 46:23–24 – Al-Ahqáf – So when they saw a cloud coming straight for their valleys, they said, "It is a passing cloud that shall give us rain." "Nay, it is that whose speedy coming ye challenged—a blast wherein is an afflictive punishment:—

It will destroy everything at the bidding of its Lord!" And at morn nought was to be seen but their empty dwellings! Thus repay we a wicked people.

Some of the passages from the Bahá'í sacred texts concerning the coming of the Promised One overshadowed by clouds:

He Who is the All-Bountiful is come, riding aloft on the clouds. Advance, O people of the earth, with shining faces and radiant hearts!

Bahá'u'lláh, Tablets of Bahá'u'lláh, pp. 115–16.

He, verily, is come with His Kingdom, and all the atoms cry aloud: "Lo! The Lord is come in His great majesty!" He who is the Father is come, and the Son (Jesus), in the holy vale, crieth out: "Here am I, here am I, O Lord, My God!" whilst Sinai circleth round the House, and the Burning Bush calleth aloud: "The All-Bounteous is come mounted upon the clouds!"

Bahá'u'lláh, The Summons of the Lord of Hosts, "Súriy-i-Haykal," ¶159.

Were the prophecies recorded in the Gospel to be literally fulfilled; were Jesus, Son of Mary, accompanied by angels, to descend from the visible heaven upon the clouds; who would dare to disbelieve, who would dare to reject the truth, and wax disdainful? Nay, such consternation would immediately seize all the dwellers of the earth that no soul would feel able to utter a word, much less to reject or accept the truth.

Bahá'u'lláh, The Book of Certitude, ¶88.

O kings of Christendom! Heard ye not the saying of Jesus, the Spirit of God, "I go away, and come again unto you"? Wherefore, then, did ye fail, when He did come again unto you in the clouds of heaven, to draw nigh unto Him, that ye might behold His face, and be of them that attained His Presence?

Bahá'u'lláh, The Summons of the Lord of Hosts,
"Súriy-i-Mulúk," ¶15.

64

It is evident that the changes brought about in every Dispensation constitute the dark clouds that intervene between the eye of man's understanding and the divine Luminary which shineth forth from the dayspring of the divine Essence. Consider how men for generations have been blindly imitating their fathers, and have been trained according to such ways and manners as have been laid down by the dictates of their Faith. Were these men, therefore, to discover suddenly that a Man, Who hath been living in their midst, Who, with respect to every human limitation, hath been their equal, had risen to abolish every established principle imposed by their Faith—principles by which for centuries they have been disciplined, and every opposer and denier of which they have come to regard as infidel, profligate and wicked—they would of a certainty be veiled and hindered from acknowledging His truth. Such things are as "clouds" that veil the eyes of those whose inner being hath not tasted the Salsabíl of detachment, nor drunk from the Kaw<u>th</u>ar of the knowledge of God.

Bahá'u'lláh, The Book of Certitude, ¶81.

By the term "clouds" is meant those things that are contrary to the ways and desires of men. . . . These "clouds" signify, in one sense, the annulment of laws, the abrogation of former Dispensations, the repeal of rituals and customs current amongst men, the exalting of the illiterate faithful above the learned opposers of the Faith. In another sense, they mean the appearance of that immortal Beauty in the image of mortal man, with such human limitations as eating and drinking, poverty and riches, glory and abasement, sleeping and waking, and such other things as cast doubt in the minds of men, and cause them to turn away. All such veils are symbolically referred to as "clouds."

These are the "clouds" that cause the heavens of the knowledge and understanding of all that dwell on earth to be cloven asunder. Even as He hath revealed: "On that day shall the heaven be cloven by the clouds." Even as the clouds prevent the eyes of men from beholding the sun, so do these things hinder the souls of men from recognizing the light of the divine Luminary.

Bahá'u'lláh, The Book of Certitude, ¶79–80.

And they are waiting for Him to come down from there again, riding upon a cloud, and they imagine that there are clouds in that infinite space and that He will ride thereon and by that means He will descend. Whereas the truth is that a cloud is but a vapor that riseth out of the earth, and it doth not come down from heaven. Rather, the cloud referred to in the Gospel is the human body, so called because the body is as a veil to man, which, even as a cloud, preventeth him from beholding the Sun of Truth that shineth from the horizon of Christ.

'Abdu'l-Bahá, *Selections from the Writings of 'Abdu'l-Bahá*, no. 143.3.

Praise ye the Lord of Hosts for He, riding upon the clouds, hath come down to this world out of the heaven of the invisible realm, so that East and West were lit by the glory of the Sun of Truth, and the call of the Kingdom was raised, and the heralds of the realm above, with melodies of the Concourse on high, sang out the glad tidings of the Coming. Then the whole world of being did quiver for joy, and still the people, even as the Messiah saith, slept on: for the day of the Manifestation, when the Lord of Hosts descended, found them wrapped in the slumber of unknowing. As He saith in the Gospel, My coming is even as when the thief is in the house, and the goodman of the house watcheth not.

'Abdu'l-Bahá, *Selections from the Writings of 'Abdu'l-Bahá*, no. 17.1.

4

The Place where He Appears

The Holy Scriptures conspicuously indicate the place where the Promised One is to appear. The details of the history of the Bahá'í Faith, as well as the verses selected here, indicate the banishments of Bahá'u'lláh inflicted upon Him by the Persian and Ottoman Empires were foretold in the sacred scriptures. From Tehran, the capital of Iran, Bahá'u'lláh was banished to Baghdad. From Baghdad, He was sent to Constantinople (Istanbul), then to Adrianople (Edirne), and finally—by way of Egypt—to the prison city of 'Akká.

The importance Isaiah, Hosea, and Ezekiel gave to the valley of Achor, to Mount Carmel, and the plain of Sharon (south of Mt. Carmel), and to "'Akká," the "door of hope," "the gate that looketh towards the East,"—which they promised will see the "Glory of the Lord"—provides an indication of the location where the Promised One, "Bahá'u'lláh," was to appear (Bahá'u'lláh's name translates as the "Glory of God" or "Glory of the Lord").*

One will note from the verses quoted that the name "Bahá'u'lláh" or "Glory of the Lord" is used as a person in the visions recorded in Hosea,

---

* See footnote under the chapter "He Comes with a New Name."

Jeremiah, Ezekiel, Isaiah, and Acts. For example, we will read below, "the *glory of the Lord* entered the temple by the gate facing east," "behold, the *glory of the God* of Israel came from the east," "Carmel and Sharon, they shall see *the glory of the Lord*," "and, lo, *the glory of the Lord* stood there," and "looked up steadfastly into heaven, and saw *the glory of God*, and Jesus standing on the right hand of God."

In Islam, there are numerous references to the city of 'Akká, how blessed and special 'Akká would become, and the blessings that would be bestowed upon those who visit 'Akká as pilgrims. With the passing of Bahá'u'lláh in 'Akká and His burial there, 'Akká became the Qiblih and the place of pilgrimage for the Bahá'ís of the world.

Some of the verses from the Holy Bible concerning the place where the Promised One would appear:

Hosea 2:15 – And I will give her vineyards from thence, and the valley of Achor for a door of hope: and she shall sing there, as in the days of her youth, and as in the day when she came up out of the land of Egypt.

Jeremiah 46:18 – As I live, saith the King, whose name is the *Lord of hosts,* Surely as Tabor is among the mountains, and as Carmel by the sea, so shall he come.

Amos 1:2 – The Lord roars from Zion, and utters his voice from Jerusalem; the pastures of the shepherds mourn, and the top of Carmel withers.

Acts 7:55 – But he, being full of the Holy Ghost, looked up steadfastly into heaven, and saw *the glory of God,* and Jesus standing on the right hand of God.

Ezekiel 43:1–2 – Afterward he brought me to the gate, the gate facing east. And behold, *the glory of the God* of Israel came from the east . . .

Ezekiel 43:4–5 – As the *glory of the Lord* entered the temple by the gate facing east, the Spirit lifted me up, and brought me into the inner court; and behold, *the glory of the Lord* filled the temple.

Ezekiel 44:4 – Then brought he me the way of the north gate before the house: and I looked, and, behold, the *glory of the Lord* filled the house of the Lord: and I fell upon my face.

Ezekiel 3:22–23 – And the hand of the Lord was there upon me; and he said to me, "Arise, go forth into the plain, and there I will speak with you."

So I arose and went forth into the plain; and, lo, *the glory of the Lord* stood there, like the *glory* which I had seen by the river Chebar; and I fell on my face.

Ezekiel 10:4 – Then the *glory of the Lord* went up from the cherub, and stood over the threshold of the house; and the house was filled with the cloud, and the court was full of the brightness of the LORD's glory.

Ezekiel 10:18 – Then the *glory of the Lord* departed from off the threshold of the house, and stood over the cherubims.

Ezekiel 11:23 – And the *glory of the Lord* went up from the midst of the city, and stood upon the mountain which is on the east side of the city.

Isaiah 40:5 – And the *glory of the Lord* shall be revealed, and all flesh shall see it together: for the mouth of the LORD hath spoken it.

Micah 7:11–13 – In the day that thy walls are to be built, in that day shall the decree be far removed.

In that day also he shall come even to thee from Assyria, and from the fortified cities, and from the fortress even to the river, and from sea to sea, and from mountain to mountain.

Notwithstanding the land shall be desolate because of them that dwell therein, for the fruit of their doings.

Micah 4:1 – But in the last days it shall come to pass, that the mountain of the house of the Lord shall be established in the top of the mountains, and it shall be exalted above the hills; and people shall flow unto it.

Isaiah 2:2–3 – And it shall come to pass in the last days, that the mountain of the Lord's house shall be established in the top of the mountains, and shall be exalted above the hills; and all nations shall flow unto it.

And many people shall go and say, Come ye, and let us go up to the mountain of the Lord, to the house of the God of Jacob; and he will teach us of his ways, and we will walk in his paths: for out of Zion shall go forth the law, and the word of the Lord from Jerusalem.

Isaiah 35:1–2 – The wilderness and the solitary place shall be glad for them; and the desert shall rejoice, and blossom as the rose.

It shall blossom abundantly, and rejoice even with joy and singing: the glory of Lebanon shall be given unto it, the excellency of Carmel and Sharon, they shall see *the glory of the Lord,* and the excellency of our God.

Isaiah 65:10 – And Sharon shall be a fold of flocks, and the valley of Achor a place for the herds to lie down in, for my people that have sought me.

Psalms 108:10–11 – Who will bring me into the strong city? who will lead me into Edom? Wilt not thou, O God, who hast cast us off?

Revelation 21:10–11 – And he carried me away in the spirit to a great and high mountain, and shewed me that great city, the holy Jerusalem, descending out of heaven from God, Having *the glory of God*: and her light was like unto a stone most precious, even like a jasper stone, clear as crystal.

Some of the verses from the Holy Qur'án and Hadíth concerning the place where the Promised One would appear:

Sura 10:26 – Yúnis – And God calleth to the abode of peace; and He guideth whom He will into the right way.

Sura 50:40 – Qáf – And list for the day whereon the crier shall cry from a place near to every one alike.

'Abdu'l-'Azíz, quoted in Bahá'u'lláh, Epistle to the Son of the Wolf, p. 178 – 'Abdu'l-'Azíz, son of 'Abdu'l-Salám, hath related unto us that the Prophet— may the blessings of God and His salutations be upon Him—hath said: "Akká is a city in Syria to which God hath shown His special mercy."

Anas, quoted in Bahá'u'lláh, Epistle to the Son of the Wolf, pp. 178–81 – Anas, son of Málik—may God be pleased with him—hath said: "The Apostle of God—may the blessings of God and His salutations be upon Him—hath said: '. . . I announce unto you a city, on the shores of the sea, white, whose whiteness is pleasing unto God—exalted be He! It is called 'Akká. He that hath been bitten by one of its fleas is better, in the estimation of God than he who hath received a grievous blow in the path of God. And he that raiseth therein the call to prayer, his voice will be lifted up unto Paradise. . . . There are kings and princes in Paradise. The poor of 'Akká are the kings of Paradise and the princes thereof. A month in 'Akká is better than a thousand years elsewhere . . .'

"Blessed the man that hath visited 'Akká, and blessed he that hath visited the visitor of 'Akká. . . . And he that saith in 'Akká: 'Glorified be God, and praise be unto God, and there is none other God but God, and most great is God, the Exalted, the Mighty,' God will write down for him a thousand good deeds, and blot out from him a thousand evil deeds, and will uplift him a thousand grades in Paradise, and will forgive him his transgressions. And whoso saith in 'Akká: 'I beg forgiveness of God,' God will forgive all his trespasses. And he that remembereth God in 'Akká at morn and at eventide, in the night-season and at dawn, is better in the sight of God than he who beareth swords, spears and arms in the path of God—exalted be He!"

The Apostle of God—may the blessings of God and His salutations be upon Him—hath also said: "He that looketh upon the sea at eventide, and said: 'God is Most Great!' at sunset, God will forgive his sins, though they be heaped as piles of sand. And he that counteth forty waves, while repeating: 'God is Most Great!'—exalted be He—God will forgive his sins, both past and future."

Some of the passages from the Bahá'í sacred texts concerning the place where the Promised One would appear:

Haste thee, O Carmel, for lo, the light of the countenance of God, the Ruler of the Kingdom of Names and Fashioner of the heavens, hath been lifted upon thee.

Bahá'u'lláh, Tablets of Bahá'u'lláh, p. 3.

Call out to Zion, O Carmel, and announce the joyful tidings: He that was hidden from mortal eyes is come! His all-conquering sovereignty is manifest; His all-encompassing splendour is revealed. Beware lest thou hesitate or halt. Hasten forth and circumambulate the City of God that hath descended from heaven, the celestial Kaaba round which have circled in adoration the favoured of God, the pure in heart, and the company of the most exalted angels.

Bahá'u'lláh, Tablets of Bahá'u'lláh, p. 4.

No sooner had her voice reached that most exalted Spot than We made reply: "Render thanks unto thy Lord, O Carmel. The fire of thy separation from Me was fast consuming thee, when the ocean of My presence surged before thy face, cheering thine eyes and those of all creation, and filling with delight all things visible and invisible. Rejoice, for God hath in this Day established upon thee His throne, hath made thee the dawning-place of His signs and the dayspring of the evidences of His Revelation. Well is it with him that circleth around thee, that proclaimeth the revelation of thy glory, and recounteth that which the bounty of the Lord thy God hath showered upon thee. Seize thou the Chalice of Immortality in the name of thy Lord, the All-Glorious, and give thanks unto Him, inasmuch as He, in token of His mercy unto thee, hath turned thy sorrow into gladness, and transmuted thy grief into blissful joy. He, verily, loveth the spot which hath been made the seat of His throne, which His footsteps have trodden, which hath been honoured by His presence, from which He raised His call, and upon which He shed His tears."

Bahá'u'lláh, *Tablets of Bahá'u'lláh*, p. 4.

He, for Whose sake the world was called into being, hath been imprisoned in the most desolate of cities ('Akká), by reason of that which the hands of the wayward have wrought. From the horizon of His prison-city He summoneth mankind unto the Dayspring of God, the Exalted, the Great.

Bahá'u'lláh, Epistle to the Son of the Wolf, p. 56

The Sun of Truth shineth resplendently, at the bidding of the Lord of the kingdom of utterance, and the King of the heaven of knowledge, above the horizon of the prison-city of 'Akká. Repudiation hath not veiled it, and ten thousand hosts arrayed against it were powerless to withhold it from shining. Thou canst excuse thyself no longer. Either thou must recognize it, or—God forbid—arise and deny all the Prophets!

Bahá'u'lláh, Epistle to the Son of the Wolf, p. 119.

. . . a Voice was raised from the direction of Ḥijáz, calling aloud and saying: "Great is thy blessedness, O 'Akká, in that God hath made thee the dayspring of His Most Sweet Voice, and the dawn of His most mighty signs. Happy art thou in that the Throne of Justice hath been established upon thee, and the Daystar of God's loving-kindness and bounty hath shone forth above thy horizon. Well it is with every fair-minded person that hath judged fairly Him Who is the Most Great Remembrance, and woe betide him that hath erred and doubted."

Bahá'u'lláh, Epistle to the Son of the Wolf, p. 79.

Carmel, in the Book of God, hath been designated as the Hill of God, and His Vineyard. It is here that, by the grace of the Lord of Revelation, the Tabernacle of Glory hath been raised. Happy are they that attain thereunto; happy they that set their faces towards it.

Bahá'u'lláh, Epistle to the Son of the Wolf, p. 145.

Indeed all the Prophets have yearned to attain this Day. David saith: "Who will bring me into the Strong City?" [Psalms 59:9; 108:10.] By Strong City is meant 'Akká. Its fortifications are very strong and this Wronged One is imprisoned within its walls. Likewise it is revealed in the Qur'án: "Bring forth thy people from the darkness into the light and announce to them the days of God." [Qur'án 14:5]

Bahá'u'lláh, *Tablets of Bahá'u'lláh*, p. 259.

Hearken with thine inner ear unto the Voice of Jeremiah, Who saith: "Oh, for great is that Day, and it hath no equal." Wert thou to observe with the eye of fairness, thou wouldst perceive the greatness of the Day. Incline thine ear unto the Voice of this All-Knowing Counsellor, and suffer not thyself to be deprived of the mercy that hath surpassed all created things, visible and invisible. Lend an ear unto the song of David. He saith: "Who will bring me into the Strong City?" The Strong City is 'Akká, which hath been named the Most Great Prison, and which possesseth a fortress and mighty ramparts.

Bahá'u'lláh, Epistle to the Son of the Wolf, p. 144.

It is recorded in the Torah: And I will give you the valley of Achor for a door of hope. This valley of Achor is the city of 'Akká, and whoso hath interpreted this otherwise is of them who know not.

'Abdu'l-Bahá, *Selections from the Writings of 'Abdu'l-Bahá*, no. 139.9.

. . . Bahá'u'lláh's tent, the *"Tabernacle of Glory,"* was raised on Mt. Carmel, *"the Hill of God and His Vineyard,"* the home of Elijah, extolled by Isaiah as the *"mountain of the Lord,"* to which *"all nations shall flow."*

Shoghi Effendi, *God Passes By*, p. 194.

'Akká, itself, flanked by the *"glory of Lebanon,"* and lying in full view of the *"splendor of Carmel,"* at the foot of the hills which enclose the home of Jesus Christ Himself, had been described by David as *"the Strong City,"* designated by Hosea as *"a door of hope,"* and alluded to by Ezekiel as *"the gate that looketh towards the East,"* whereunto *"the glory of the God of Israel came from the way of the East,"* His voice *"like a noise of many waters."* To it the Arabian Prophet had referred as *"a city in Syria to which God hath shown His special mercy,"* situated *"betwixt two mountains . . . in the middle of a meadow,"* *"by the shore of the sea . . . suspended beneath the Throne,"* *"white, whose whiteness is pleasing unto God."*

Shoghi Effendi, *God Passes By*, p. 184.

5

The Time of His Coming

Although both the Bible and the Qur'án contain many references to the time of the coming of the Promised One, this chapter deals with only a few.

One of the well-known prophecies in the Bible is found in the Book of Daniel (chapter 8) and was confirmed by Jesus in the Gospel of Matthew (chapter 24). Daniel says that from the edict of Artaxerxes to Ezra (457 B.C.)—which ordered the restoration and rebuilding of Jerusalem—to the coming of the Messiah, there would be seventy weeks, and from that same edict to the end of the abomination of desolation, there would be 2,300 days. According to the Bible, each day counts as a year (Numbers 14:34; Ezekiel 4:6). 'Abdu'l-Bahá explains these dates by saying, *"Seventy weeks make four hundred and ninety days. Each day, according to the text of the Holy Book, is a year. . . . Therefore, four hundred and ninety days are four hundred and ninety years. The third edict of Artaxerxes was issued four hundred and fifty-seven years before the birth of Christ, and Christ when He was martyred and ascended was thirty-three years of age. When you add thirty-three to four hundred and fifty-seven, the result is four hundred and ninety, which is the time announced by Daniel for the manifestation of Christ."** As for the 2,300 days, which signals

---

* 'Abdu'l-Bahá, *Some Answered Questions,* pp. 40–41.

the coming of the Lord of Hosts and is calculated by the same edict that signaled the birth of the Christian dispensation, 'Abdu'l-Bahá says, "*Then from the date of issuing of the edict of Artaxerxes to rebuild Jerusalem until the day of the birth of Christ there are 456 years, and from the birth of Christ until the day of the manifestation of the Báb there are 1844 years. When you add 456 years to this number it makes 2300 years. That is to say, the fulfillment of the vision of Daniel took place in the year A.D. 1844, and this is the year of the Báb's manifestation according to the actual text of the Book of Daniel.*"*

In Islam, the Qur'án states, "to each age its Book" (Sura 13:38) and "Every nation [Umma] hath its set time" (Sura 7:33). To the Muḥammadan dispensation He hath ordained "a day whose length shall be a thousand of such years as ye reckon" (Sura 32:4). The reckoning of the day stated was after the last of the twelve Imams had passed away, i.e. the year 260 A.H. By adding the period of 1,000 years previously mentioned to the year 260, results to 1260 A.H., which is equivalent to 1844 A.D., the year the Báb declared His mission.

---

* Ibid., p. 42.

Some of the verses from the Holy Bible
concerning the time of His coming:

Daniel 8:13–14 – Then I heard a holy one speaking and another holy one said to the one that spoke, "For how long is the vision concerning the continual burnt offering, the transgression that makes desolate, and the giving over of the sanctuary and host to be trampled under foot?" And he said to him, "For two thousand and three hundred evenings and mornings; then the sanctuary shall be restored to its rightful state."

Daniel 9:24–25 – Seventy weeks are determined upon thy people and upon thy holy city, to finish the transgression, and to make an end of sins, and to make reconciliation for iniquity, and to bring in everlasting righteousness, and to seal up the vision and prophecy, and to anoint the most Holy.

Know therefore and understand, that from the going forth of the commandment to restore and to build Jerusalem unto the Messiah the Prince shall be seven weeks, and threescore and two weeks: the street shall be built again, and the wall, even in troublous times.

Matthew 24:2–3, 15 – Truly, I say to you, there will not be left here one stone upon another, that will not be thrown down.

As he sat on the Mount of Olives, the disciples came to him privately, saying, 'Tell us, when will this be, and what will be the sign of your coming and of the close of the age?'

So when you see the desolating sacrilege spoken of by the prophet Daniel, standing in the holy place (let the reader understand).

Daniel 12:6–7 – And I said to the man clothed in linen, who was above the waters of the stream, "How long shall it be till the end of these wonders?" The man clothed in linen, who was above the waters of the stream, raised his right hand and his left hand toward heaven; and I heard him swear by him who lives for ever that it would be for a time, two times, and half a time. . . .

Daniel 12:11–12 – And from the time that the continual burnt offering is taken away, and the abomination that makes desolate is set up, there shall be a thousand two hundred and ninety days. Blessed is he who waits and comes to the thousand three hundred and thirty-five days.

Revelation 11:1–2 – I was given a long cane, a kind of measuring-rod, and told: 'Now go and measure the temple of God, the altar, and the number of the worshippers. But have nothing to do with the outer court of the temple; do not measure that; for it has been given over to the Gentiles, and they will trample the Holy City underfoot for forty-two months.

Revelation 11:8–9 – Their corpses will lie in the street of the great city, whose name in allegory is Sodom; or Egypt; where also their Lord was crucified. For three days and a half, men of every people and tribe, of every language and nation, gaze upon their corpses and refuse them burial.

Revelation 12:5–6 – . . . she brought forth a male child, one who is to rule all the nations with a rod of iron, but her child was caught up to God and to his throne, and the woman fled into the wilderness, where she has a place prepared by God, in which to be nourished for one thousand two hundred and sixty days.

Some of the verses from the Holy Qur'án and Hadíth concerning the time of His coming:

Sura 13:38–39 – Al-Ra'd – To each age its Book. What He pleaseth will God abrogate or confirm: for with Him is the source of revelation.

Sura 7:33 – Al-A'ráf – Every nation [Umma] hath its set time. And when their time is come, they shall not retard it an hour; and they shall not advance it.

Sura 10:48–50 – Yunis – And every people [Umma]* hath had its apostle. And when their apostle came, a rightful decision took place between them, and they were not wronged. . . . Every people [Umma] hath its time: when their time is come, they shall neither retard nor advance it an hour.

Sura 32:4 – Al-Sajdah – From the Heaven to the Earth He governeth all things: hereafter shall they come up to him on a day whose length shall be a thousand of such years as ye reckon.

Sura 22:46 – Al-Haj – And they will bid thee to hasten the chastisement. But God cannot fail His threat. And verily, a day with thy Lord is as a thousand years, as ye reckon them!

Sura 22:56–57 – Al-Haj – But the Infidels will not cease to doubt concerning it, until 'the Hour' come suddenly upon them, or until the chastisement of the day of desolation come upon them.

---

* The Arabic text uses the word *Umma* as followers of Islam. In the above verses, it has been translated once as nation and the other time as people.

On that day the Kingdom shall be God's: He shall judge between them: and they who shall have believed and done the things that are right, shall be in gardens of delight.

Sura 23:45–46 – Al-Mu'minún – Neither too soon nor too late, shall a people reach its appointed time. Then sent we our apostles one after another.

Imám Ja'far, quoted in Nabíl-i-A'zam, The Dawn-breakers, p. 49 – "Verily, in the year sixty His Cause shall be revealed, and His name shall be noised abroad."

Muḥyi'd-Dín-i-'Arabí, quoted in Nabíl-i-A'zam, The Dawn-breakers, p. 49 – "The year of His Revelation is identical with half of that number which is divisible by nine [2520]."

Muḥammad-i-Akhbári, quoted in Nabíl-i-A'zam, The Dawn-breakers, p. 50 – "In the year G̲h̲árs* (the numerical value of the letters of which is 1260) the earth shall be illumined by His light, and in G̲h̲árasih (1265) the world shall be suffused with its glory. If thou livest until the year G̲h̲árasi (1270), thou shall witness how the nations, the rulers, the peoples, and the Faith of God shall all have been renewed."

Imám 'Alí, quoted in Nabíl-i-A'zam, The Dawn-breakers, p. 50 – "In G̲h̲árs the Tree of Divine guidance shall be planted."

---

* In Arabic, the word *G̲h̲árs* means to plant, and in numerology, its numerical value is Gha=1000, R=200, S=60—i.e., the year 1260 Hejira, or the Islamic Calendar.

Some of the passages from the Bahá'í sacred texts concerning the time of His coming:

Once in about a thousand years shall this City be renewed and re-adorned. . . . That city is none other than the Word of God revealed in every age and dispensation. In the days of Moses it was the Pentateuch; in the days of Jesus the Gospel; in the days of Muḥammad the Messenger of God the Qur'án; in this day the Bayán; and in the dispensation of Him Whom God will make manifest His own Book—the Book unto which all the Books of former Dispensations must needs be referred . . .

Bahá'u'lláh, The Book of Certitude, ¶218–19.

According to the tradition, Mufaḍḍal asked Ṣádiq saying: "What of the sign of His manifestation, O my master?" He made reply: "In the year sixty, His Cause shall be made manifest, and His Name shall be proclaimed."

Bahá'u'lláh, The Book of Certitude, ¶281.

. . . in the Book of Daniel, from the rebuilding of Jerusalem to the martyrdom of Christ, seventy weeks are appointed; for by the martyrdom of Christ the sacrifice is accomplished and the altar destroyed. This is a prophecy of the manifestation of Christ. These seventy weeks begin with the restoration and the rebuilding of Jerusalem, concerning which four edicts were issued by three kings.

The first was issued by Cyrus in the year 536 B.C.; this is recorded in the first chapter of the Book of Ezra. The second edict, with reference to the rebuilding of Jerusalem, is that of Darius of Persia in the year 519 B.C.; this is recorded in the sixth chapter of Ezra. The third is that of Artaxerxes in the seventh year of his reign—that is, in 457 B.C.; this is recorded in the seventh chapter of Ezra. The fourth is that of Artaxerxes in the year 444 B.C.; this is recorded in the second chapter of Nehemiah.

But Daniel refers especially to the third edict which was issued in the year 457 B.C.

'Abdu'l-Bahá, *Some Answered Questions*, p. 40.

. . . Daniel mentions two dates. One of these dates begins with the command of Artaxerxes to Ezra to rebuild Jerusalem; this is the seventy weeks which came to an end with the ascension of Christ, when by His martyrdom the sacrifice and oblation ceased.

The second period, which is found in the twenty-sixth verse, means that after the termination of the rebuilding of Jerusalem until the ascension of Christ, there will be sixty-two weeks: the seven weeks are the duration of the rebuilding of Jerusalem, which took forty-nine years. When you add these seven weeks to the sixty-two weeks, it makes sixty-nine weeks, and in the last week (69–70) the ascension of Christ took place. These seventy weeks are thus completed, and there is no contradiction.

Now that the manifestation of Christ has been proved by the prophecies of Daniel, let us prove the manifestation of Bahá'u'lláh and the Báb. Up to the present we have only mentioned rational proofs; now we shall speak of traditional proofs.

In the eighth chapter of the Book of Daniel, verse thirteen, it is said: "Then I heard one saint speaking, and another saint said unto that certain saint which spake, How long shall be the vision concerning the daily sacrifice, and the transgression of desolation, to give both the sanctuary and the host to be trodden under foot?" Then he answered (v. 14): "Unto two thousand and three hundred days; then shall the sanctuary be cleansed"; (v. 17) "But he said unto me . . . at the time of the end shall be the vision."

That is to say, how long will this misfortune, this ruin, this abasement and degradation last? Meaning, when will be the dawn of the Manifestation? Then he answered, "Two thousand and three hundred days; then shall the sanctuary be cleansed." Briefly, the purpose of this passage is that he appoints two thousand three hundred years, for in the text of the Bible each days is a year. Then from the date of the issuing of the decree of Artaxerxes to rebuild Jerusalem until the day of the birth of Christ there are 456 years and from the birth of Christ until the day of the manifestation of the Báb there are 1844 years. When you add 456 years to this number it makes 2300 years. That is to say, the fulfillment of the vision of Daniel took place in the year A.D. 1844, and this is the year of the Báb's manifestation according to the actual text of the Book of Daniel. Consider how clearly he determines the year of the manifestation; there could be no clearer prophecy for a manifestation than this.

In Matthew, chapter 24 verse 3, Christ clearly says that what Daniel meant by this prophecy was the date of the manifestation, and this is the verse: "And he sat upon the mount of Olives, the disciples came unto him privately, saying, Tell us, when shall these things be? and what shall be the sign of thy coming, and of the end of the world?" One of the explanations he gave them in reply was this (v. 15): "When ye therefore shall see the abomination of desolation, spoken of by Daniel the prophet, stand in the holy place, (whoso readeth let him understand)." In this answer he referred them to the eighth chapter of the Book of Daniel, saying that every one who reads it will understand that it is this time that is spoken of. Consider how clearly the manifestation of the Báb is spoken of in the Old Testament and in the Gospel.

To conclude, let us now explain the date of the manifestation of Bahá'u'lláh from the Bible. The date of Bahá'u'lláh is calculated according to lunar years from the mission of and the Hejira of Muḥammad; for in the religion of

Muḥammad the lunar year is in use, as also it is the lunar year which is employed concerning all commands of worship.

In Daniel, chapter 12, verse 6, it is said: "And one said to the man clothed in linen, which was upon the waters of the river, How long shall it be to the end of these wonders? And I heard the man clothed in linen, which was upon the waters of the river, when he held up his right hand and his left hand unto heaven, and swear by him that liveth for ever that it shall be for a time, [two] times, and a half; and that when he shall have accomplished to scatter the power of the holy people, all these things shall be finished."

As I have already explained the signification of one day, it is not necessary to explain it further; but we will say briefly that each day of the Father counts as a year, and in each year there are twelve months. Thus three years and a half make forty-two months, and forty-two months are twelve hundred and sixty days. The Báb, the precursor to Bahá'u'lláh, appeared in the year 1260 from the Hejira of Muḥammad, by the reckoning of Islám.

Afterwards, in verse 11, it is said: "And from the time that the daily sacrifice shall be taken away, and the abomination that maketh desolation be set up, there shall be a thousand two hundred and ninety days. Blessed is he that waiteth and cometh to the thousand three hundred and five-and-thirty days."

The beginning of this lunar reckoning is from the day of the proclamation of the prophethood of Muḥammad in the country of Ḥijáz; and that was three years after his mission, because in the beginning the prophethood of Muḥammad was kept secret, and no one knew it save Khadíjah and Ibn Nawfal. After three years it was announced. And Bahá'u'lláh in the year 1290 from the proclamation of the mission of Muḥammad, caused His manifestation to be known.

'Abdu'l-Bahá, *Some Answered Questions*,
pp. 41–44.

In the beginning of the seventh century after Christ, when Jerusalem was conquered, the Holy of Holies was outwardly preserved—that is to say, the house which Solomon built; but outside the Holy of Holies the outer court was taken and given to the Gentiles. "And the holy city shall they tread under foot forty and two months"—that is to say, the Gentiles shall govern and control Jerusalem forty and two months, signifying twelve hundred and sixty days; and as each day signifies a year, by this reckoning it becomes twelve hundred and sixty years, which is the duration of the cycle of the Qur'án. For in the texts of the Holy Book, each day is a year; as it is said in the fourth chapter of Ezekiel, verse 6: "Thou shalt bear the iniquity of the house of Judah forty days: I have appointed thee each day for a year."

This prophesies the duration of the Dispensation of Islám when Jerusalem was trodden under foot, which means that it lost its glory—but the Holy of Holies was preserved, guarded and respected—until the year 1260. This twelve hundred and sixty years is a prophecy of the manifestation of the Báb, the "Gate" of Bahá'u'lláh, which took place in the year 1260 of the Hejira of Muḥammad, and as the period of twelve hundred and sixty years has expired, Jerusalem, the Holy City, is now beginning to become prosperous, populous and flourishing.

'Abdu'l-Bahá, *Some Answered Questions,*

p. 46.

"And their dead bodies shall lie in the street of the great city, which spiritually is called Sodom and Egypt, where also our Lord was crucified" (Revelation 11:8). "Their bodies" means the Religion of God, and "the street" means in public view. The meaning of "Sodom and Egypt," the place "where also our Lord was crucified," is this region of Syria, and especially Jerusalem, where the Umayyads then had their dominions; and it was here that the Religion

89

of God and the divine teachings first disappeared, and a body without spirit remained. "Their bodies" represents the Religion of God, which remained like a dead body without spirit.

"And they of the people and kindreds and tongues and nations shall see their dead bodies three days and a half, and shall not suffer their dead bodies to be put in graves" [Revelation 11:9].

As it was before explained, in the terminology of the Holy Books three days and a half signify three years and a half, and three years and a half are forty and two months, and forty and two months twelve hundred and sixty days; and as each day by the text of the Holy Book signifies one year, the meaning is that for twelve hundred and sixty years, which is the cycle of the Qur'án, the nations, tribes and peoples would look at their bodies—that is to say, that they would make a spectacle of the Religion of God: though they would not act in accordance with it, still, they would not suffer their bodies—meaning the Religion of God—to be put in the grave. That is to say, that in appearance they would cling to the Religion of God and not allow it to completely disappear from their midst, nor the body of it to be entirely destroyed and annihilated. Nay, in reality they would leave it, while outwardly preserving its name and remembrance.

Those "kindreds, people and nations" signify those who are gathered under the shadow of the Qur'án, not permitting the Cause and Law of God to be, in outward appearance, entirely destroyed and annihilated—for there are prayer and fasting among them—but the fundamental principles of the Religion of God, which are morals and conduct, with the knowledge of divine mysteries, have disappeared; the light of the virtues of the world of humanity, which is the result of the love and knowledge of God, is extinguished; and the darkness of tyranny, oppression, satanic passions and desires has become victorious. The body of the Law of God, like a corpse, has been exposed to the public view for twelve hundred and sixty days, each day being counted as a year, and this period is the cycle of Muḥammad.

'Abdu'l-Bahá, Some Answered Questions, pp. 51–53.

Consider how the prophecies correspond to one another. In the Apocalypse, the appearance of the Promised One is appointed after forty-two months, and Daniel expresses it as three times and a half, which is also forty-two months, which are twelve hundred and sixty days. In another passage of John's Revelation it is clearly spoken of as twelve hundred and sixty days, and in the Holy Book it is said that each day signifies one year. Nothing could be clearer than this agreement of the prophecies with one another. The Báb appeared in the year 1260 of the Hejira of Muḥammad, which is the beginning of the universal era reckoning of all Islám. There are no clearer proofs than this in the Holy Books for any Manifestation. For him who is just, the agreement of the times indicated by the tongues of the Great Ones is the most conclusive proof. There is no other possible explanation of these prophecies. Blessed are the just souls who seek the truth.

'Abdu'l-Bahá, Some Answered Questions, p. 71.

6

He Comes as a Thief

Although the scriptures indicate the time of the coming of the Promised One, we also read, "If you will not awake, I will come like a thief, and you will not know at what hour I will come upon you."* By using the conditional phrase, "if you will not awake," the scriptures anticipate that the majority of people will be asleep when the Promised One comes like a thief in the night, that He will be inside the house, and that those in the house will be unaware. The verses in both the Bible and the Qur'án indicate that He will come "while they are sunk in heedlessness and while they believe not." That is, the Promised One will come secretly, at a time when the people are "heedless" and occupied with their own fancies. Then He will be in their midst, and the people will be unaware. For this reason, in addition to the parables given in the holy scriptures, the advice is to be "awake," to "take heed," to "watch and pray," and to be "attentive" and not "heedless."

When Bahá'u'lláh appeared, the Promised One was in the world, and as was the case in previous Dispensations, the people were unaware of His presence. Even among those who were informed, the majority of them did not recognize the Manifestation of God.

---

* Revelation 3:3.

Some of the verses from the Holy Bible concerning the coming of the Promised One when people are unaware:

Mark 13:33–37 – Take ye heed, watch and pray: for ye know not when the time is.

For the Son of Man is as a man taking a far journey, who left his house, and gave authority to his servants, and to every man his work, and commanded the porter to watch.

Watch ye therefore: for ye know not when the master of the house cometh, at even, or at midnight, or at the cockcrowing, or in the morning: Lest coming suddenly he find you sleeping.

And what I say unto you I say unto all, Watch.

Luke 17:20–21 — Being asked by the Pharisees when the kingdom of God was coming, he answered them, "The kingdom of God is not coming with signs to be observed; nor will they say, 'Lo, here it is!' or 'There!' for behold, the kingdom of God is in the midst of you."

Luke 12:37–40 – Blessed are those servants, whom the lord when he cometh shall find watching: verily I say unto you, that he shall gird himself, and make them to sit down to meat, and will come forth and serve them.

And if he shall come in the second watch, or come in the third watch, and find them so, blessed are those servants.

And this know, that if the good man of the house had known what hour the thief would come, he would have watched, and not have suffered his house to be broken through.

Be ye therefore ready also: for the Son of man cometh at an hour when ye think not.

Revelation 3:3 – If you will not awake, I will come like a thief, and you will not know at what hour I will come upon you.

Revelation 16:15 – "Lo, I am coming like a thief! Blessed is he who is awake, keeping his garments that he may not go naked and be seen exposed!"

2ⁿᵈ Peter 3:10 – But the day of the Lord will come like a thief in the night; . . .

1ˢᵗ Thessalonians 5:2–3 – For you yourselves know well that the day of the Lord will come like a thief in the night. When people say, "There is peace and security," then sudden destruction will come upon them as travail comes upon a woman with child, and there will be no escape.

Matthew 24:42–44 – Watch therefore, for you do not know on what day your Lord is coming. But know this, that if the householder had known in what part of the night the thief was coming, he would have watched and would not have let this house be broken into. Therefore you also must be ready; for the Son of man is coming at an hour you do not expect.

Matthew 25:1–13 – Then the kingdom of heaven shall be compared to ten maidens who took their lamps and went to meet the bridegroom. Five of them were foolish, and five were wise. For when the foolish took their lamps, they took no oil with them; but the wise took flasks of oil with their lamps. As the bridegroom was delayed, they all slumbered and slept. But at midnight there was a cry, "Behold, the bridegroom! Come out to meet him." Then all those maidens rose and trimmed their lamps. And the foolish said to the wise, "Give us some of your oil, for our lamps are going out." But the wise replied, "Perhaps there will not be enough for us and for you; go rather to the dealers and buy for yourselves." And while they went to buy, the bridegroom came, and those who were ready went in with him to the marriage feast; and the door was shut. Afterward the other maidens came also, saying, "Lord, lord, open to us." But he replied, "Truly, I say to you, I do not know you." Watch therefore, for you know neither the day nor the hour.

Some of the verses from the Holy Qur'án concerning the coming of the Promised One when people are unaware:

Sura 7:186 – Al-A'ráf – They will ask thee of the Hour—for what time is its coming fixed! Say: The knowledge of it is only with my Lord: none shall manifest it in its time but He: it is the burden of the Heavens and of the Earth: not otherwise than on a sudden will it come on you.

Sura 12:107 – Yúsuf – What! Are they sure that the overwhelming chastisement of God shall not come upon them, or that that Hour shall not come upon them suddenly, while they are unaware?

Sura 19:40 – Maryam – Warn them of the day of sighing when the decree shall be accomplished, while they are sunk in heedlessness and while they believe not.

Sura 22:7 – Al-Haj – And that "the Hour" will indeed come—there is no doubt of it—and that God will wake up to life those who are in the tombs.

Sura 22:54 – Al-Haj – But the Infidels will not cease to doubt concerning it, until "the Hour" come suddenly upon them, or until the chastisement of the day of desolation come upon them.

Sura 40:61 – Gháfir – Aye, "the Hour" will surely come: there is no doubt of it: but most men believe it not.

Some of the passages from the Bahá'í sacred texts concerning the coming of the Promised One when people are unaware:

Day and night ye have been calling upon your Lord, the Omnipotent, but when He came from the heaven of eternity in His great glory, ye turned aside from Him and remained sunk in heedlessness.

Bahá'u'lláh, *Tablets of Bahá'u'lláh*, p. 9.

Say: O ye that envy Me and seek My hurt! The fury of your wrath against Me confound you! Lo, the Daystar of Glory hath risen above the horizon of My Revelation, and enveloped with its radiance the whole of mankind. And yet, behold how ye have shut out yourselves from its splendor and are sunk in utter heedlessness. Have mercy upon yourselves, and repudiate not the claim of Him Whose truth ye have already recognized, and be not of them that transgress.

Bahá'u'lláh, *Gleanings from the Writings of Bahá'u'lláh*, no. 121.1.

. . . and still the people, even as the Messiah saith, slept on: for the day of the Manifestation, when the Lord of Hosts descended, found them wrapped in the slumber of unknowing. As He saith in the Gospel, My coming is even as when the thief is in the house, and the goodman of the house watcheth not.

'Abdu'l-Bahá, *Selections from the Writings of 'Abdu'l-Bahá*, no. 17.1.

. . . Christ said: "Perhaps I shall come when you are yet asleep, for the coming of the Son of man is like the coming of a thief." Perhaps the thief will be in the house, and the owner will not know it.

'Abdu'l-Bahá, *Some Answered Questions*, p. 112.

All the people of the world are buried in the graves of nature, or are slumbering, heedless and unaware. Just as Christ saith: "I may come when you are not aware. The coming of the Son of Man is like the coming of a thief into a house, the owner of which is utterly unaware."

'Abdu'l-Bahá, *Selections from the Writings of 'Abdu'l-Bahá*, no. 168.1.

7

He Comes with a New Name

The holy scriptures indicate that at "the time of the end," the One expected would come with a new name. This often comes as a surprise, especially to Christians, many of whom expect Christ to return to earth in the same body, with the same name, and even speaking the same words as He did the first time. In fact, the scriptures clearly warn us about someone coming, assuming Christ's name, and saying, "I am the Christ." They clearly indicate that "another Counselor" with a "new name" would come, and they also indicate what that new name would be.

Several verses in the Bible refer to the coming of *"the glory of God"* or *"the glory of the Lord."* The Qur'án says that after the second trumpet blast, the earth shall shine with *"the light of her Lord."* In Arabic, these words translate as *Bahá'u'lláh*—the title assumed by the Founder of the Bahá'í Faith. In some of the older Arabic versions of the Bible,* the words *"glory of the Lord"* are translated as *"Bahá'u'lláh."* Bahá'u'lláh is the new name of the Promised One.

---

* The New Testament Arabic Bible was published in London on behalf of the Eastern Churches by Richard Watts, 1833, and the other was also published on behalf of the Eastern Churches by William Watts in 1958.

Some of the verses from the Holy Bible concerning the Promised One coming with a new name (italics added):

Isaiah 62:2 – The nations shall see your vindication, and all the kings your glory; and you shall be called by a new name which the mouth of the Lord will give.

Revelation 2:17 – He who has an ear, let him hear what the Spirit says to the churches. To him who conquers I will give some of the hidden manna, and I will give him a white stone, with a new name written on the stone which no one knows except him who receives it.

John 14:16–17 – And I will pray the Father, and he shall give you *another* Comforter, that he may abide with you for ever; Even the Spirit of truth; whom the world cannot receive, because it seeth him not, neither knoweth him: but ye know him; for he dwelleth with you, and shall be in you.

John 11:40 – Jesus saith unto her, Said I not unto thee, that, if thou wouldest believe, thou shouldest see *the glory of God?*

Ezekiel 43:2–5 – And behold, *the glory of the God* of Israel came from the east; and the sound of his coming was like the sound of many waters; and the earth shone with his glory.

And the vision I saw was like the vision which I had seen when he came to destroy the city, and like the vision which I had seen by the river Chebar; and I fell upon my face.

As *the glory of the Lord* entered the temple by the gate facing east, the Spirit lifted me up, and brought me into the inner court; and behold, *the glory of the Lord* filled the temple.

Acts 7:55 – But he, being full of the Holy Ghost, looked up steadfastly into heaven, and saw *the glory of God,* and Jesus standing on the right hand of God.

Revelation of Saint John the Divine: 21:22–24 – And I saw no temple therein: for the Lord God Almighty and the Lamb are the temple of it.

And the city had no need of the sun, neither of the moon, to shine in it: for *the glory of God* did lighten it, and the Lamb is the light thereof.

And the nations of them which are saved shall walk in the light of it: and the kings of the earth do bring their glory and honour into it.

Philippians 2:11 – And that every tongue should confess that Jesus Christ is Lord, to *the glory of God* the Father.

Isaiah 40:5 – And *the glory of the Lord* shall be revealed, and all flesh shall see it together, for the mouth of the Lord has spoken.

Luke 2:9 – And, lo, the angel of the Lord came upon them, and *the glory of the Lord* shone round about them: and they were sore afraid.

Matthew 24:4–5 – And Jesus answered them, "Take heed that no one leads you astray. For many will come in my name, saying, 'I am the Christ,' and they will lead many astray."

Matthew 24:23 – "Then if any one says to you, 'Lo, here is the Christ!' or 'There he is!' do not believe it."

Revelation 3:11–12 – I am coming soon; hold fast what you have, so that no one may seize your crown. He who conquers, I will make him a pillar in the temple of God; never shall he go out of it, and I will write on him the name of my God, and the name of the city of my God, the new Jerusalem which comes down from my God out of heaven, and my own new name.

Revelation 21:10–11 – And he carried me away in the spirit to a great and high mountain, and shewed me that great city, the holy Jerusalem, descending out of heaven from God, Having *the glory of God:* and her light was like unto a stone most precious, even like a jasper stone, clear as crystal . . .

Some of the verses from the Holy Qur'án and Hadíth concerning the Promised One coming with a new name:

Sura 39:68–69 – Al-Zumar – And there shall be a blast on the trumpet, and all who are in the Heavens and all who are in the Earth shall expire, save those whom God shall vouchsafe to live. Then shall there be another blast on it, and lo! arising they shall gaze around them: And the earth shall shine with the light of her Lord,* and the Book shall be set. . . .

Sura 69:13–17 – Al-Háqqah – But when one blast shall be blown on the trumpet, And the earth and the mountains shall be upheaved, and shall both be crushed into dust at a single crushing, On that day the woe that must come suddenly shall suddenly come, And the heaven shall cleave asunder, for on that day it shall be fragile; And the angels shall be on its sides, and over them on that day eight shall bear up the throne of thy Lord.

Muhyi'd-Din-i-'Arabí, quoted in Nabíl-i-A'zam, The Dawn-breakers, p. 49 – 'In His name, the name of the Guardian ['Alí] precedeth that of the Prophet [Muḥammad].'†

---

* "Light of her Lord" is in reference to Bahá'u'lláh, as Bahá means "glory," "light," or "splendor,"—the second part of Bahá'u'lláh's name "of the Lord" is equivalent to "of her Lord."

† Bahá'u'lláh's predecessor was a Manifestation of God in His own rights, and His given name was 'Alí-Muḥammad.

Some of the passages from the Bahá'í sacred texts concerning the Promised One coming with a new name:

Say, O followers of the Son! Have ye shut out yourselves from Me by reason of My Name? Wherefore ponder ye not in your hearts? Day and night ye have been calling upon your Lord, the Omnipotent, but when He came from the heaven of eternity in His great glory, ye turned aside from Him and remained sunk in heedlessness.

Bahá'u'lláh, Tablets of Bahá'u'lláh, p. 9.

Say, He Who is the Exponent of the hidden Name hath appeared, did ye but know it. He Whose advent hath been foretold in the heavenly Scriptures is come, could ye but understand it. The world's horizon is illumined by the splendours of this Most Great Revelation. Haste ye with radiant hearts and be not of them that are bereft of understanding. The appointed Hour hath struck and mankind is laid low. Unto this bear witness the honoured servants of God.

Bahá'u'lláh, Tablets of Bahá'u'lláh, p. 244.

He was formally designated Bahá'u'lláh, an appellation specifically recorded in the Persian Bayán, signifying at once the glory, the light and the splendor of God, and was styled the "Lord of Lords," the "Most Great Name," the "Ancient Beauty," the "Pen of the Most High," the "Hidden Name," the "Preserved Treasure," "He Whom God will make manifest," the "Most Great Light," the "All-Highest Horizon," the "Most Great Ocean," the "Supreme Heaven," the "Pre-Existent Root," the "Self-subsistent," the "Day-Star of the Universe," the "Great Announcement," the "Speaker on Sinai," the "Sifter of Men," the "Wronged One of the World," the "Desire of the Nations," the "Lord of the Covenant," the "Tree beyond which there is no passing."

Shoghi Effendi, God Passes By, p. 94.

To Him Isaiah, the greatest of the Jewish prophets, had alluded as the *"Glory of the Lord,"* the *"Everlasting Father,"* the *"Prince of Peace,"* the *"Wonderful,"* the *"Counsellor,"* the *"Rod come forth out of the stem of Jesse"* and the *"Branch grown out of His roots,"* Who *"shall be established upon the throne of David,"* Who *"will come with strong hand,"* Who *"shall judge among the nations,"* Who *"shall smite the earth with the rod of His mouth, and with the breath of His lips slay the wicked,"* and Who *"shall assemble the outcasts of Israel, and gather together the dispersed of Judah from the four corners of the earth."* Of Him David had sung in his Psalms, acclaiming Him as the *"Lord of Hosts"* and the *"King of Glory."*

Shoghi Effendi, God Passes By, pp. 94–95.

8

The Unity of God
and His Manifestations

All the Messengers or Manifestations of God have claimed to be one and the same. They all came from One God to fulfill a specific mission at a specific time in the history of mankind's evolution. They all reflect God's will and purpose in accordance to the needs or requirements of the time. As the Qur'án says, "To each age its Book. What He pleaseth will God abrogate or confirm."*

All the Messengers or Manifestations of God have praised each other, all have glorified each other, all have prophesied about one another. They all explained in different ways that They are, in reality, one and the same—as Jesus says, "If you believed Moses, you would believe me, for he wrote of me."† He also said: "Think not that I am come to destroy the law, or the prophets: I am not come to destroy, but to fulfil."‡ The Qur'án reads, "we make no distinction between any of His Apostles."§ Similarly, Bahá'u'lláh says: "Beware, O

---

* Sura 13:38–39.
† John 5:46.
‡ Matthew 5:17.
§ Sura 2:285.

believers in the Unity of God, lest ye be tempted to make any distinction between any of the Manifestations of His Cause, or to discriminate against the signs that have accompanied and proclaimed their Revelation."* He also says, "That they differ one from another is to be attributed to the varying requirements of the ages in which they were promulgated."† Bahá'u'lláh emphasizes the divine unity and oneness of religion of God by saying, "This is the changeless Faith of God, eternal in the past, eternal in the future."‡

To obey the Manifestations of God is to obey God Himself, and to turn away from Them is to turn away from God.

---

* Bahá'u'lláh, *Gleanings from the Writings of Bahá'u'lláh*, no. 24.1.
† Ibid., no. 132.1.
‡ Ibid., no. 70.2.

Some of the verses in the Holy Bible concerning the unity of God and His Manifestations:

Revelation 1:8 – "I am the Alpha and the Omega," says the Lord God, "who is and who was and who is to come, the Almighty."

Deuteronomy 33:2 – The Lord came from Sinai, and dawned from Seir upon us; he shone forth from Mount Paran, he came from the ten thousands of holy ones, with flaming fire at his right hand.

Deuteronomy 18:17–19 – And the Lord said to me "I will raise up for them a prophet like you from among their brethren; and I will put my words in his mouth, and he shall speak to them all that I command him. And whoever will not give heed to my words which he shall speak in my name, I myself will require it of him."

John 10:16 – "And I have other sheep, that are not of this fold; I must bring them also, and they will heed my voice. So there shall be one flock, one shepherd."

John 5:46 – "If you believed Moses, you would believe me, for he wrote of me. But if you do not believe his writings, how will you believe my words?"

Matthew 5:17 – "Think not that I am come to destroy the law, or the prophets: I am not come to destroy, but to fulfil."

John 5:22–23 – For the Father judgeth no man, but hath committed all judgment unto the Son: That all men should honour the Son, even as they honour the Father. He that honoureth not the Son honoureth not the Father which hath sent him.

John 10:30 – "I and the Father are one."

John 8:56–58 – "Your father Abraham rejoiced that he was to see my day; he saw it and was glad." The Jews then said to him, "You are not yet fifty years old, and have you seen Abraham?" Jesus said to them, "Truly, truly, I say to you, before Abraham was, I am."

The Unity of God and His Manifestations

Some of the verses in the Holy Qur'án and Hadíth concerning the unity of God and His Manifestations:

Sura 2:285 – Al-Baqarah – The apostle believeth in that which hath been sent down from his Lord, as do the faithful also. Each one believeth in God, and His Angels, and His Books, and His Apostles: we make no distinction between any of His Apostles.

Sura 2:130 – Al-Baqarah – Say ye: 'We believe in God, and that which hath been sent down to us, and that which hath been sent down to Abraham and Ismael and Isaac and Jacob and the tribes: and that which hath been given to Moses and to Jesus, and that which was given to the prophets from their Lord. No difference do we make between any of them: and to God are we resigned (Muslims).'

Sura 4:149–151 – Al-Nisá' – Of a truth they who believe not on God and his Apostles, and seek to separate God from his Apostles, and say, "Some we believe, and some we believe not," and desire to take a middle way;

These! They are veritable infidels! And for the infidels have we prepared a shameful punishment.

And they who believe on God and his Apostles, and make no difference between them—these! we will bestow on them their reward at last. God is Gracious, Merciful!

Sura 4:161 – Al-Nisá' – Verily we have revealed to thee as we revealed to Noah and the Prophets after him, and as we revealed to Abraham, and Ismail, and

113

Isaac, and Jacob, and the tribes, and Jesus, and Job, and Jonah, and Aaron, and Solomon; and to David gave we Psalms.

Sura 2:100 – Al-Baqarah – Whatever verses we cancel, or cause thee to forget, we bring a better or its like. Knowest thou not that God hath power over all things?

Sura 2:254 – Al-Baqarah – Some of the apostles we have endowed more highly than others: Those to whom God hath spoken, He hath raised to the loftiest grade, and to Jesus the Son of Mary we gave manifest signs, and we strengthened him with the Holy Spirit.

Sura 42:11 – Al-Shúra – To you hath He prescribed the faith which He commanded unto Noah, and which we have revealed to thee, and which we commanded unto Abraham and Moses and Jesus, saying, 'Observe this faith, and be not divided into sects therein.'

Sura 5:50–51 – Al-Má'idah – And in the footsteps of the prophets caused we Jesus, the son of Mary, to follow, confirming the law which was before him: and we gave him the Evangel with its guidance and light, confirmatory of the preceding Law; a guidance and warning to those who fear God;—

And that the people of the Evangel may judge according to what God hath sent down therein. And whoso will not judge by what God hath sent down— such are the perverse.

Sura 5:72 – Al-Má'idah – Say: O People of the Book! ye have no ground to stand on, until ye observe the Law and the Evangel, and that which hath been sent down to you from your Lord.

Ḥadíth, quoted in Bahá'u'lláh, Gleanings from the Writings of Bahá'u'lláh, no. 27.4 – "Manifold and mysterious is My relationship with God. I am He, Himself and He is I, Myself, except that I am that I am, and He is that He is."

Ḥadíth, quoted in Bahá'u'lláh, Gleanings from the Writings of Bahá'u'lláh, no. 27.4 – "There is no distinction whatsoever between Thee and Them, except that They are Thy Servants."

Ḥadíth, quoted in Bahá'u'lláh, The Book of Certitude, ¶161 – "I am all the Prophets." "I am the first Adam, Noah, Moses, and Jesus."

Some of the passages in the Bahá'í sacred texts concerning the unity of God and His Manifestations:

This is the changeless Faith of God, eternal in the past, eternal in the future.

Bahá'u'lláh, The Kitáb-í-Aqdas, ¶181.

The essence of belief in Divine unity consisteth in regarding Him Who is the Manifestation of God and Him Who is the invisible, the inaccessible, the unknowable Essence as one and the same. By this is meant that whatever pertaineth to the former, all His acts and doings, whatever He ordaineth or forbiddeth, should be considered, in all their aspects, and under all circumstances, and without any reservation, as identical with the Will of God Himself. This is the loftiest station to which a true believer in the unity of God can ever hope to attain. Blessed is the man that reacheth this station, and is of them that are steadfast in their belief.

Bahá'u'lláh, *Gleanings from the Writings of Bahá'u'lláh*,

no. 84.4.

The door of the knowledge of the Ancient Being hath ever been, and will continue for ever to be, closed in the face of men. No man's understanding shall ever gain access unto His holy court. As a token of His mercy, however, and as a proof of His loving-kindness, He hath manifested unto men the Daystars of His divine guidance, the Symbols of His divine unity, and hath ordained the knowledge of these sanctified Beings to be identical with the knowledge of His own Self. Whoso recognizeth them hath recognized God. Whoso hearkeneth to their call, hath hearkened to the Voice of God, and whoso testifieth to the truth of their Revelation, hath testified to the truth of God Himself. Whoso turneth away from them, hath turned away from God, and whoso disbelieveth in them, hath disbelieved in God. Every one of them is the Way of God that connecteth this world with the realms above, and the Standard of His Truth unto every one in the kingdoms of earth and heaven. They are the Manifestations of God amidst men, the evidences of His Truth, and the signs of His glory.

Bahá'u'lláh, Gleanings from the Writings of Bahá'u'lláh, no. 21.1.

Know thou assuredly that the essence of all the Prophets of God is one and the same. Their unity is absolute. God, the Creator, saith: There is no distinction whatsoever among the Bearers of My Message. They all have but one purpose; their secret is the same secret. To prefer one in honor to another, to exalt certain ones above the rest, is in no wise to be permitted. Every true Prophet hath regarded His Message as fundamentally the same as the Revelation of every other Prophet gone before Him.

Bahá'u'lláh, Gleanings from the Writings of Bahá'u'lláh, no. 34.3.

The Bearers of the Trust of God are made manifest unto the peoples of the earth as the Exponents of a new Cause and the Revealers of a new Message. . . .

These Manifestations of God have each a twofold station. One is the station of pure abstraction and essential unity. In this respect, if thou callest them all by one name, and dost ascribe to them the same attributes, thou hast not erred from the truth. . . .

. . . The other station is the station of distinction, and pertaineth to the world of creation, and to the limitations thereof. In this respect, each Manifestation of God hath a distinct individuality, a definitely prescribed mission, a predestined revelation, and specially designated limitations. Each one of them is known by a different name, is characterized by a special attribute, fulfils a definite mission, and is entrusted with a particular Revelation.

Bahá'u'lláh, Gleanings from the Writings of Bahá'u'lláh,
nos. 22.1, 22.2, 22.4.

It is because of this difference in their station and mission that the words and utterances flowing from these Wellsprings of divine knowledge appear to diverge and differ. Otherwise, in the eyes of them that are initiated into the mysteries of divine wisdom, all their utterances are in reality but the expressions of one Truth. As most of the people have failed to appreciate those stations to which We have referred, they therefore feel perplexed and dismayed at the varying utterances pronounced by Manifestations that are essentially one and the same.

It hath ever been evident that all these divergences of utterance are attributable to differences of station. Thus, viewed from the standpoint of their oneness and sublime detachment, the attributes of Godhead, Divinity, Supreme Singleness, and Inmost Essence, have been and are applicable to those Essences of being, inasmuch as they all abide on the throne of divine Revelation, and are established upon the seat of divine Concealment. Through their appearance the Revelation of God is made manifest, and by their countenance the Beauty of God is revealed. Thus it is that the accents of God Himself have been heard uttered by these Manifestations of the divine Being.

Bahá'u'lláh, The Book of Certitude, ¶192–93.

Beware, O believers in the Unity of God, lest ye be tempted to make any distinction between any of the Manifestations of His Cause, or to discriminate against the signs that have accompanied and proclaimed their Revelation. This indeed is the true meaning of Divine Unity, if ye be of them that apprehend and believe this truth. Be ye assured, moreover, that the works and acts of each and every one of these Manifestations of God, nay whatever pertaineth unto them, and whatsoever they may manifest in the future, are all ordained by God, and are a reflection of His Will and Purpose. Whoso maketh the slightest possible difference between their persons, their words, their messages, their acts and manners, hath indeed disbelieved in God, hath repudiated His signs, and betrayed the Cause of His Messengers.

Bahá'u'lláh, *Gleanings from the Writings of Bahá'u'lláh*, no. 24.1.

He, the Revealer of the unseen Beauty, addressing one day His disciples, referred unto His passing and, kindling in their hearts the fire of bereavement, said unto them: "I go away and come again unto you." And in another place He said: "I go and another will come, Who will tell you all that I have not told you, and will fulfill all that I have said." Both these sayings have but one meaning, were ye to ponder upon the Manifestations of the Unity of God with Divine insight.

Every discerning observer will recognize that in the Dispensation of the Qur'án both the Book and the Cause of Jesus were confirmed. As to the matter of names, Muḥammad, Himself, declared: "I am Jesus." He recognized the truth of the signs, prophecies, and words of Jesus, and testified that they were all of God. In this sense, neither the person of Jesus nor His writings hath differed from that of Muḥammad and of His holy Book, inasmuch as both have championed the Cause of God, uttered His praise, and revealed His commandments. Thus it is that Jesus, Himself, declared: "I go away and come again unto you." Consider the sun. Were it to say now, "I am the sun of yesterday," it would speak the truth.

Bahá'u'lláh, *Gleanings from the Writings of Bahá'u'lláh*, nos. 13.5–6.

These sanctified Mirrors, these Daysprings of ancient glory, are, one and all, the Exponents on earth of Him Who is the central Orb of the universe, its Essence and ultimate Purpose. From Him proceed their knowledge and power; from Him is derived their sovereignty. . . . These Tabernacles of Holiness, these Primal Mirrors which reflect the light of unfading glory, are but expressions of Him Who is the Invisible of the Invisibles. By the revelation of these Gems of Divine virtue all the names and attributes of God, such as knowledge and power, sovereignty and dominion, mercy and wisdom, glory, bounty, and grace, are made manifest . . . all the Prophets of God, His well-favored, His holy and chosen Messengers are, without exception, the bearers of His names, and the embodiments of His attributes. They only differ in the intensity of their revelation, and the comparative potency of their light.

Bahá'u'lláh, *Gleanings from the Writings of Bahá'u'lláh*, no. 19.3–4.

The Purpose of the one true God, exalted be His glory, in revealing Himself unto men is to lay bare those gems that lie hidden within the mine of their true and inmost selves. That the divers communions of the earth, and the manifold systems of religious belief, should never be allowed to foster the feelings of animosity among men, is, in this Day, of the essence of the Faith of God and His Religion. These principles and laws, these firmly established and mighty systems, have proceeded from one Source, and are the rays of one Light. That they differ one from another is to be attributed to the varying requirements of the ages in which they were promulgated.

Bahá'u'lláh, *Gleanings from the Writings of Bahá'u'lláh*, no. 132.1.

O Jews! If ye be intent on crucifying once again Jesus, the Spirit of God, put Me to death, for He hath once more, in My person, been made manifest unto you. Deal with Me as ye wish, for I have vowed to lay down My life in the path of God. I will fear no one, though the powers of earth and heaven be leagued against Me. Followers of the Gospel! If ye cherish the desire to slay Muḥammad, the Apostle of God, seize Me and put an end to My life, for I am He, and My Self is His Self. Do unto Me as ye like, for the deepest longing of Mine heart is to attain the presence of My Best-Beloved in His Kingdom of Glory. Such is the Divine decree, if ye know it. Followers of Muḥammad! If it be your wish to riddle with your shafts the breast of Him

Who hath caused His Book the Bayán to be sent down unto you, lay hands on Me and persecute Me, for I am His Well-Beloved, the revelation of His own Self, though My name be not His name. I have come in the shadows of the clouds of glory, and am invested by God with invincible sovereignty. He, verily, is the Truth, the Knower of things unseen. I, verily, anticipate from you the treatment ye have accorded unto Him that came before Me. To this all things, verily, witness, if ye be of those who hearken.

Bahá'u'lláh, *Gleanings from the Writings of Bahá'u'lláh*, no. 47.1.

The knowledge of Him, Who is the Origin of all things, and attainment unto Him, are impossible save through knowledge of, and attainment unto, these luminous Beings who proceed from the Sun of Truth. By attaining, therefore, to the presence of these holy Luminaries, the "Presence of God" Himself is attained. From their knowledge, the knowledge of God is revealed, and from the light of their countenance, the splendor of the Face of God is made manifest. Through the manifold attributes of these Essences of Detachment, Who are both the first and the last, the seen and the hidden, it is made evident that He Who is the Sun of Truth is "the First and the Last, the Seen, and the Hidden" [Qur'án 57:3]. Likewise the other lofty names and exalted attributes of God. Therefore, whosoever, and in whatever Dispensation, hath recognized and attained unto the presence of these glorious, these resplendent and most excellent Luminaries, hath verily attained unto the "Presence of God" Himself, and entered the city of eternal and immortal life.

Bahá'u'lláh, The Book of Certitude, ¶151.

"Know of a certainty," Bahá'u'lláh explains in this connection, *"that in every Dispensation the light of Divine Revelation hath been vouchsafed to men in direct proportion to their spiritual capacity. Consider the sun. How feeble its rays the moment it appeareth above the horizon. How gradually its warmth and potency*

121

increase as it approacheth its zenith, enabling meanwhile all created things to adapt themselves to the growing intensity of its light. How steadily it declineth until it reacheth its setting point. Were it all of a sudden to manifest the energies latent within it, it would no doubt cause injury to all created things . . . In like manner, if the Sun of Truth were suddenly to reveal, at the earliest stages of its manifestation, the full measure of the potencies which the providence of the Almighty hath bestowed upon it, the earth of human understanding would waste away and be consumed; for men's hearts would neither sustain the intensity of its revelation, nor be able to mirror forth the radiance of its light. Dismayed and overpowered, they would cease to exist."

Bahá'u'lláh, quoted in Shoghi Effendi,
The World Order of Bahá'u'lláh, p. 117.

"God hath sent down His Messengers to succeed to Moses and Jesus, and He will continue to do so till 'the end that hath no end'; so that His grace may, from the heaven of Divine bounty, be continually vouchsafed to mankind."

Bahá'u'lláh, quoted in Shoghi Effendi,
The World Order of Bahá'u'lláh, p. 116.

The holy Manifestations Who have been the Sources or Founders of the various religious systems were united and agreed in purpose and teaching. Abraham, Moses, Zoroaster, Buddha, Jesus, Muḥammad, the Báb and Bahá'u'lláh are one in spirit and reality. Moreover, each Prophet fulfilled the promise of the One Who came before Him and, likewise, Each announced the One Who would follow.

'Abdu'l-Bahá, *The Promulgation of Universal Peace*, p. 276.

Religion, moreover, is not a series of beliefs, a set of customs; religion is the teachings of the Lord God, teachings which constitute the very life of humankind, which urge high thoughts upon the mind, refine the character, and lay the groundwork for man's everlasting honor.

'Abdu'l-Bahá, *Selections from the Writings of 'Abdu'l-Bahá*,
no. 23.6.

The different religions have one truth underlying them; therefore, their reality is one.

Each of the divine religions embodies two kinds of ordinances. The first is those which concern spiritual susceptibilities, the development of moral principles and the quickening of the conscience of man. . . .

The second kind of ordinances in the divine religions is those which relate to the material affairs of humankind. These are the material or accidental laws which are subject to change in each day of manifestation, according to exigencies of the time, conditions and differing capacities of humanity. . . .

In brief, every one of the divine religions contains essential ordinances, which are not subject to change, and material ordinances, which are abrogated according to the exigencies of time.

'Abdu'l-Bahá, *The Promulgation of Universal Peace*,
pp. 146–47.

All these holy, divine Manifestations are one. They have served one God, promulgated the same truth, founded the same institutions and reflected the same light. Their appearances have been successive and correlated; each One has announced and extolled the One Who was to follow, and all laid the foundation of reality. They summoned and invited the people to love and made the human world a mirror of the Word of God. Therefore, the divine religions They established have one foundation; Their teachings, proofs and evidences are one; in name and form They differ, but in reality They agree and are the same. These holy Manifestations have been as the coming of springtime in the world. Although the springtime of this year is designated by another name according to the changing calendar, yet as regards its life and quickening it is the same as the springtime of last year. . . .

Likewise, the divine religions of the holy Manifestations of God are in reality one, though in name and nomenclature they differ. Man must be a lover of the light, no matter from what dayspring it may appear . . . Attachment to the lantern is not loving the light.

'Abdu'l-Bahá, *The Promulgation of Universal Peace*, pp. 209–10.

Nor does the Bahá'í Revelation, claiming as it does to be the culmination of a prophetic cycle and the fulfillment of the promise of all ages, attempt, under any circumstances, to invalidate those first and everlasting principles that animate and underlie the religions that have preceded it. The God-given authority, vested in each one of them, it admits and establishes as its firmest and ultimate basis. It regards them in no other light except as different stages in the eternal history and constant evolution of one religion, Divine and indivisible, of which it itself forms but an integral part.

Shoghi Effendi, *The World Order of Baha'u'llah*, p. 11.

— PART 2 —

SOME CHRISTIAN TOPICS

9

The Word of God

Jesus says, "In the beginning was the Word and the Word was with God, and the Word was God."* He also says, "Heaven and earth shall pass away; but my words shall not pass away."† As the "Word was God," and God exists from the beginning that has no beginning, therefore "His Word" existed from the beginning that has no beginning. Bahá'u'lláh says, *"Know assuredly that God's creation hath existed from eternity, and will continue to exist forever. Its beginning hath had no beginning, and its end knoweth no end. His name, the Creator, presupposeth a creation, even as His title, the Lord of Men, must involve the existence of a servant."‡* Bahá'u'lláh further states, *"That which hath been in existence had existed before, but not in the form thou seest today."§*

Hence, this contingent world was not the beginning of God's creation, nor will it be the end, as God has no beginning or end. When Christ said, "heaven and earth shall pass away; but my words shall not pass away;" this is of course true, because the "Word was God," and God was from the beginning that has

---

* John 1:1.
† Luke 21:33.
‡ Bahá'u'lláh, *Gleanings from the Writings of Bahá'u'lláh*, no. 78.1.
§ Bahá'u'lláh, *Tablets of Bahá'u'lláh*, p. 140.

no beginning, and "His Word" will remain to the end that has no end, even after the passing away of "heaven and earth." Furthermore, Bahá'u'lláh says that the Word of God was *"the Cause of the entire creation, while all else besides His Word are but the creatures and the effects thereof."**

There was never a time when the Word of God and His bounties were withheld from the world of being, nor was there ever a time when the Creator did not have a creation. 'Abdu'l-Bahá explains this by saying, *". . . the earth has not always existed, but the world of existence has always been, for the universe is not limited to this terrestrial globe."†* He further states, *"The Creator always had a creation; the rays have always shone and gleamed from the reality of the sun, for without the rays the sun would be opaque darkness. The names and attributes of God require the existence of beings, and the Eternal Bounty does not cease. If it were to, it would be contrary to the perfections of God."‡*

The reality of Christ, as well as the reality of all the Manifestations of God, is the Word of God, which is eternal and has no beginning or end. Through the instrumentality of the Divine Messengers, or Manifestations of God, mankind is enabled to receive the Word of God. 'Abdu'l-Bahá describes the Word of God before manifesting itself through the Divine Manifestations by saying, "Before appearing in the human form, the Word of God was in the utmost sanctity and glory, existing in perfect beauty and splendor in the height of its magnificence. When through the wisdom of God the Most High it shone from the heights of glory in the world of the body, the Word of God, through this body, became oppressed . . ."§

The Word of God was revealed in stages through the Prophets, or Manifestations of God. It is likened to the rain of spring; mankind continually needs

---

* Ibid.
† 'Abdu'l-Bahá, *Some Answered Questions*, p. 151.
‡ Ibid., p. 181.
§ Ibid., p. 117.

the rain for its sustenance, growth, and development. The Word of God will always produce results; however, the results or reaction will depend on the type of soil or substance the rain falls upon. The early Hebrew prophets, such as Abraham, Noah, and Jacob, guided the people by the Word of God. Then Moses appeared, spoke the Word of God, and brought about new laws, raising man to a higher stage. After Him, the prophets of Israel continued to guide the people with the Word of God—Isaiah, Jeremiah, Ezekiel, and others. When Jesus Christ began His ministry, He represented the Word of God for His day, and so did Muḥammad, the Báb, and Bahá'u'lláh.

Bahá'ís call this periodic dispensation of God's will and purpose for man "progressive revelation" or "evolution" of religion. In every age, the Word of God is renewed and regenerated by the appearance of a new Messenger, or Manifestation of God, whose coming brings about a new spiritual spring-time, new teachings, and a divinely revealed new Revelation or religion from God suited to the requirements of the time. As Bahá'u'lláh says, *"It hath been decreed by Us that the Word of God and all the potentialities thereof shall be manifested unto men in strict conformity with such conditions as have been foreordained by Him Who is the All-Knowing, the All-Wise . . . Should the Word be allowed to release suddenly all the energies latent within it, no man could sustain the weight of so mighty a revelation . . . ."* All the revealed religions from God have been given to man in direct proportion to mankind's capacities and requirements of the age in which humanity was living. The progress of mankind throughout history can be compared to the life-span of a human being. As 'Abdu'l-Baha says, ". . . *there are periods and stages in the collective life of humanity. At one time it was passing through its stage of childhood, at another its period of youth, but now it has entered its long-predicted phase of*

---

* Bahá'u'lláh, quoted by Shoghi Effendi in *The World Order of Bahá'u'lláh*, p. 164.

maturity. . . ."* Shoghi Effendi, Guardian of the Bahá'í Faith, writes, "These divinely-revealed religions, as a close observer has graphically expressed it, 'are doomed not to die, but to be reborn . . . Does not the child succumb in the youth and the youth in the man; yet neither child nor youth perishes?'"† For this reason, the Divine Educators bring to mankind at every age the "Word of God" in proportion to the needs and requirements of the time. As Jesus said: "I have fed you with milk, and not with meat: for hitherto ye were not able to bear it, neither yet now are ye able."‡ The Qur'án says, "To each age its Book. What He pleaseth will God abrogate or confirm: for with Him is the source of revelation."§

The divine reality is one, and His Manifestations are one. They renew the Word of God in accordance to the requirements of the time, in a process that has no beginning and no end.

---

* 'Abdu'l-Bahá, quoted by Shoghi Effendi in *The World Order of Bahá'u'lláh*, pp. 164–65.
† Shoghi Effendi, *The World Order of Bahá'u'lláh*, p. 114.
‡ I Corinthians 3:2.
§ Sura 13:39–40.

The Word of God

Some of the verses in the Holy Bible concerning the Word of God:

John 1:1 – In the beginning was the Word, and the Word was with God, and the Word was God.

John 1:14 – And the Word became flesh and dwelt among us, full of grace and truth. . . .

Luke 21:33 – Heaven and earth shall pass away; but my words shall not pass away.

John 3:31–36 – He who comes from above is above all; he who is of the earth belongs to the earth, and of the earth he speaks; he who comes from heaven is above all. He bears witness to what he has seen and heard, yet no one receives his testimony; he who receives his testimony sets his seal to this, that God is true. For he whom God has sent utters the words of God, for it is not by measure that he gives the Spirit; the Father loves the Son, and has given all things into his hand. He who believes in the Son has eternal life. . . .

Isaiah 55:10–11 – For as the rain cometh down, and the snow from heaven, and returneth not thither, but watereth the earth, and maketh it bring forth and bud, that it may give seed to the sower, and bread to the eater: So shall my word be that goeth forth out of my mouth: it shall not return unto me void, but it shall accomplish that which I please, and it shall prosper in the thing whereto I sent it.

John 3:12–13 – If I have told you earthly things and you do not believe, how can you believe if I tell you heavenly things?

I Corinthians 3:2 – I have fed you with milk, and not with meat: for hitherto ye were not able to bear it, neither yet now are ye able.

John 16:12 – I have yet many things to say to you, but you cannot bear them now. When the Spirit of truth comes, he will guide you into all the truth.

Some of the verses in the Holy Qur'án concerning the Word of God:

Sura 3:40–41 – Ál-'Imrán – Remember when the angel said, 'O Mary! Verily God announceth to thee the Word from Him: His name shall be, Messiah Jesus the son of Mary, illustrious in this world, and in the next, and one of those who have near access to God; And He shall speak to men alike when in the cradle and when grown up; And he shall be one of the just.'

Sura 4:169 – Al-Nisá' – O ye people of the Book! overstep not bounds in your religion; and of God, speak only truth. The Messiah, Jesus, son of Mary, is only an apostle of God, and his Word which he conveyed into Mary, and a Spirit proceeding from himself. Believe therefore in God and his apostles, and say not, 'Three:' (there is a Trinity)—Forbear—it will be better for you. God is only one God! Far be it from His glory that He should have a son! His, whatever is in the Heavens, and whatever is in the Earth! And God is a sufficient Guardian.

Sura 18:109 – Al-Kahf – SAY: Should the sea become ink, to write the words of my Lord, the sea would surely fail ere the words of my Lord would fail, though we brought its like in aid.

Some of the passages from the Bahá'í sacred texts concerning the Word of God:

Every thing must needs have an origin and every building a builder. Verily, the Word of God is the cause which hath preceded the contingent world—a world which is adorned with the splendours of the Ancient of Days, yet is being renewed and regenerated at all times. Immeasurably exalted is the God of Wisdom Who hath raised this sublime structure.

Bahá'u'lláh, *Tablets of Bahá'u'lláh*,
p. 141.

Know thou, moreover, that the Word of God—exalted be His glory—is higher and far superior to that which the senses can perceive, for it is sanctified from any property or substance. It transcendeth the limitations of known elements and is exalted above all the essential and recognized substances. It became manifest without any syllable or sound and is none but the Command of God which pervadeth all created things. It hath never been withheld from the world of being. It is God's all-pervasive grace, from which all grace doth emanate. It is an entity far removed above all that hath been and shall be.

Bahá'u'lláh, *Tablets of Bahá'u'lláh*,
pp. 140–41.

When the Word of God is revealed unto all created things whoso then giveth ear and heedeth the Call is, indeed, reckoned among the most distinguished souls, though he be a carrier of ashes. And he who turneth away is accounted as the lowliest of His servants, though he be a ruler amongst men and the possessor of all the books that are in the heavens and on earth.

Bahá'u'lláh, *Tablets of Bahá'u'lláh*, p. 186.

The understanding of His words and the comprehension of the utterances of the Birds of Heaven are in no wise dependent upon human learning. They depend solely upon purity of heart, chastity of soul, and freedom of spirit.

Bahá'u'lláh, The Book of Certitude, ¶233.

None apprenhendeth the meaning of these utterances except them whose hearts are assured, whose souls have found favor with God, and whose minds are detached from all else but Him.

Bahá'u'lláh, The Book of Certitude, ¶283.

The Word of God is the king of words and its pervasive influence is incalculable. It hath ever dominated and will continue to dominate the realm of being. The Great Being saith: The Word is the master key for the whole world, inasmuch as through its potency the doors of the hearts of men, which in reality are the doors of heaven, are unlocked. No sooner had but a glimmer of its effulgent splendour shone forth upon the mirror of love than the blessed word "I am the Best-Beloved" was reflected therein. It is an ocean inexhaustible in riches, comprehending all things. Every thing which can be perceived is but an emanation therefrom. High, immeasurably high is this sublime station, in whose shadow moveth the essence of loftiness and splendour, wrapt in praise and adoration.

Bahá'u'lláh, *Tablets of Bahá'u'lláh*, p. 173.

The Book of God is wide open, and His Word is summoning mankind unto Him. No more than a mere handful, however, hath been found willing to cleave to His Cause, or to become the instruments for its promotion. These few have been endued with the Divine Elixir that can, alone, transmute into purest gold the dross of the world, and have been empowered to administer the infallible remedy for all the ills that afflict the children of men. No man can obtain everlasting life, unless he embraceth the truth of this inestimable, this wondrous and sublime Revelation.

Bahá'u'lláh, *Gleanings from the Writings of Bahá'u'lláh*, no. 92.1.

Every word that proceedeth out of the mouth of God is endowed with such potency as can instill new life into every human frame, if ye be of them that comprehend this truth. All the wondrous works ye behold in this world have been manifested through the operation of His supreme and most exalted Will, His wondrous and inflexible Purpose. Through the mere revelation of the word "Fashioner," issuing forth from His lips and proclaiming His attribute to mankind, such power is released as can generate, through successive ages, all the manifold arts which the hands of man can produce. This, verily, is a certain truth. No sooner is this resplendent word uttered, than its animating energies, stirring within all created things, give birth to the means and instruments whereby such arts can be produced and perfected. All the wondrous achievements ye now witness are the direct consequences of the Revelation of this Name. In the days to come, ye will, verily, behold things of which ye have never heard before. Thus hath it been decreed in the Tablets of God, and none can comprehend it except them whose sight is sharp. In like manner, the moment the word expressing My attribute "The Omniscient" issueth forth from My mouth, every created thing will, according to its capacity and limitations, be invested with the power to unfold the knowledge of the most marvelous sciences, and will be empowered to manifest them in the course of time at the bidding of Him Who is the Almighty, the All-Knowing. Know thou of a certainty that the Revelation of every other Name is accompanied by a similar manifestation of Divine power. Every single letter proceeding out of the mouth of God is indeed a mother letter, and every word uttered by Him Who is the Wellspring of Divine Revelation is a mother word, and His Tablet a Mother Tablet. Well is it with them that apprehend this truth.

Bahá'u'lláh, *Gleanings from the Writings of Bahá'u'lláh*, no. 74.1.

Adam is the cause of man's physical life; but the Reality of Christ—that is to say, the Word of God—is the cause of spiritual life. It is "a quickening spirit," meaning that all the imperfections which come from the requirements of the physical life of man are transformed into human perfections by the teachings and education of that spirit. Therefore, Christ was a quickening spirit, and the cause of life in all mankind.

Adam was the cause of physical life, and as the physical world of man is the world of imperfections, and imperfections are the equivalent of death, Paul compared the physical imperfections to death.

'Abdu'l-Bahá, *Some Answered Questions*, pp. 119–20.

As it is said in the Gospel of John, "In the beginning was the Word, and the Word was with God" [John 1:1]; then the Holy Spirit and the Word are the appearance of God. The Spirit and the Word mean the divine perfections that appeared in the Reality of Christ, and these perfections were with God; so the sun manifests all its glory in the mirror. For the Word does not signify the body of Christ, no, but the divine perfections manifested in Him. For Christ was like a clear mirror which was facing the Sun of Reality; and the perfections of the Sun of Reality—that is to say, its light and heat—were visible and apparent in this mirror. If we look into the mirror, we see the sun, and we say, "It is the sun." Therefore, the Word and the Holy Spirit, which signify the perfections of God, are the divine appearance. This is the meaning of the verse in the Gospel which says: "The Word was with God, and the Word was God"; for the divine perfections are not different from the

Essence of Oneness. The perfections of Christ are called the Word because all the beings are in the condition of letters, and one letter has not a complete meaning, while the perfections of Christ have the power of the word because a complete meaning can be inferred from a word. As the Reality of Christ was the manifestation of the divine perfections, therefore, it was like the word. Why? Because He is the sum of perfect meanings. This is why He is called the Word.

'Abdu'l-Bahá, *Some Answered Questions*, pp. 206–7.

The third station is that of the divine appearance and heavenly splendor: it is the Word of God, the Eternal Bounty, the Holy Spirit. It has neither beginning nor end, for these things are related to the world of contingencies and not to the divine world. For God the end is the same thing as the beginning. So the reckoning of days, weeks, months and years, of yesterday and today, is connected with the terrestrial globe; but in the sun there is no such thing—there is neither yesterday, today nor tomorrow, neither months nor years: all are equal. In the same way the Word of God is purified from all these conditions and is exempt from the boundaries, the laws and the limits of the world of contingency. Therefore, the reality of prophethood, which is the Word of God and the perfect state of manifestation, did not have any beginning and will not have any end; its rising is different from all others and is like that of the sun. For example, its dawning in the sign of Christ was with the utmost splendor and radiance, and this is eternal and everlasting.

'Abdu'l-Bahá, *Some Answered Questions*, p. 152.

In the Gospel it is said, "In the beginning was the Word, and the Word was with God." Then it is evident and clear that Christ did not reach to the station of Messiahship and its perfections at the time of baptism, when the

Holy Spirit descended upon Him in the likeness of a dove. Nay, the Word of God from all eternity has always been, and will be, in the exaltation of sanctification.

'Abdu'l-Bahá, *Some Answered Questions*, p. 153.

The Word of God is sanctified from time. The past, the present, the future, all, in relation to God, are equal. Yesterday, today, tomorrow do not exist in the sun.

In the same way there is priority with regard to glory—that is to say, the most glorious precedes the glorious. Therefore, the Reality of Christ, Who is the Word of God, with regard to essence, attributes and glory, certainly precedes the creatures. Before appearing in the human form, the Word of God was in the utmost sanctity and glory, existing in perfect beauty and splendor in the height of its magnificence. When through the wisdom of God the Most High it shone from the heights of glory in the world of the body, the Word of God, through this body, became oppressed, so that it fell into the hands of the Jews, and became the captive of the tyrannical and ignorant, and at last was crucified.

'Abdu'l-Bahá, *Some Answered Questions*,
pp. 116–17.

Yet the Sun of Reality, the Word of God, shone from the Messianic mirror through the wonderful channel of Jesus Christ more fully and more wonderfully. Its effulgences were manifestly radiant, but even to this day the Jews are holding to the Mosaic mirror. Therefore, they are bereft of witnessing the lights of eternity in Jesus.

'Abdu'l-Bahá, *The Promulgation of Universal Peace*,
p. 159.

There is no intrinsic meaning in the leaves of a book, but the thought they convey leads you to reflect upon reality. The reality of Jesus was the perfect meaning, the Christhood in Him which in the Holy Books is symbolized as the Word.

'Abdu'l-Bahá, The Promulgation of Universal Peace, p. 214.

"The Word was with God." The Christhood means not the body of Jesus but the perfection of divine virtues manifest in Him. Therefore, it is written, "He is God." This does not imply separation from God, even as it is not possible to separate the rays of the sun from the sun. The reality of Christ was the embodiment of divine virtues and attributes of God. For in Divinity there is no duality. All adjectives, nouns and pronouns in that court of sanctity are one; there is neither multiplicity nor division. The intention of this explanation is to show that the Words of God have innumerable significances and mysteries of meanings—each one a thousand and more.

'Abdu'l-Bahá, The Promulgation of Universal Peace, p. 214.

Thus, if there was a time when God did not manifest His qualities, then there was no God, because the attributes of God presuppose the creation of phenomena. For example, by present consideration we say that God is the creator. Then there must always have been a creation—since the quality of creator cannot be limited to the moment when some man or men realize this attribute. The attributes that we discover one by one—these attributes themselves necessarily anticipated our discovery of them. Therefore, God has no beginning and no ending; nor is His creation limited ever as to degree. Limitations of time and degree pertain to things created, never to the creation as a whole. They pertain to the forms of things, not to their realities. The effulgence of God cannot be suspended. The sovereignty of God cannot be interrupted.

As long as the sovereignty of God is immemorial, therefore the creation of our world throughout infinity is presupposed. When we look at the reality of this subject, we see that the bounties of God are infinite, without beginning and without end.

'Abdu'l-Bahá, *Foundations of World Unity*, p. 53.

10

Salvation

Most Christians believe that Christ came to die on the cross for the remission of our sins, and that in Christ's crucifixion we can find our salvation. Of course, this is true—and this is the case with all the Manifestations of God—if our faith is supported by virtues and goodly deeds.

We find salvation in the sacrifices of the Manifestations of God for us and also in Their lives and teachings through which we can be enabled to overcome all sin, such as anger, hatred, prejudice, greed, and selfishness. However, if these sins cannot be overcome and replaced with Divine virtues such as the knowledge and love of God, holiness, faithfulness, mastery of self, purity, detachment, truthfulness, steadfastness, selflessness and self-sacrifice, which are the fruit or essential components of one's faith; then the sacrifices of all the Prophets and Manifestations of God are of no benefit to us. As James points out, "So faith by itself, if it has no works, is dead."*

On the other hand, goodly deeds by themselves are not sufficient and are not the cause of eternal salvation. For example, Bahá'u'lláh says, *"The first duty prescribed by God for His servants is the recognition of Him Who is the Day Spring of His Revelation and the Fountain of His laws, Who representeth the*

---

* James 2:17.

143

*Godhead in both the Kingdom of His Cause and the world of creation. Whoso achieveth this duty hath attained unto all good; and whoso is deprived thereof hath gone astray, though he be the author of every righteous deed. It behoveth every one who reacheth this most sublime station, this summit of transcendent glory, to observe every ordinance of Him Who is the Desire of the world. These twin duties are inseparable. Neither is acceptable without the other."** Recognition of the Manifestation of God is "the first duty," as the knowledge and love of God is the foundation of all goodly deeds and virtues; they are the basis from which one can knowledgeably observe His ordinances. Recognition of the Manifestation of God for the age in which we live and abiding by His teachings are as a tree and its fruit, and we cannot have one without the other. 'Abdu'l-Bahá says, "... *good actions alone, without the knowledge of God, cannot be the cause of eternal salvation, everlasting success, and prosperity, and entrance into the Kingdom of God."*†

---

* Bahá'u'lláh, The Kitáb-i-Aqdas, ¶1.
† 'Abdu'l-Bahá, *Some Answered Questions*, p. 238.

Selected verses from the Holy Bible
concerning the meaning of salvation:

John 6:51 – I am the living bread which came down from heaven: if any man eat of this bread, he shall live for ever: and the bread which I will give is my own flesh, which I will give for the life of the world.

Matthew 7:21 – Not everyone who says to me, "Lord, Lord," shall enter the kingdom of heaven, but he who does the will of my Father who is in heaven.

First Corinthians 15:22 – As in Adam all men die, so in Christ all will be brought to life.

John 3:3–6 – Jesus answered and said unto him, Verily, verily, I say unto thee, Except a man be born again, he cannot see the kingdom of God. Nicodemus saith unto him, How can a man be born when he is old? Can he enter the second time into his mother's womb, and be born? Jesus answered, Verily, verily, I say unto thee, except a man be born of water and of the Spirit, he cannot enter into the kingdom of God. That which is born of the flesh is flesh; and that which is born of the Spirit is spirit.

John 6:63 – It is the spirit that quickeneth; the flesh profiteth nothing: the words that I speak unto you, they are spirit, and they are life.

Matthew 19:16–17 – And behold, one came up to him, saying, "Teacher, what good deed must I do, to have eternal life?" And he said to him, "Why do you ask me about what is good? One there is who is good. If you would enter life, keep the commandments."

John 3:16–17 – For God so loved the world, that he gave his only begotten Son, that whosoever believeth in him should not perish, but have everlasting life. For God sent not his Son into the world to condemn the world; but that the world through him might be saved.

Ezekiel 18:20–21 – The soul that sinneth, it shall die. The son shall not bear the iniquity of the father, neither shall the father bear the iniquity of the son. The righteousness of the righteous shall be upon him, and the wickedness of the wicked shall be upon him. But if the wicked will turn from his sins that he has committed, and keep all my statutes, and do that which is lawful and right, he shall surely live, he shall not die.

James 2:14–17 – What does it profit, my brethren, if a man says he has faith but has not works? Can his faith save him? If a brother or sister is ill clad and in lack of daily food, and one of you says to them, "Go in peace, be warmed and filled," without giving them the things needed for the body, what does it profit? So faith by itself, if it has no works, is dead.

James 2:26 – For as the body without the spirit is dead, so faith without works is dead also.

John 15:22 – If I had not come and spoken to them, they would not be guilty of sin. Now, however, they have no excuse for their sin.

Selected verses from the Holy Qur'án concerning the meaning of salvation:

Sura 2:23 – Al-Baqarah – But announce to those who believe and do the things that are right, that for them are gardens 'neath which the rivers flow!

Sura 22:57 – Al-Haj – . . . and they who shall have believed and done the things that are right, shall be in gardens of delight.

Sura 20:77–78 – Tá' Há' – But he who shall come before Him, a believer, with righteous works,—these! the loftiest grades await them: Gardens of Eden, beneath whose trees the rivers flow: therein shall they abide for ever. This, the reward of him who hath been pure.

Sura 29:19 – Al-'Ankabút – Say, Go through the earth, and see how he hath brought forth created beings. Hereafter, with a second birth will God cause them to be born again; for God is Almighty.

Sura 8:2-4 – Al-Anfál – Believers are they only whose hearts thrill with fear when God is named, and whose faith increaseth at each recital of his signs, and who put their trust in their Lord;

Who observe the prayers, and give alms out of that with which we have supplied them;

These are the believers: their due grade awaiteth them in the presence of their Lord, and forgiveness, and a generous provision.

Sura 14:27–28 – Ibráhím – Blame not me then, but blame yourselves: I cannot aid you, neither can ye aid me . . . As for the evil doers, a grievous torment doth await them.

But they who shall have believed and done the things that be right, shall be brought into gardens beneath which the rivers flow: therein shall they abide for ever by the permission of their Lord: their greeting therein shall be 'Peace.'

Sura 9:20 – Al-Tawbah – They who have believed, and fled their homes, and striven with their substance and with their persons on the path of God, shall be of highest grade with God: and these are they who shall be happy!

Sura 49:13 – Al-Hujurát – Truly, the most worthy of honor in the sight of God is he who feareth Him most.

Sura 16:99 – Al-Nahl – Whoso doeth that which is right, whether male or female, if a believer, him will we surely quicken to a happy life, and recompense them with a reward meet for their best deeds.

Sura 29:69 – Al-'Ankabút – And whoso maketh efforts for us, in our ways will we guide them: for God is assuredly with those who do righteous deeds.

Selected verses from the Bahá'í sacred texts
concerning the meaning of salvation:

The first duty prescribed by God for His servants is the recognition of Him Who is the Dayspring of His Revelation and the Fountain of His laws, Who representeth the Godhead in both the Kingdom of His Cause and the world of creation. Whoso achieveth this duty hath attained unto all good; and whoso is deprived thereof, hath gone astray, though he be the author of every righteous deed. It behooveth every one who reacheth this most sublime station, this summit of transcendent glory, to observe every ordinance of Him Who is the Desire of the world. These twin duties are inseparable. Neither is acceptable without the other. Thus hath it been decreed by Him Who is the Source of Divine Inspiration.

Bahá'u'lláh, The Kitáb-i-Aqdas, ¶1.

True belief in God and recognition of Him cannot be complete save by acceptance of that which He hath revealed and by observance of whatsoever hath been decreed by Him and set down in the Book by the Pen of Glory.

Bahá'u'lláh, *Tablets of Bahá'u'lláh*, p. 50.

Say: Because He bore injustice, justice hath appeared on earth, and because He accepted abasement, the majesty of God hath shone forth amidst mankind.

Bahá'u'lláh, The Kitáb-i-Aqdas, ¶158.

The Ancient Beauty hath consented to be bound with chains that mankind may be released from its bondage, and hath accepted to be made a prisoner within this most mighty Stronghold that the world may attain unto true liberty. He hath drained to its dregs the cup of sorrow, that all the people of the earth may attain unto abiding joy, and be filled with gladness. This is of the mercy of your Lord, the Compassionate, the Most Merciful. We have accepted to be abased, O believers in the Unity of God, that ye may be exalted, and have suffered manifold afflictions, that ye might prosper and flourish. He Who hath come to build anew the whole world, behold, how they that have joined partners with God have forced Him to dwell within the most desolate of cities!

Bahá'u'lláh, Gleanings from the Writings of Bahá'u'lláh, no. 45.1.

Say, strive ye to attain that which ye have been promised in the Books of God, and walk not in the way of the ignorant. My body hath endured imprisonment that ye may be released from the bondage of self. Set your faces then towards His countenance and follow not the footsteps of every hostile oppressor.

Bahá'u'lláh, Tablets of Bahá'u'lláh, pp. 11–12.

When the sanctified breezes of Christ and the Holy light of the Greatest Luminary were spread abroad, the human realities—that is to say, those who turned toward the Word of God and received the profusion of His bounties—were saved from this attachment and sin, obtained everlasting life, were delivered from the chains of bondage, and attained to the world of liberty. They were freed from the vices of the human world, and were blessed by the virtues of the Kingdom.

'Abdu'l-Bahá, Some Answered Questions, p. 125.

Adam is the cause of man's physical life; but the Reality of Christ—that is to say, the Word of God—is the cause of spiritual life. It is "a quickening spirit," meaning that all the imperfections which come from the requirements of the physical life of man are transformed into human perfections by the teachings and education of that spirit. Therefore, Christ was a quickening spirit, and the cause of life in all mankind.

Adam was the cause of physical life, and as the physical world of man is the world of imperfections, and imperfections are the equivalent of death, Paul compared the physical imperfections to death.

'Abdu'l-Bahá, *Some Answered Questions*, pp. 119–20.

Thou didst ask whether, at the advent of the Kingdom of God, every soul was saved. The Sun of Truth hath shone forth in splendor over all the world, and its luminous rising is man's salvation and his eternal life—but only he is of the saved who hath opened wide the eye of his discernment and beheld that glory.

'Abdu'l-Bahá, *Selections from the Writings of 'Abdu'l-Bahá*, no. 160.5.

Know that such actions, such efforts and such words are praiseworthy and approved, and are the glory of humanity. But these actions alone are not sufficient; they are a body of the greatest loveliness, but without spirit. No, that which is the cause of everlasting life, eternal honor, universal enlightenment, real salvation and prosperity is, first of all, the knowledge of God. It is known that the knowledge of God is beyond all knowledge, and it is the greatest glory of the human world. For in the existing knowledge of the reality of things there is material advantage, and through it outward civilization progresses; but the knowledge of God is the cause of spiritual progress and attraction, and through it the perception of truth, the exaltation of humanity, divine civilization, rightness of morals and illumination are obtained.

'Abdu'l-Bahá, *Some Answered Questions*, p. 300.

The kernel of Christian doctrine as taught in the churches is that redemption comes through Christ alone, that He is a unique figure in the world's history, that no one was ever like Him or will be like Him until He comes again. Every single logical tendency of our twentieth-century minds, educated to understand the nature of the universe we live in, should revolt against such a narrow concept as this. We know that man has been for millions of years on this planet as a self-conscious thinking form of life. Are we to believe he had no redemption until the year one? What became of all the souls that left this world before Christ was born? And what has become of all the others that have not accepted Him since He appeared? What is the matter with God, that when He could produce so many other marvels, dozens, hundreds, millions of times, He could only produce one Son and one way to Himself, and this at such an arbitrary point in history as two thousand years ago? Why did He not do it in the beginning so we could all, all these thousands of years, have had a chance of redemption; or if He did it at just the right time, why is it that just two thousand years later the whole world is not only unconverted to Christianity, but those who do profess it are living up to almost the exact opposite of its teachings? We might ask ourselves what, if after two thousand years we are in this mess, will our condition be in the year 3000 or 6000 A.D. if we must rely solely on the legacy of Christianity?

Rúhíyyih Rabbani, *Prescription for Living*, p. 139.

11

Baptism

Most Christian churches require baptism in water before one can be considered a true Christian. There are various customs and practices associated with baptism, and these have become an important part of church life. However, Bahá'ís believe that these ceremonies in themselves have no effect on the soul. Originally, baptism was intended to be a symbol of repentance and remission of sins, but the way that it is practiced today is quite different.

John the Baptist exhorted the people to repent. Only after they had done so did he baptize them—using water as a symbol of spiritual cleansing. The people that he baptized were Jews, and they remained Jews after baptism. John promised that Christ would baptize his followers "with the Holy Spirit and with fire."* This baptism is, of course, allegorical, since baptism with the Holy Spirit or with fire is physically impossible.

'Abdu'l-Bahá explains the symbolic meaning of baptism and its allegorical association with the Holy Spirit, water, and fire by saying: "Man cannot free himself from the rage of the carnal passions except by the help of the Holy Spirit. That is why He says baptism with the spirit, with water and with

---

* Matthew 3:11.

153

fire is necessary, and that it is essential—that is to say, the spirit of divine bounty, the water of knowledge and life, and the fire of the love of God. Man must be baptized with this spirit, this water and this fire so as to become filled with the eternal bounty. Otherwise, what is the use of baptizing with material water? No, this baptism with water was a symbol of repentance, and of seeking forgiveness of sins."* He also said: "Water is the cause of life, and when Christ speaks of water, He is symbolizing that which is the cause of *Everlasting Life.*"†

Although the ritual of baptism with water is not practiced in the Bahá'í Faith, the need for a cleansing of the spirit and the renewal of one's inner life through the divine teachings and the knowledge and love of God is recognized and understood.

---

* 'Abdu'l-Bahá, *Some Answered Questions*, p. 92.
† 'Abdu'l-Bahá, *Paris Talks*, no. 27.3.

Baptism

Some of the verses from the Holy Bible concerning baptism:

Acts 19:4–5 – Then said Paul, John verily baptized with the baptism of repentance, saying unto the people, that they should believe on him which should come after him, that is, on Christ Jesus. When they heard this, they were baptized in the name of the Lord Jesus.

Matthew 3:11 – "I baptize you with water for repentance, but he who is coming after me is mightier than I, whose sandals I am not worthy to carry; he will baptize you with the Holy Spirit and with fire."

Mark 1:4–5 – John did baptize in the wilderness, and preach the baptism of repentance for the remission of sins. And there went out unto him all the land of Judaea, and they of Jerusalem, and were all baptized of him in the river of Jordan, confessing their sins.

Matthew 3:5–8 – Then went out to him Jerusalem, and all Judaea, and all the region round about Jordan, And were baptized of him in Jordan, confessing their sins. But when he saw many of the Pharisees and Sadducees come to his baptism, he said unto them, O generation of vipers, who hath warned you to flee from the wrath to come? Bring forth therefore fruits meet for repentance.

John 1:29–33 – The next day he saw Jesus coming toward him, and said, "Behold, the Lamb of God, who takes away the sin of the world! This is he of whom I said, 'After me comes a man who ranks before me, for he was before me.' I myself did not know him; . . . but he who sent me to baptize with water said to me, 'He on whom you see the Spirit descend and remain, this is he who baptizes with the Holy Spirit.'"

Matthew 3:16–17 – And Jesus, when he was baptized, went up straightway out of the water: and, lo, the heavens were opened unto him, and he saw the Spirit of God descending like a dove, and lighting upon him: And lo a voice from heaven, saying, This is my beloved Son, in whom I am well pleased.

A verse from the Holy Qur'án concerning baptism:

Sura 2:132 – Al-Baqarah – Islam is the Baptism of God, and who is better to baptise than God? And Him do we serve.

Baptism

Some of the passages from the Bahá'í sacred texts concerning baptism:

As Christ desired that this institution of John should be used at that time by all, He Himself conformed to it in order to awaken the people and to complete the law of the former religion. Although the ablution of repentance was the institution of John, it was in reality formerly practiced in the religion of God.

Christ was not in need of baptism; but as at that time it was an acceptable and praiseworthy action, and a sign of the glad tidings of the Kingdom, therefore, He confirmed it. However, afterward He said the true baptism is not with material water, but it must be with spirit and with water. In this case water does not signify material water, for elsewhere it is explicitly said baptism is with spirit and with fire, from which it is clear that the reference is not to material fire and material water, for baptism with fire is impossible.

Therefore, the spirit is the bounty of God, the water is knowledge and life, and the fire is the love of God. For material water does not purify the heart of man; no, it cleanses his body. But the heavenly water and spirit, which are knowledge and life, make the human heart good and pure. . . .

'Abdu'l-Bahá, Some Answered Questions, pp. 91–92.

The principle of baptism is purification by repentance. John admonished and exhorted the people, and caused them to repent; then he baptized them. Therefore, it is apparent that this baptism is a symbol of repentance from all sin: its meaning is expressed in these words: "O God! As my body has become purified and cleansed from physical impurities, in the same way purify and sanctify my spirit from the impurities of the world of nature, which are not worthy of the Threshold of Thy Unity!"

'Abdu'l-Bahá, Some Answered Questions, p. 91.

Reflect, also, that baptism in the days of John the Baptist was used to awaken and admonish the people to repent from all sin, and to watch for the appearance of the Kingdom of Christ. But at present in Asia, the Catholics and the Orthodox Church plunge newly born children into water mixed with olive oil, and many of them become ill from the shock; at the time of baptism they struggle and become agitated. In other places, the clergy sprinkle the water of baptism on the forehead. But neither from the first form nor from the second do the children derive any spiritual benefit.

'Abdu'l-Bahá, *Some Answered Questions*, pp. 94–95.

The immortality of the spirit is mentioned in the Holy Books; it is the fundamental basis of the divine religions. Now punishments and rewards are said to be of two kinds: first, the rewards and punishments of this life; second those of the other world. But the paradise and hell of existence are found in all the worlds of God, whether in this world or in the spiritual heavenly worlds. Gaining these rewards is the gaining of eternal life. That is why Christ said, "Act in such a way that you may find eternal life, and that you may be born of water and the spirit, so that you may enter into the Kingdom" [John 3:5].

'Abdu'l-Bahá, *Some Answered Questions*, p. 223.

In the Gospel according to St. John, Christ has said: "Except a man be born of water and the Spirit, he cannot enter into the Kingdom of Heaven" [John 3:5]. The priests have interpreted this into meaning that baptism is necessary for salvation. In another Gospel it is said: "He shall baptize you with the Holy Ghost and with fire" [Matthew 3:11].

Thus the water of baptism and the fire are one! It cannot mean that the "water" spoken of is *physical* water, for it is the direct opposite of "fire," and one destroys the other. When in the Gospels, Christ speaks of "water," He means *that which causes life,* for without water no worldly creature can

158

live—mineral, vegetable, animal and man, one and all, depend upon water for their very being. Yes, the latest scientific discoveries prove to us that even mineral has some form of life, and that it also needs water for its existence.

Water is the cause of life, and when Christ speaks of water, He is symbolizing that which is the cause of *Everlasting Life*.

'Abdu'l-Bahá, *Paris Talks*, no. 27.1–27.3.

Man cannot free himself from the rage of the carnal passions except by the help of the Holy Spirit. That is why He says baptism with the spirit, with water and with fire is necessary, and that it is essential—that is to say, the spirit of divine bounty, the water of knowledge and life, and the fire of the love of God. Man must be baptized with this spirit, this water and this fire so as to become filled with the eternal bounty. Otherwise, what is the use of baptizing with material water? No, this baptism with water was a symbol of repentance, and of seeking forgiveness of sins.

But in the cycle of Bahá'u'lláh there is no longer need of this symbol; for its reality, which is to be baptized with the spirit and love of God, is understood and established.

'Abdu'l-Bahá, *Some Answered Questions*, p. 92.

During the time Jesus Christ was upon the earth mankind sought nearness to God, but in that day no one attained it save a very few—His disciples. Those blessed souls were confirmed with divine nearness through the love of God. Divine nearness is dependent upon attainment to the knowledge of God, upon severance from all else save God. It is contingent upon self-sacrifice and to be found only through forfeiting wealth and worldly possessions. It is made possible through the baptism of water and fire revealed in the Gospels. Water symbolizes the water of life, which is knowledge, and fire is the fire of the love of God; therefore, man must be baptized with the water of life, the

159

Holy Spirit and the fire of the love of the Kingdom. Until he attains these three degrees, nearness to God is not possible.

'Abdu'l-Bahá, *The Promulgation of Universal Peace*, p. 203.

This is why, in Holy Scriptures, the counsels of heaven are likened to water, even as the Qur'án saith: "And pure water send We down from Heaven," [Qur'án 25:50] and the Gospel: "Except a man be baptized of water and of the spirit, he cannot enter into the Kingdom of God." [John 3:5] Thus is it clear that the Teachings which come from God are heavenly outpourings of grace; they are rain-showers of divine mercy, and they cleanse the human heart.

'Abdu'l-Bahá, *Selections from the Writings of 'Abdu'l-Bahá*, no. 129.3.

12

The Lord's Supper

Holy Communion, or the sacrament of the Eucharist, is another practice that is observed by most Christian churches. Again, Bahá'ís see this ritual as symbolic, rather than having in itself any effect on the soul. Christ said, "I am the bread of life: he that cometh to me shall never hunger; and he that believeth on me shall never thirst."* He was talking in allegorical terms about the heavenly food—the knowledge and love of God, purity, sanctity, and faith and benevolence, rather than His flesh and blood. As He also said, "It is the spirit that quickeneth; the flesh profiteth nothing: the words that I speak unto you, they are spirit, and they are life."†

---

* John 6:35.
† John 6:63.

Some of the verses from the Holy Bible concerning the Lord's Supper:

Matthew 4:4 – Man shall not live by bread alone, but by every word that proceedeth out of the mouth of God.

Matthew 26:26–28 – And as they were eating, Jesus took bread, and blessed it, and brake it, and gave it to the disciples, and said, Take, eat; this is my body. And he took the cup, and gave thanks, and gave it to them, saying, Drink ye all of it; For this is my blood of the new testament, which is shed for many for the remission of sins.

Mark 14:22–25 – And as they were eating, he took bread, and blessed, and broke it, and gave it to them, and said, "Take; this is my body." And he took a cup, and when he had given thanks he gave it to them, and they all drank of it. And he said to them, "This is my blood of the covenant, which is poured out for many. Truly, I say to you, I shall not drink again of the fruit of the vine until that day when I drink it new in the kingdom of God."

Luke 22:17–20 – And he took the cup, and gave thanks, and said, Take this, and divide it among yourselves: For I say unto you, I will not drink of the fruit of the vine, until the kingdom of God shall come. And he took bread, and gave thanks, and brake it, and gave unto them, saying, This is my body which is given for you: this do in remembrance of me. Likewise also the cup after supper, saying, This cup is the new testament in my blood, which is shed for you.

John 6:47–63 – "Truly, truly, I say to you, he who believes has eternal life. I am the bread of life. Your fathers ate the manna in the wilderness, and they

162

died. This is the bread which comes down from heaven, that a man may eat of it and not die. I am the living bread which came down from heaven; if any one eats of this bread, he will live for ever; and the bread which I shall give for the life of the world is my flesh."

The Jews then disputed among themselves, saying, "How can this man give us his flesh to eat?" So Jesus said to them, "Truly, truly, I say to you unless you eat the flesh of the Son of man and drink his blood, you have no life in you; he who eats my flesh and drinks my blood has eternal life, and I will raise him up at the last day. For my flesh is food indeed, and my blood is drink indeed. He who eats my flesh and drinks my blood abides in me, and I in him. As the living Father sent me, and I live because of the Father, so he who eats me will live because of me. This is the bread which came down from heaven, not such as the fathers ate and died; he who eats this bread will live for ever." This he said in the synagogue, as he taught at Capernum.

Many of his disciples, when they heard it, said, "This is a hard saying; who can listen to it?" But Jesus, knowing in himself that his disciples murmured at it, said to them, "Do you take offense at this? Then what if you were to see the Son of man ascending where he was before? It is the spirit that gives life, the flesh is of no avail; the words that I have spoken to you are spirit and life."

John 6:33 – For the bread of God is that which comes down from heaven, and gives life to the world.

Some of the passages from the Bahá'í sacred texts concerning the Lord's Supper:

The position of Christ was that of absolute perfection; He made His divine perfections shine like the sun upon all believing souls, and the bounties of the light shone and radiated in the reality of men. This is why He says: "I am the bread which descended from heaven; whosoever shall eat of this bread will not die." [John 6:41, 50, 58]—that is to say, that whosoever shall partake of this divine food will attain unto eternal life: that is, every one who partakes of this bounty and receives these perfections will find eternal life, will obtain preexistent favors, will be freed from the darkness of error, and will be illuminated by the light of His guidance.

'Abdu'l-Bahá, Some Answered Questions, p. 121.

This is the meaning of the words of Christ, "I gave My blood for the life of the world" [John 6:51]—that is to say, I have chosen all these troubles, these sufferings, calamities, and even the greatest martyrdom, to attain this object, the remission of sins (that is, the detachment of spirits from the human world, and their attraction to the divine world) in order that souls may arise who will be the very essence of the guidance of mankind, and the manifestations of the perfections of the Supreme Kingdom.

'Abdu'l-Bahá, Some Answered Questions, p. 125.

Christ had an elemental body and a celestial form. The elemental body was crucified, but the heavenly form is living and eternal, and the cause of everlasting life; the first was the human nature, and the second is the divine nature. It is thought by some that the Eucharist is the reality of Christ, and that the Divinity and the Holy Spirit descend into and exist in it. Now when once the Eucharist is taken, after a few moments it is simply disintegrated and entirely transformed. Therefore, how can such a thought be conceived? God forbid! certainly it is an absolute fantasy.

To conclude: through the manifestation of Christ, the divine teachings, which are an eternal bounty, were spread abroad, the light of guidance shone forth, and the spirit of life was conferred on man. Whoever found guidance became living; whoever remained lost was seized by enduring death. This bread which came down from heaven was the divine body of Christ, His spiritual elements, which the disciples ate, and through which they gained eternal life.

The disciples had taken many meals from the hand of Christ; why was the last supper distinguished from the others? It is evident that the heavenly bread did not signify this material bread, but rather the divine nourishment of the spiritual body of Christ, the divine graces and heavenly perfections of which His disciples partook, and with which they became filled.

In the same way, reflect that when Christ blessed the bread and gave it to His disciples, saying, "This is My body," [Matt. 26:26] and gave grace to them, He was with them in person, in presence, and form. He was not transformed into bread and wine; if He had been turned into bread and wine, He could not have remained with the disciples in body, in person and in presence.

'Abdu'l-Bahá, *Some Answered Questions,* pp. 98–99.

13

The Meaning of "Life" and "Death"

Bahá'u'lláh explains the meaning of "life" and "death" by saying, *"By the terms 'life' and 'death,' spoken of in the scriptures, is intended the life of faith and the death of unbelief."** The true and everlasting life is the life of the spirit—whereas the physical life is, of course, only temporary. Jesus said, "It is the spirit that gives life; the flesh is of no avail."† He also said, "The hour is coming, and now is, when the dead shall hear the voice of the Son of God: and they that hear shall live."‡ Bahá'u'lláh says, *"Whoso hath been reborn in this Day, shall never die; whoso remaineth dead, shall never live."§*

The purpose of our life on this planet is to acquire what is termed the "spirit of faith" or spiritual birth—that is, to be reborn spiritually while still on earth. As Christ said, "Except a man be born again, he cannot see the kingdom of God."** This second or spiritual birth can be attained through our recognition of the Manifestation of God in the Day in which we live, our

---

* Bahá'u'lláh, The Book of Certitude, ¶120.
† John 6:63.
‡ John 5:25.
§ John 3:3.
** Bahá'u'lláh, *Gleanings from the Writings of Bahá'u'lláh,* no. 106.3.

obedience to His eachings, our knowledge and love of God, our prayers and meditation, our study of the sacred text, and our facing the tests this physical world provides. It is the Word of God, the divine teachings brought to man in every Dispensation that bestows upon us life eternal. For this reason, the Qur'án states, "Make answer to the appeal of God and his apostle when he calleth you to that which giveth you life."*

Without acquiring the "spirit of faith" in this world, that is, without our "spiritual birth," we are as dead—though we may be physically alive, as Jesus said, "Follow me; and let the dead bury their dead."†

---

* Sura 8:24.
† Matthew 8:22.

The Meaning of "Life" and "Death"

Some of the verses from the Holy Bible concerning the meaning of "Life" and "Death":

Matthew 8:21–22 – And another of his disciples said unto him, Lord, suffer me first to go and bury my father. But Jesus said unto him, Follow me; and let the dead bury their dead.

John 3:3–6 – Jesus answered and said unto him, Verily, verily, I say unto thee, Except a man be born again, he cannot see the kingdom of God.

Nicodemus saith unto him, How can a man be born when he is old? Can he enter the second time into his mother's womb, and be born? Jesus answered, Verily, verily, I say unto thee, Except a man be born of water and of the Spirit, he cannot enter into the kingdom of God.

That which is born of the flesh is flesh; and that which is born of the Spirit is spirit.

John 5:24–25 – Verily, verily, I say unto you, He that heareth my word, and believeth on him that sent me, hath everlasting life, and shall not come into condemnation; but is passed from death unto life. Verily, verily, I say unto you, The hour is coming, and now is, when the dead shall hear the voice of the Son of God: and they that hear shall live.

John 8:51 – Verily, verily, I say unto you, If a man keep my saying, he shall never see death.

Revelation 3:1–2 – I know your works; you have the name of being alive, and you are dead. Awake, and strengthen what remains and is on the point of death, for I have not found your works perfect in the sight of God.

Matthew 4:4 – Man shall not live by bread alone, but by every word that proceedeth out of the mouth of God.

John 6:63 – "It is the spirit that gives life, the flesh is of no avail; the words that I have spoken to you are spirit and life."

John 1:12–13 – But to all who did receive him, to those who have yielded him their allegiance, he gave the right to become children of God, not born of any human stock, or by the fleshly desire of a human father, but the offspring of God himself.

I Peter 4:6 – The gospel was preached to the dead so that they may be judged according to men in flesh, but live according to men in spirit.

I John 3:14 – We know that we have passed from death unto life, because we love the brethren. He that loveth not his brother abideth in death.

John 11:25–26 – Jesus said to her, "I am the resurrection and the life; he who believes in me though he die, yet shall he live, and whoever lives and believes in me shall never die."

John 3:16–17 – God loved the world so much that he gave his only Son, that everyone who has faith in him may not die but have eternal life. It was not to judge the world that God sent his Son into the world, but that through him the world might be saved.

James 5:20 – Let him know, that he which converts a sinner from his error, shall save him from death; and shall hide a great number of sins.

Romans 8:6 – For to be worldly minded is death, but to be spiritually minded is life and peace.

Some of the verses from the Holy Qur'án concerning the meaning of "Life" and "Death":

Sura 8:24 – Al-Anfál – O ye faithful! – Make answer to the appeal of God and his apostle when he calleth you to that which giveth you life.

Sura 29:19 – Al-'Ankabút – Say, Go through the earth, and see how he hath brought forth created beings. Hereafter, with a second birth will God cause them to be born again; for God is Almighty.

Sura 2:258–59 – Al-Baqarah – God is the patron of believers: He shall bring them out of darkness into light:

As to those who believe not, their patrons are Thagout: they shall bring them out of light into darkness: they shall be given over to the fire: they shall abide therein for ever.

Sura 6:122 – Al-An'ám – Shall the dead, whom have quickened, and for whom we have ordained a light whereby he may walk among men, be like him, whose likeness is in the darkness, whence he will not come forth?

Sura 35:20–21– Al-Fátir – And the blind and the seeing are not alike; neither darkness and light; nor the shade and the hot wind;

Nor are the living and the dead the same thing! God indeed shall make whom He will to hearken, but thou shalt not make those who are in their graves to hearken; for only with warning art thou charged.

Sura 30:18 – Al-Rúm – He bringeth forth the living out of the dead, and He bringeth forth the dead out of the living: and He quickeneth the earth when dead. Thus is it that ye too shall be brought forth.

Some of the passages from the Bahá'í sacred texts concerning the meaning of "Life" and "Death":

The first duty prescribed by God for His servants is the recognition of Him Who is the Dayspring of His Revelation and the Fountain of His laws, Who representeth the Godhead in both the Kingdom of His Cause and the world of creation. Whoso achieveth this duty hath attained unto all good; and whoso is deprived thereof hath gone astray, though he be the author of every righteous deed. It behooveth every one who reacheth this most sublime station, this summit of transcendent glory, to observe every ordinance of Him Who is the Desire of the world. These twin duties are inseparable. Neither is acceptable without the other. Thus hath it been decreed by Him Who is the Source of Divine inspiration.

Bahá'u'lláh, The Kitáb-i-Aqdas, ¶1.

By the terms "life" and "death," spoken of in the scriptures, is intended the life of faith and the death of unbelief. The generality of the people, owing to their failure to grasp the meaning of these words, rejected and despised the person of the Manifestation, deprived themselves of the light of His divine guidance, and refused to follow the example of that immortal Beauty.

Bahá'u'lláh, The Book of Certitude, ¶120.

. . . true life is not the life of the flesh but the life of the spirit. For the life of the flesh is common to both men and animals, whereas the life of the spirit is possessed only by the pure in heart who have quaffed from the ocean of faith and partaken of the fruit of certitude. This life knoweth no death, and this existence is crowned by immortality. Even as it hath been said: "He who is a true believer liveth both in this world and in the world to come." If by "life" be meant this earthly life, it is evident that death must needs overtake it.

Bahá'u'lláh, The Book of Certitude, ¶128.

No man can obtain everlasting life, unless he embraceth the truth of this inestimable, this wondrous, and sublime Revelation.

Bahá'u'lláh, *Gleanings from the Writings of Bahá'u'lláh*, no. 92.1.

Know then that "life" hath a twofold meaning. The first pertaineth to the appearance of man in an elemental body, and is as manifest to thine eminence and to others as the midday sun. This life cometh to an end with physical death, which is a God-ordained and inescapable reality. That life, however, which is mentioned in the Books of the Prophets and the Chosen Ones of God is the life of knowledge; that is to say, the servant's recognition of the sign of the splendors wherewith He Who is the Source of all splendor hath Himself invested him, and his certitude of attaining unto the presence of God through the Manifestations of His Cause. This is that blessed and everlasting life that perisheth not: whosoever is quickened thereby shall never die, but will endure as long as His Lord and Creator will endure.

The first life, which pertaineth to the elemental body, will come to an end, as hath been revealed by God: "Every soul shall taste of death." But the second life, which ariseth from the knowledge of God, knoweth no death, as hath been revealed aforetime: "Him will We surely quicken to a blessed life." And in another passage concerning the martyrs: "Nay, they are alive and sustained by their Lord." And from the Traditions: "He who is a true believer liveth both in this world and in the world to come." Numerous examples of similar words are to be found in the Books of God and of the Embodiments of His justice.

Bahá'u'lláh, *The Pen of Glory*, nos. 1.64–1.65.

Such things have come to pass in the days of every Manifestation of God. Even as Jesus said: "Ye must be born again." Again He saith: "Except a man be born of water and of the Spirit, he cannot enter into the Kingdom of God. That which is born of the flesh is flesh; and that which is born of the Spirit is spirit." The purport of these words is that whosoever in every dispensation is born of the Spirit and is quickened by the breath of the Manifestation of Holiness, he verily is of those that have attained unto "life" and "resurrection" and have entered into the "paradise" of the love of God. And whosoever is not of them, is condemned to "death" and "deprivation," to the "fire" of unbelief, and to the "wrath" of God.

Bahá'u'lláh, The Book of Certitude, ¶125.

In like manner, two of the people of Kúfih went to 'Alí, the Commander of the Faithful. One owned a house and wished to sell it; the other was to be the purchaser. They had agreed that this transaction should be effected and the contract be written with the knowledge of 'Alí. He, the exponent of the law of God, addressing the scribe, said: "Write thou: 'A dead man hath bought from another dead man a house. That house is bounded by four limits. One extendeth toward the tomb, the other to the vault of the grave, the third to the Ṣiráṭ, the fourth to either Paradise or hell.'" Reflect, had these two souls been quickened by the trumpet-call of 'Alí, had they risen from the grave of error by the power of his love, the judgment of death would certainly not have been pronounced against them.

Bahá'u'lláh, The Book of Certitude, ¶127.

Arise, and lift up your voices, that haply they that are fast asleep may be awakened. Say: O ye who are as dead! The Hand of Divine bounty proffereth unto you the Water of Life. Hasten and drink your fill. Whoso hath been reborn in this Day, shall never die; whoso remaineth dead, shall never live.

Bahá'u'lláh, *Gleanings from the Writings of Bahá'u'lláh*, no. 106.3.

Whoso, while reading the Sacred Scriptures, is tempted to choose therefrom whatever may suit him with which to challenge the authority of the Representative of God among men, is, indeed, as one dead, though to outward seeming he may walk and converse with his neighbors, and share with them their food and their drink.

Bahá'u'lláh, *Gleanings from the Writings of Bahá'u'lláh*, no. 89.

Observe: those who in appearance were physically alive, Christ considered dead; for life is the eternal life, and existence is the real existence. Wherever in the Holy Books they speak of raising the dead, the meaning is that the dead were blessed by eternal life; where it is said that the blind received sight, the signification is that he obtained the true perception; where it is said a deaf man received hearing, the meaning is that he acquired spiritual and heavenly hearing.

'Abdu'l-Bahá, *Some Answered Questions*, pp. 101–2.

That is why those who were heedless and denied God were said by Christ to be dead, although they were apparently living; in relation to the people of faith they were dead, blind, deaf and dumb. This is what Christ meant when He said, "Let the dead bury their dead."

'Abdu'l-Bahá, *Some Answered Questions*, p. 279.

. . . for the perfect man there are two kinds of birth: the first, physical birth, is from the matrix of the mother; the second, or spiritual birth, is from the world of nature. In both he is without knowledge of the new world of existence he is entering. Therefore, rebirth means his release from the captivity of nature, freedom from attachment to this mortal and material life. This is the second, or spiritual, birth of which Jesus Christ spoke in the Gospels.

'Abdu'l-Bahá, *The Promulgation of Universal Peace*, p. 424.

What is he in need of in the Kingdom which transcends the life and limitation of this mortal sphere? That world beyond is a world of sanctity and radiance; therefore, it is necessary that in this world he should acquire these divine attributes. In that world there is need of spirituality, faith, assurance, the knowledge and love of God. These he must attain in this world so that after his ascension from the earthly to the heavenly Kingdom he shall find all that is needful in that eternal life ready for him.

That divine world is manifestly a world of lights; therefore, man has need of illumination here. That is a world of love; the love of God is essential. It is a world of perfections; virtues, or perfections, must be acquired. That world is vivified by the breaths of the Holy Spirit; in this world we must seek them. That is the Kingdom of everlasting life; it must be attained during this vanishing existence.

By what means can man acquire these things? How shall he obtain these merciful gifts and powers? First, through the knowledge of God. Second, through the love of God. Third, through faith. Fourth, through philanthropic deeds. Fifth, through self-sacrifice. Sixth, through severance from this world. Seventh, through sanctity and holiness. Unless he acquires these forces and attains to these requirements, he will surely be deprived of the life that is eternal. But if he possesses the knowledge of God, becomes ignited through the fire of the love of God, witnesses the great and mighty signs of the Kingdom, becomes the cause of love among mankind and lives in the utmost state of sanctity and holiness, he shall surely attain to second birth, be baptized by the Holy Spirit and enjoy everlasting existence.

'Abdu'l-Bahá, *The Promulgation of Universal Peace*, p. 316.

The rewards of this life are the virtues and perfections which adorn the reality of man. For example, he was dark and becomes luminous; he was ignorant and becomes wise; he was neglectful and becomes vigilant; he was asleep and becomes awakened; he was dead and becomes living; he was blind and becomes a seer; he was deaf and becomes a hearer; he was earthly and becomes heavenly; he was material and becomes spiritual. Through these rewards he gains spiritual birth and becomes a new creature. He becomes the manifestation of the verse in the Gospel where it is said of the disciples that they "were born, not of blood, nor of the will of the flesh, nor of the will of man, but of God"—that is to say, they were delivered from the animal characteristics and qualities which are the characteristics of human nature, and they became qualified with the divine characteristics, which are the bounty of God. This is the meaning of the second birth.

'Abdu'l-Bahá, *Some Answered Questions*, pp. 223–24.

. . . the human spirit, unless assisted by the spirit of faith, does not become acquainted with the divine secrets and the heavenly realities.

'Abdu'l-Bahá, *Some Answered Questions*, p. 208.

14

The Symbolic Meanings of Parables

The Holy Books use parables to express—through metaphor and colorful imagery—certain spiritual concepts that would otherwise have been difficult or impossible to explain.

However, parables can either guide or mislead a person from the truth, depending on the individual's spiritual capacity and perception. Taking parables literally will always be misleading, as the apostle Paul writes, "the letter killeth, but the spirit giveth life."* Christ says, "the words that I speak unto you, they are spirit, and they are life."† When Christ was asked by the disciples as to why He spoke in parables, He replied, "Unto you it is given to know the mystery of the kingdom of God: but unto them that are without, all these things are done in parables: that seeing they may see, and not perceive; and hearing they may hear, and not understand; lest at any time they should be converted, and their sins should be forgiven them."‡ Similarly the Qur'án reads, "Hearts have they with which they understand not, and eyes have they with which they see not, and ears have they with which they

---

* 2 Corinthians 3:6.
† John 6:63.
‡ Mark 4:11–12.

hearken not. They are like the brutes: Yea, they go more astray: these are the heedless."* Furthermore, the Qur'án explains whom He will guide or mislead by such parables by saying: "Many will He mislead by such parables and many guide: but none will He mislead thereby except the wicked."†

Bahá'u'lláh explains the requisites needed to understand the sacred scriptures, He says, *"The understanding of His words and the comprehension of the utterances of the Birds of Heaven are in no wise dependent upon human learning. They depend solely upon purity of heart, chastity of soul, and freedom of spirit."‡* He further states, *"In such utterances, the literal meaning, as generally understood by the people, is not what hath been intended."§*

The Holy Books have their own special terminology in conveying figurative or allegorical concepts. They require reflection, prayer, meditation, careful study, and comparison of verses and concepts to uncover the inner spiritual verities found in parables and/or figurative verses. 'Abdu'l-Bahá talked about the inner meanings of parables by saying, *"When the spiritually minded dive deeply into the ocean of their meaning they bring to the surface the pearls of their inner significance."*** Examples of such parables are quoted in this chapter where Christ compares the "Kingdom of Heaven" to the "marriage feast," the "ten maidens," and the parable of the "vineyard."

---

* Sura 7:178.
† Sura 2:24.
‡ Bahá'u'lláh, The Book of Certitude, ¶233.
§ Bahá'u'lláh, The Book of Certitude, ¶283.
** 'Abdu'l-Bahá, *'Abdu'l-Bahá in London,* p. 80.

Some of the verses from the Holy Bible concerning the symbolic meanings of parables:

Matthew 13:34–35 – All these things spake Jesus unto the multitude in parables; and without a parable spake he not unto them: That it might be fulfilled which was spoken by the prophet, saying, I will open my mouth in parables; I will utter things which have been kept secret from the foundation of the world.

Matthew 13:10–16 – And the disciples came and said to him, "Why speakest thou unto them in parables?" He answered and said unto them, "Because it is given unto you to know the mysteries of the kingdom of heaven, but to them it is not given. For whosoever hath, to him shall be given, and he shall have more abundance: but whosoever hath not, from him shall be taken away even that he hath. Therefore speak I to them in parables: because they seeing see not; and hearing they hear not, neither do they understand. And in them is fulfilled the prophecy of Isaiah which saith, By hearing ye shall hear, and shall not understand; and seeing ye shall see, and shall not perceive: For this people's heart is waxed gross, and their ears are dull of hearing, and their eyes they have closed; lest at any time they should see with their eyes, and hear with their ears, and should understand with their heart, and should be converted, and I should heal them. But blessed are your eyes, for they see: and your ears, for they hear."

Isaiah 6:9–10 – And he said, Go, and tell this people, Hear ye indeed, but understand not; and see ye indeed, but perceive not.

Make the heart of this people fat, and make their ears heavy, and shut their eyes; lest they see with their eyes, and hear with their ears, and understand with their heart, and convert, and be healed.

Mark 4:10–12 – And when he was alone, they that were about him with the twelve asked of him the parable.

And he said unto them, "Unto you it is given to know the mystery of the kingdom of God: but unto them that are without, all these things are done in parables: That seeing they may see, and not perceive; and hearing they may hear, and not understand; lest at any time they should be converted, and their sins should be forgiven them."

Luke 8:9–10 – And when his disciples asked him what this parable meant, he said, "To you has been given to know the secrets of the kingdom of God; but for others they are in parables, so that seeing they may not see, and hearing they may not understand."

Mark 4:33–34 – And with many such parables spake he the word unto them, as they were able to hear it. But without a parable spake he not unto them: and when they were alone, he expounded all things to his disciples.

Matthew 22:1–14 – And again Jesus spoke to them in parables, saying: "The kingdom of heaven may be compared to a king who gave a marriage feast for his son, and sent his servants to call those who were invited to the marriage feast; but they would not come. Again he sent other servants, saying, 'Tell those who are invited, Behold, I have made ready my dinner, my oxen and my fat calves are killed, and everything is ready; come to the marriage feast.' But they made light of it and went off, one to his farm, another to his business, while the rest seized his servants, treated them shamefully, and killed them. The king was angry, and he sent his troops and destroyed those murderers and burned their city. Then he said to his servants, 'The wedding is ready, but those invited were not worthy. Go therefore to the thoroughfares, and invite to the marriage feast as many as you find.' And those servants went out into the streets and gathered all whom they found, both bad and good; so the wedding hall was filled with guests.

But when the king came in to look at the guests, he saw there a man who had no wedding garment; and he said to him, 'Friend, how did you get in here without a wedding garment!' And he was speechless. Then the king said to the attendants, 'Bind him hand and foot, and cast him into the outer darkness; there men will weep and gnash their teeth.' For many are called, but few are chosen.

Matthew 25:1–13 – Then the kingdom of heaven shall be compared to ten maidens who took their lamps and went to meet the bridegroom. Five of them were foolish, and five were wise. For when the foolish took their lamps, they took no oil with them; but the wise took flasks of oil with their lamps. As the bridegroom was delayed, they all slumbered and slept. But at midnight there was a cry, "Behold, the bridegroom! Come out to meet him." Then all those maidens rose and trimmed their lamps. And the foolish said to the wise, "Give us some of your oil, for our lamps are going out." But the wise replied, "Perhaps there will not be enough for us and for you; go rather to the dealers and buy for yourselves." And while they went to buy, the bridegroom came, and those who were ready went in with him to the marriage feast; and the door was shut. Afterward the other maidens came also, saying, "Lord, lord, open to us." But he replied, "Truly, I say to you, I do not know you." Watch therefore, for you know neither the day nor the hour.

Matthew 21:33–43 – Hear another parable. There was a householder who planted a vineyard, and set a hedge around it, and dug a wine press in it, and built a tower, and let it out to tenants, and went into another country.

When the season of fruit drew near, he sent his servants to the tenants, to get his fruit; and the tenants took his servants and beat one, killed another, and stoned another. Again he sent other servants, more than the first; and they did the same to them. Afterward he sent his son to them, saying: "They will respect my son." But when the tenants saw the son, they said to themselves, "This is the heir; come, let us kill him and have his inheritance." And they took him and cast him out of the vineyard, and killed him. When therefore the owner of the vineyard comes, what will he do to those tenants? They said to him, "He will put those wretches to a miserable death, and let out the vineyard to other tenants who will give him the fruits in their seasons."

Jesus said to them, "Have you never read in the scriptures: 'The very stone which the builders rejected has become the head of the corner; this was the Lord's doing, and it is marvelous in our eyes'?

Therefore I tell you, the kingdom of God will be taken away from you and given to a nation producing the fruits of it."

Some of the verses from the Holy Qur'án concerning the symbolic meanings of parables:

Sura 2:24 – Al-Baqarah – Many will He mislead by such parables and many guide: but none will He mislead thereby except the wicked.

Sura 74:33–34 – Al-Muddaththir – And that the infirm of heart and the unbelievers may say, What meaneth God by this parable?

Thus God misleadeth whom He will, and whom He will doth He guide aright: and none knoweth the armies of thy Lord but Himself: and this is no other than a warning to mankind.

Sura 40:36 – The Believer – Thus God misleadeth him who is the transgressor, the doubter.

Sura 3:5 – Ál-'Imrán – He it is who hath sent down to thee "the Book." Some of its signs are of themselves perspicuous;—these are the basis of the Book—and others are figurative. But they whose hearts are given to err, follow its figures, craving discord, craving an interpretation; yet none knoweth its interpretation but God. And the stable in knowledge say, "We believe in it: it is all from our Lord." But none will bear this in mind, save men endued with understanding.

Sura 39:28–29 – Al-Zumar – Now have we set before man in this Qur'án every kind of parable for their warning. An Arabic Qur'án, free from tortuous wording, to the intent that they may fear God.

Sura 30:58–59 – Al-Rúm – And now have we set before men, in this Qur'án, every kind of parable: yet if thou bring them a single verse of it, the infidels will surely say, "Ye are only utterers of vain things."

It is thus that God hath sealed up the hearts of those who are devoid of knowledge.

Sura 59:21 – Al-Hashra – Had we sent down this Qur'án on some mountain, thou wouldst certainly have seen it humbling itself and cleaving asunder for the fear of God. Such are the parables we propose to men in order that they may reflect.

Some of the passages from the Bahá'í sacred text concerning the symbolic meanings of parables:

Whatever proceeded from the tongue of the Son was revealed in parables, whilst He Who proclaimeth the Truth in this Day speaketh without them. Take heed lest thou cling to the cord of idle fancy and withhold thyself from that which hath been ordained in the Kingdom of God, the Almighty, the All-Bountiful.

Bahá'u'lláh, "Súriy-i-Haykal," The Summons of the Lord of Hosts, ¶120.

The understanding of His words and the comprehension of the utterances of the Birds of Heaven are in no wise dependent upon human learning. They depend solely upon purity of heart, chastity of soul, and freedom of spirit. This is evidenced by those who, today, though without a single letter of the accepted standards of learning, are occupying the loftiest seats of knowledge; and the garden of their hearts is adorned, through the showers of divine grace, with the roses of wisdom and the tulips of understanding. Well is it with the sincere in heart for their share of the light of a mighty Day!

Bahá'u'lláh, The Book of Certitude, ¶233.

It is evident unto thee that the Birds of Heaven and Doves of Eternity speak a twofold language. One language, the outward language, is devoid of allusions, is unconcealed and unveiled; that it may be a guiding lamp and a beaconing light whereby wayfarers may attain the heights of holiness, and seekers may advance into the realm of eternal reunion. . . . The other language is veiled and concealed, so that whatever lieth hidden in the heart of the malevolent may be made manifest and their innermost being be disclosed. . . . This is the divine standard, this is the Touchstone of God, wherewith He proveth His servants. None apprehendeth the meaning of these utterances except

189

them whose hearts are assured, whose souls have found favor with God, and whose minds are detached from all else but Him. In such utterances, the literal meaning, as generally understood by the people, is not what hath been intended.

Bahá'u'lláh, The Book of Certitude, ¶283.

The Holy Books have their special terminologies which must be known and understood. Physicians have their own peculiar terms; architects, philosophers have their characteristic expressions; poets have their phrases; and scientists, their nomenclatures. In the scripture we read the Zion is dancing. It is evident that this has other than literal interpretation.

'Abdu'l-Bahá, *The Promulgation of Universal Peace*, p. 344.

The generality of mankind are unable to grasp a sequence of logical arguments. For this reason they stand in need of symbols and parables telling of rewards and punishments in the next world.

'Abdu'l-Bahá, *The Secret of Divine Civilization*, p. 84.

. . . Their expressions, Their parables and Their instructions have a spiritual and divine signification, and have no connection with material things.

'Abdu'l-Bahá, *Some Answered Questions*, p. 103.

Christ spoke a parable in which He said His words were like the seeds of the sower; some fall upon stony ground, some upon sterile soil, some are choked by thorns and thistles, but some fall upon the ready, receptive and fertile ground of human hearts. When seeds are cast upon sterile soil, no growth follows. Those cast upon stony ground will grow a short time, but lacking deep roots will wither away. Thorns and thistles destroy others completely, but the seed cast in good ground brings forth harvest and fruitage.

In the same way, the words I speak to you here tonight may produce no effect whatever. Some hearts may be affected, then soon forget; others owing to superstitious ideas and imaginations may even fail to hear and understand; but the blessed souls who are attentive to my exhortation and admonition, listening with the ear of acceptance, allowing my words to penetrate effectively, will advance day by day toward full fruition, yea even to the Supreme Concourse. Consider how the parable makes attainment dependent upon capacity. Unless capacity is developed, the summons of the Kingdom cannot reach the ear, the light of the Sun of Truth will not be observed, and the fragrances of the rose garden of inner significance will be lost.

'Abdu'l-Bahá, *The Promulgation of Universal Peace*, pp. 205–6.

Another asked why the teachings of all religions are expressed largely by parables and metaphors and not in the plain language of the people.

'Abdu'l-Bahá replied:—"Divine things are too deep to be expressed by common words. The heavenly teachings are expressed in parable in order to be understood and preserved for ages to come. When the spiritually minded dive deeply into the ocean of their meaning they bring to the surface the pearls of their inner significance. There is no greater pleasure than to study God's Word with a spiritual mind."

'Abdu'l-Bahá, *'Abdu'l-Bahá in London,* pp. 79–80.

15

The Mission of Christ

Although Christ's mission centered on the redemption of the individual and the development of a virtuous moral character, He also said that He was sent to mankind to "preach the good news of the Kingdom of God."* Christ, as well as all the other Messengers or Manifestations of God, came as a divine teacher to educate man about the knowledge and love of God, sanctity, holiness, detachment, the development of a virtuous character, and the remission of sins. He also came to prepare mankind to develop a spiritual civilization for the coming of the "Kingdom of God." This promised "Day of God," foretold by the Prophets and Messengers of God, has been ushered in—the coming of which They all yearned to attain.

The coming of the "Day of God" or the "Kingdom of God on earth" could not have come about without the sacrifices of the blessed Divine Educators such as Abraham, Moses, Jesus and Muḥammad, who brought the Word of God to humanity at successive stages in preparation for this Promised Day. This Promised Day was announced by the Báb in 1844, and inaugurated by the declaration of Bahá'u'lláh in 1863. The bounties and perfections of God are in this Day being reflected on His creation and are illuminating all things.

---

* Luke 4:43.

Some of the verses from the Holy Bible concerning the mission of Christ:

Matthew 6:9–10 – Our Father in heaven, hallowed be Thy name, Thy kingdom come, Thy will be done on earth as it is in heaven.

Luke 4:43 – I must preach the good news of the kingdom of God to the other cities also; for I was sent for this purpose.

John 18:37 – Pilate said to him, "So you are a king?" Jesus answered, "You say that I am a king. For this I was born, and for this I have come into the world, to bear witness to the truth."

Matthew 26:28 – For this is my blood of the new testament, which is shed for many for the remission of sins.

John 11:25–26 – I am the resurrection and the life; he who believes in me, though he die, yet shall he live, and whoever lives and believes in me shall never die.

John 9:39 – Jesus said, For judgment I am come into this world, that they which see not might see; and that they which see might be made blind.

Matthew 10:34 – Do not think that I have come to bring peace on earth; I have not come to bring peace, but a sword.

Luke 12:51 – Suppose ye that I am come to give peace on earth? I tell you, Nay; but rather division.

Some of the verses from the Holy Qur'án concerning the mission of Christ:

Sura 2:81 – Al-Baqarah – . . . and to Jesus, son of Mary, gave we clear proofs of his mission, and strengthened him by the Holy Spirit.

Sura 5:79 – Al-Má'idah – The Messiah, Son of Mary, is but an Apostle; other Apostles have flourished before him; and his mother was a just person: they both ate food.

Sura 61:6 – Al-Saff – And remember when Jesus the son of Mary said, "O children of Israel! of a truth I am God's apostle to you to confirm the law which was given before me, and to announce an apostle that shall come after me whose name shall be Ahmad!"

Sura 43:63-64 – Al-Zukhruf – And when Jesus came with manifest proofs, he said, "Now am I come to you with wisdom; and a part of those things about which ye are at variance I will clear up to you; fear ye God therefore and obey me.

Verily, God is my Lord and your Lord; wherefore worship ye him: this is a right way."

Some of the passages from the Bahá'í sacred texts concerning the mission of Christ:

. . . is not the object of every Revelation to effect a transformation in the whole character of mankind, a transformation that shall manifest itself, both outwardly and inwardly, that shall affect both its inner life and external conditions? For if the character of mankind be not changed, the futility of God's universal Manifestations would be apparent.

Bahá'u'lláh, The Book of Certitude, ¶270.

The purpose underlying this Revelation, as well as those that preceded it, has, in like manner, been to announce the advent of the Faith of Him Whom God will make manifest. And this Faith—the Faith of Him Whom God will make manifest—in its turn, together with all the Revelations gone before it, have as their object the Manifestation destined to succeed it. And the latter, no less than all the Revelations preceding it, prepare the way for the Revelation which is yet to follow. The process of the rise and setting of the Sun of Truth will thus indefinitely continue—a process that hath had no beginning and will have no end.

The Báb, quoted in Shoghi Effendi,
The World Order of Bahá'u'lláh, p. 117.

Jesus Christ came to teach the people of the world this heavenly civilization and not material civilization. He breathed the breath of the Holy Spirit into the body of the world and established an illumined civilization. Among the principles of divine civilization He came to proclaim is the Most Great Peace of mankind. Among His principles of spiritual civilization is the oneness of the kingdom of humanity. Among the principles of heavenly civilization He brought is the virtue of the human world. Among the principles of celestial civilization He announced is the improvement and betterment of human morals.

'Abdu'l-Bahá, *The Promulgation of Universal Peace*, p. 15.

Christ appeared in this world nineteen hundred years ago to establish ties of unity and bonds of love between the various nations and different communities. He cemented together the sciences of Rome and the splendors of the civilization of Greece. He also accomplished affiliation between the Assyrian kingdom and the power of Egypt. The blending of these nations in unity, love and agreement had been impossible, but Christ through divine power established this condition among the children of men.

'Abdu'l-Bahá, *The Promulgation of Universal Peace*, p. 25.

Jesus Christ was an Educator of humanity. His teachings were altruistic; His bestowal, universal. He taught mankind by the power of the Holy Spirit and not through human agency, for the human power is limited, whereas the divine power is illimitable and infinite. The influence and accomplishment of Christ will attest this.

'Abdu'l-Bahá, *The Promulgation of Universal Peace*, p. 118.

When the sanctified breezes of Christ and the holy light of the Greatest Luminary [Bahá'u'lláh] were spread abroad, the human realities—that is to say, those who turned toward the Word of God and received the profusion of His bounties—were saved from this attachment and sin, obtained everlasting life, were delivered from the chains of bondage, and attained to the world of liberty. They were freed from the vices of the human world, and were blessed by the virtues of the Kingdom. This is the meaning of the words of Christ, "I gave My blood for the life of the world" [John 6:51]—that is to say, I have chosen all these troubles, these sufferings, calamities, and even the greatest martyrdom, to attain this object, the remission of sins (that is, the detachment of spirits from the human world, and their attraction to the divine world) in order that souls may arise who will be the very essence of the guidance of mankind, and the manifestations of the perfections of the Supreme Kingdom.

'Abdu'l-Bahá, *Some Answered Questions*, p. 125.

This young man, Christ, by the help of a supernatural power, abrogated the ancient Mosaic Law, reformed the general morals, and once again laid the foundation of eternal glory for the Israelites. Moreover, He brought to humanity the glad tidings of universal peace, and spread abroad teachings which were not for Israel alone but were for the general happiness of the whole human race.

'Abdu'l-Bahá, *Some Answered Questions*, p. 16.

The Revelation associated with the Faith of Jesus Christ focused attention primarily on the redemption of the individual and the molding of his conduct, and stressed, as its central theme, the necessity of inculcating a high standard of morality and discipline into man, as the fundamental unit in human society. Nowhere in the Gospels do we find any reference to the unity of nations or the unification of mankind as a whole. When Jesus spoke to those around Him, He addressed them primarily as individuals rather than as component parts of one universal, indivisible entity. The whole surface of the earth was as yet unexplored, and the organization of all its peoples and nations as one unit could, consequently, not be envisaged, how much less proclaimed or established. What other interpretation can be given to these words, addressed specifically by Bahá'u'lláh to the followers of the Gospel, in which the fundamental distinction between the Mission of Jesus Christ, concerning primarily the individual, and His own Message, directed more particularly to mankind as a whole, has been definitely established: *"Verily, He [Jesus] said: 'Come ye after Me, and I will make you to become fishers of men.' In this day, however, We say: 'Come ye after Me, that We may make you to become the quickeners of mankind.'"*

Shoghi Effendi, The Promised Day is Come, pp. 195–96.

16

The Miracles of Christ

Most of the miracles mentioned in the holy scriptures have an inner spiritual significance that goes beyond their outward form. As is the case with parables, one should not take them literally. Of course, it is not beyond the power of an omnipotent God to raise the dead, for instance, or to cure a leper of his disease. But, the Prophets of God do not come into the world to provide a sideshow of miracles to entertain the crowd. The Prophets come to teach spiritual truths that will influence the souls of all people.

If Christ raised bodies from the dead, as is recorded in the Gospels, of what real significance is this? Did not these same persons who were raised die again at some later date? Similarly, if the blind were given sight, the deaf hearing, and the lame made to walk, were these physical miracles not also only temporary?

But when the spiritually dead were given eternal life through the Word of God, or the spiritually blind were given permanent sight by His teachings, weren't these the true and lasting miracles? Aren't those the miracles we can experience today?

Some of the verses from the Holy Bible concerning the miracles of Christ:

John 9:39–41 – Jesus said, "For judgement I came into this world, that those who do not see may see, and that those who see may become blind." Some of the Pharisees near him heard this, and they said to him, "Are we also blind?" Jesus said to them, "If you were blind, you would have no guilt; but now that you say, 'We see,' your guilt remains."

Matthew 16:6–12 – Jesus said to them, "Beware, be on your guard against the leaven of the Pharisees and Sadducees," they began to say among themselves, "It is because we have brought no bread!" Knowing what was in their minds, Jesus said to them: "Why do you talk about bringing no bread? Where is your faith? Do you not understand even yet? Do you not remember the five loaves for the five thousand, and how many basketfuls you picked up? Or the seven loaves for the four thousand, and how many basketfuls you picked up? How can you fail to see that I was not speaking about bread? Be on your guard, I said, against the leaven of the Pharisees and Sadducees." Then they understood: they were to be on their guard, not against baker's leaven, but against the teaching of the Pharisees and Sadducees.

Matthew 4:3–4 – And when the tempter came to him, he said, If thou be the Son of God, command that these stones be made bread. But he answered and said, It is written, Man shall not live by bread alone, but by every word that proceedeth out of the mouth of God.

Luke 7:20–23 – And when the men had come to him, they said, "John the Baptist has sent us to you saying, 'Are you he who is to come, or shall we look for another?'" In that hour he cured many of diseases and plagues and evil spirits, and on many that were blind he bestowed sight. And he answered them, "Go tell John what you have seen and heard: the blind receive their sight, the lame walk, lepers are cleased, and the deaf hear, the dead are raised up, the poor have good news preached to them. And blessed is he who takes no offense at me."

Matthew 9:35–38 – And Jesus went about all the cities and villages, teaching in their synagogues, and preaching the gospel of the kingdom, and healing every sickness and every disease among the people. But when he saw the multitudes, he was moved with compassion on them, because they fainted, and were scattered abroad, as sheep having no shepherd. Then saith he unto his disciples, The harvest truly is plenteous, but the labourers are few; Pray ye therefore the Lord of the harvest, that he will send forth labourers into his harvest.

Matthew 10:1 – And when he had called unto him his twelve disciples, he gave them power against unclean spirits, to cast them out, and to heal all manner of sickness and all manner of disease.

Some of the verses from the Holy Qur'án concerning the miracles of Christ:

Sura 5:109–10 – Al-Má'idah – When He shall say: O Jesus! Son of Mary! call to mind my favour upon thee and upon thy mother, when I strengthened thee with the Holy Spirit, . . .

And when I taught thee the Scripture, and Wisdom, and the Law, and the Evangel: and thou didst create of clay, as it were, the figure of a bird, by my leave, and didst breathe into it, and by my leave it became a bird; and thou didst heal the blind and the leper, by my leave; and when, by my leave, thou didst bring forth the dead; and when I withheld the children of Israel from thee, when thou hadst come to them with clear tokens; and such of them as believed not said, "This is nought but plain sorcery."

Sura 40:78 – Al-Gháfir – And we have already sent apostles before thee: of some we have told thee, and of others we have told you nothing: but no apostle had the power to work a miracle unless by the leave of God.

Sura 29:48–50 – Al-'Ankabut – But it is a clear sign in the hearts of those whom "the knowledge" hath reached. None except the wicked reject our signs.

And they say, "Unless a sign be sent down to him from his Lord. . . ." Say: Signs are in the power of God alone. I am only a plain spoken warner.

Is it not enough for them that we have sent down to thee the Book to be recited to them? In this verily is a mercy and a warning to those who believe.

Sura 3:180 – Ál-'Imrán – Say: Already have apostles before me come to you with miracles, and with that of which ye speak. Wherefore slew ye them? Tell me, if ye are men of truth.

Sura 17:61 – Al-Isrá' – Nothing hindered us from sending thee with the power of working miracles, except that the people of old treated them as lies. We gave to Themoud the she-camel before their very eyes, yet they maltreated her! We send not a prophet with miracles but to strike terror.

Sura 13:39 – Al-Ra'd – Apostles truly have we already sent before thee, and wives and offspring have we given them. Yet no apostle had come with miracles unless by the leave of God.

Sura 2:57–58 – Al-Baqarah – And when Moses asked drink for his people, we said, "Strike the rock with the rod;" and from it there gushed twelve fountains: each tribe knew their drinking-place: "Eat and drink," said we, "of what God hath supplied, and do no wrong on the earth by licentious deeds."

And when ye said, "O Moses! we will not put up with one sort of food: pray, therefore, thy Lord for us, that He would bring forth for us of that which the earth groweth, its herbs and its cucumbers and its garlic and its lentils and its onions:" He said, "What! will ye exchange that which is worse for what is better? Get ye down into Egypt;—for ye shall have what ye have asked:" Vileness and poverty were stamped upon them, and they returned with wrath from God: This, for that they disbelieved the signs of God, and slew the Prophets unjustly: this, for that they rebelled and transgressed!

Sura 54:3 – Al-Qamar – But whenever they see a miracle they turn aside and say, This is well-devised magic.

Some of the passages from the Bahá'í sacred texts explaining the miracles of Christ:

We testify that when He (Jesus) came into the world, He shed the splendor of His glory upon all created things. Through Him the leper recovered from the leprosy of perversity and ignorance. Through Him, the unchaste and wayward were healed. Through His power, born of Almighty God, the eyes of the blind were opened, and the soul of the sinner sanctified.

Leprosy may be interpreted as any veil that interveneth between man and the recognition of the Lord, his God. Whoso alloweth himself to be shut out from Him is indeed a leper, who shall not be remembered in the Kingdom of God, the Mighty, the All-Praised. We bear witness that through the power of the Word of God every leper was cleansed, every sickness was healed, every human infirmity was banished. He it is Who purified the world. Blessed is the man who, with a face beaming with light, hath turned towards Him.

Bahá'u'lláh, *Gleanings from the Writings of Bahá'u'lláh*, no. 36.2–3.

. . . most of the miracles of the Prophets which are mentioned have an inner significance.

'Abdu'l-Bahá, *Some Answered Questions*, p. 37.

I do not wish to mention the miracles of Bahá'u'lláh, for it may perhaps be said that these are traditions, liable both to truth and to error, like the accounts of the miracles of Christ in the Gospel, which come to us from the apostles, and not from anyone else, and are denied by the Jews.

'Abdu'l-Bahá, *Some Answered Questions*, p. 37.

The meaning is not that the Manifestations are unable to perform miracles, for They have all power. But for Them inner sight, spiritual healing and eter-

206

nal life are the valuable and important things. Consequently, whenever it is recorded in the Holy Books that such a one was blind and recovered his sight, the meaning is that he was inwardly blind, and that he obtained spiritual vision, or that he was ignorant and became wise, or that he was negligent and became heedful, or that he was worldly and became heavenly.

'Abdu'l-Bahá, *Some Answered Questions*, p. 102.

The Holy Manifestations are the sources of miracles and the originators of wonderful signs. For Them, any difficult and impracticable thing is possible and easy. For through a supernatural power wonders appear from Them; and by this power, which is beyond nature, They influence the world of nature. From all the Manifestations marvelous things have appeared.

'Abdu'l-Bahá, *Some Answered Questions*, p. 100.

. . . if we relate to a seeker, a stranger to Moses and Christ, marvelous signs, he will deny them and will say: "Wonderful signs are also continually related of false gods by the testimony of many people, and they are affirmed in the Books. The Brahmans have written a book about wonderful prodigies from Brahma." He will also say: "How can we know that the Jews and the Christians speak the truth, and that the Brahmans tell a lie?" . . . Therefore, miracles are not a proof. For if they are proofs for those who are present, they fail as proofs to those who are absent."

'Abdu'l-Bahá, *Some Answered Questions*, pp. 100–101.

These are the counsels of 'Abdu'l-Bahá. It is my hope that out of the bestowals of the Lord of Hosts ye will become the spiritual essence and the very radiance of humankind, binding the hearts of all with bonds of love; that through the power of the Word of God ye will bring to life the dead now buried in the graves of their sensual desires; that ye will, with the rays of the

Sun of Truth, restore the sight of those whose inner eye is blind; that ye will bring spiritual healing to the spiritually sick. These things do I hope for, out of the bounties and the bestowals of the Beloved.

'Abdu'l-Bahá, *Selections from the Writings of 'Abdu'l-Bahá*, no. 17.7.

Recollect that Christ, solitary and alone, without a helper or protector, without armies and legions, and under the greatest oppression, uplifted the standard of God before all the people of the world, and withstood them, and finally conquered all, although outwardly He was crucified. Now this is a veritable miracle which can never be denied. There is no need of any other proof of the truth of Christ.

'Abdu'l-Bahá, *Some Answered Questions*, p. 101.

17

The Ascension of Christ

Jesus said, "And no man hath ascended up to heaven, but he that came down from heaven, even the Son of man which is in heaven."* This verse does not exclude anybody, not even the Son of man. The physical body of Christ did not descend from heaven but was born from the womb of His mother. It was the holy divine spirit of Jesus Christ that came down from heaven. Hence, His ascension was not that of the elemental body, but of the spirit.[†]

By crucifying Jesus, His enemies believed that they had destroyed Him and that His teachings would vanish. They counted His death as a victory, yet in reality His spirit was never touched. The verse revealed in the Qur'án even denied the killing or crucifixion of Jesus and reads, ". . . they slew him not, and they crucified him not, but they had only his likeness . . . they did not really slay him, but God took him up to Himself."[‡] 'Abdu'l-Bahá in explaining this apparent discrepancy, said that the verse in the Qur'án was referring to the "reality" of Christ, a reality which is eternal and protected from any worldly oppression.[§] This sanctified spiritual reality of Jesus Christ after its

---

* John 3:13.
† 'Abdu'l-Bahá, *Some Answered Questions*, pp. 103–5.
‡ Sura 4:156.
§ Star of the West, Vol. II, 7–8, p. 13.

ascension revived the disciples and conquered the world. Jesus said, "It is the spirit that gives life, the flesh is of no avail; the words that I have spoken to you are spirit and life."*

Some of the resurrection stories in the Bible explain that the disciples, after the crucifixion of Jesus Christ, were sad and discouraged. Only after speaking about Jesus, going over the prophecies and scriptures concerning the Messiah, and breaking bread together did they realize that Jesus was alive in spirit and was guiding them.

---

* John 6:63.

Some of the verses from the Holy Bible concerning the ascension of Christ:

John 3:13 – And no man hath ascended up to heaven, but he that came down from heaven, even the Son of man which is in heaven.

John 6:38 – "I have come down from heaven, not to do my own will, but the will of him who sent me."

John 6:42 – They said, "Surely this is Jesus son of Joseph; we know his father and mother. How can he now say, 'I have come down from heaven'?"

Luke 23:35–46 – The people stood looking on, and their rulers jeered at him: "He saved others: now let him save himself, if this is God's Messiah, his Chosen." The soldiers joined in the mockery and came forward offering him their sour wine. "If you are the king of the Jews," they said, "save yourself." There was an inscription above his head which ran: "This is the king of the Jews."

One of the criminals who hung there with him taunted him: "Are not you the Messiah? Save yourself, and us." But the other rebuked him: "Have you no fear of God? You are under the same sentence as he. For us it is plain justice; we are paying the price for our misdeeds; but this man has done nothing wrong." And he said, "Jesus, remember me when you come to your throne." He answered, "I tell you this: today you shall be with me in Paradise."

By now it was about midday and a darkness fell over the whole land, which lasted until three in the afternoon; the sun's light failed. And the curtain of the temple was torn in two. Then Jesus gave a loud cry and said, "Father, into thy hands I commit my spirit"; and with these words he died.

Matthew 27:39–42 – And they that passed by reviled him, wagging their heads, And saying, Thou that destroyest the temple, and buildest it in three days, save thyself. If thou be the Son of God, come down from the cross.

Likewise also the chief priests mocking him, with the scribes and elders, said, He saved others; himself he cannot save. If he be the King of Israel, let him now come down from the cross, and we will believe him.

Luke 24:13–31 – That very day two of them were going to a village named Emmaus, about seven miles from Jerusalem, and talking with each other about all these things that had happened. While they were talking and discussing together, Jesus himself drew near and went with them. But their eyes were kept from recognizing him. And he said to them, "What is this conversation which you are holding with each other as you walk?" And they stood still, looking sad. Then one of them named Cleopas, answered him, "Are you only a visitor to Jerusalem who does not know the things that have happened there in these days?" And he said to them, "What things?" And they said to him, "Concerning Jesus of Nazareth, who was a prophet mighty in deed and word before God and all the people, and how our chief priests and rulers delivered him up to be condemned to death, and crucified him. But we had hoped that he was the one to redeem Israel. Yes, and besides all this, it is now the third day since this happened. Moreover, some women of our company amazed us. They were at the tomb early in the morning and did not find his body; and they came back saying that they had even seen a vision of angels, who said that he was alive. Some of those who were with us went to the tomb, and found it just as the women had said; but him they did not see."

And he said to them, "O foolish men, and slow of heart to believe all that the prophets have spoken! Was it not necessary that the Christ should suffer these things and enter into his glory?" And beginning with Moses and all the prophets, he interpreted to them in all the scriptures the things concerning himself.

So they drew near to the village to which they were going. He appeared to be going further, but they constrained him, saying, "Stay with us, for it is toward evening and the day is now far spent." So he went in to stay with them. When he was at table with them, he took the bread and blessed, and broke it, and gave it to them. And their eyes were opened and they recognized him; and he vanished out of their sight.

The Acts of the Apostles 1:2–3 – Until the day in which he was taken up, after that he through the Holy Ghost had given commandments unto the apostles whom he had chosen:

To whom also he shewed himself alive after his passion by many infallible proofs, being seen of them forty days, and speaking of the things pertaining to the kingdom of God.

Verses from the Holy Qur'án concerning the ascension of Christ:

Sura 3:48 – Ál-'Imrán – Remember when God said, "O Jesus! Verily I will cause thee to die, and will take thee up to myself and deliver thee from those who believe not; and I will place those who follow thee above those who believe not, until the day of resurrection. Then, to me is your return, and wherein ye differ will I decide between you."

Sura 4:156 – Al-Nisá' – And for their saying, "Verily we have slain the Messiah, Jesus the Son of Mary, an Apostle of God." Yet they slew him not, and they crucified him not, but they had only his likeness. And they who differed about him were in doubt concerning him: No sure knowledge had they about him, but followed only an opinion, and they did not really slay him, but God took him up to Himself. And God is Mighty, Wise!

Some of the verses from the Bahá'í sacred texts concerning the ascension of Christ:

Know thou that when the Son of Man yielded up His breath to God, the whole creation wept with a great weeping. By sacrificing Himself, however, a fresh capacity was infused into all created things. Its evidences, as witnessed in all the peoples of the earth, are now manifest before thee. The deepest wisdom which the sages have uttered, the profoundest learning which any mind hath unfolded, the arts which the ablest hands have produced, the influence exerted by the most potent of rulers, are but manifestations of the quickening power released by His transcendent, His all-pervasive, and resplendent Spirit.

Bahá'u'lláh, *Gleanings from the Writings of Bahá'u'lláh*, no. 36.1.

That which thou hast heard concerning Abraham, the Friend of the All-Merciful, is the truth, and no doubt is there about it. The Voice of God commanded Him to offer up Ishmael as a sacrifice, so that His steadfastness in the Faith of God and His detachment from all else but Him may be demonstrated unto men. The purpose of God, moreover, was to sacrifice him as a ransom for the sins and iniquities of all the peoples of the earth. This same honor, Jesus, the Son of Mary, besought the one true God, exalted be His name and glory, to confer upon Him. For the same reason was Ḥusayn offered up as a sacrifice by Muḥammad, the Apostle of God.

Bahá'u'lláh, *Gleanings from the Writings of Bahá'u'lláh*, no. 32.1.

The resurrections of the Divine Manifestations are not of the body. All Their states, Their conditions, Their acts, the things They have established, Their teachings, Their expressions, Their parables and Their instructions have a spiritual and divine signification, and have no connection with material things. For example, there is the subject of Christ's coming from heaven: it is clearly stated in many places in the Gospel that the Son of man came from heaven, He is in heaven, and He will go to heaven. So in chapter 6, verse 38, of the Gospel of John it is written: "For I came down from heaven"; and also in verse 42 we find: "And they said, Is not this Jesus, the son of Joseph, whose father and mother we know? how is it then that he saith, I came down from heaven?" Also in John, chapter 3, verse 13: "And no man hath ascended up to heaven, but He that came down from heaven, even the Son of man which is in heaven."

'Abdu'l-Bahá, *Some Answered Questions*, p. 103.

And as it has become evident that Christ came from the spiritual heaven of the Divine Kingdom, therefore, His disappearance under the earth for three days has an inner signification and is not an outward fact. In the same way, His resurrection from the interior of the earth is also symbolical; it is a spiritual and divine fact, and not material; and likewise His ascension to heaven is a spiritual and not material ascension.

'Abdu'l-Bahá, *Some Answered Questions*, p. 104.

Therefore, we say that the meaning of Christ's resurrection is as follows: the disciples were troubled and agitated after the martyrdom of Christ. The Reality of Christ, which signifies His teachings, His bounties, His perfections and His spiritual power, was hidden and concealed for two or three days after His martyrdom, and was not resplendent and manifest. No, rather it was lost, for the believers were few in number and were troubled and agitated. The Cause of Christ was like a lifeless body; and when after three days the disciples became assured and steadfast, and began to serve the Cause of Christ, and resolved to spread the divine teachings, putting His counsels into practice, and arising to serve Him, the Reality of Christ became resplendent and His bounty appeared; His religion found life; His teachings and His admonitions became evident and visible. In other words, the Cause of Christ was like a lifeless body until the life and the bounty of the Holy Spirit surrounded it.

'Abdu'l-Bahá, *Some Answered Questions*, p. 104.

Such is the meaning of the resurrection of Christ, and this was a true resurrection. But as the clergy have neither understood the meaning of the Gospels nor comprehended the symbols, therefore, it has been said that religion is in contradiction to science, and science in opposition to religion, as, for example, this subject of the ascension of Christ with an elemental body to the visible heaven is contrary to the science of mathematics. But when the truth of this subject becomes clear, and the symbol is explained, science in no way contradicts it; but, on the contrary, science and the intelligence affirm it.

'Abdu'l-Bahá, *Some Answered Questions*, pp.104–5.

Know that the Holy Manifestations, though They have the degrees of endless perfections, yet, speaking generally, have only three stations. The first station is the physical; the second station is the human, which is that of the rational soul; the third is that of the divine appearance and the heavenly splendor.

The physical station is phenomenal; it is composed of elements, and necessarily everything that is composed is subject to decomposition. It is not possible that a composition should not be disintegrated.

The second is the station of the rational soul, which is the human reality. This also is phenomenal, and the Holy Manifestations share it with all mankind. . . .

The third station is that of the divine appearance and heavenly splendor: it is the Word of God, the Eternal Bounty, the Holy Spirit. It has neither beginning nor end. . . .

'Abdu'l-Bahá, *Some Answered Questions*, pp. 151–52.

Then it is evident that the Manifestations possess three conditions: the physical condition, the condition of the rational soul, and the condition of the divine appearance and heavenly splendor. The physical condition will certainly become decomposed, but the condition of the rational soul, though it has a beginning, has no end: nay, it is endowed with everlasting life. But the Holy Reality, of which Christ says, "The Father is in the Son," [Cf. John 14:11; 17:21.] has neither beginning nor end. When beginning is spoken of, it signifies the state of manifesting; and, symbolically, the condition of silence is compared to sleep. For example, a man is sleeping—when he begins to speak, he is awake—but it is always the same individual, whether he be asleep or awake; no difference has occurred in his station, his elevation, his glory, his reality or his nature.

'Abdu'l-Bahá, Some Answered Questions, p. 153.

Verily the heaven into which the Messiah rose up was not this unending sky, rather was His heaven the Kingdom of His beneficent Lord. Even as He Himself hath said, "I came down from heaven," [John 6:38] and again, "The Son of Man is in heaven." [John 3:13] Hence it is clear that His heaven is beyond all directional points; it encircleth all existence, and is raised up for those who worship God. Beg and implore thy Lord to lift thee up into that heaven, and give thee to eat of its food, in this age of majesty and might.

'Abdu'l-Bahá, Selections from the Writings of 'Abdu'l-Bahá, pp. 167–68.

In regard to the verse, which is revealed in the Qur'án, that, Christ was not killed and was not crucified, by this is meant the Reality of Christ. Although they crucified this elemental body, yet the merciful reality and the heavenly existence remain eternal and undying, and it was protected from the oppression and persecution of the enemies, for Christ is Eternal and Everlasting.

How can He die? This death and crucifixion were imposed on the physical body of Christ, and not upon the Spirit of Christ.

'Abdu'l-Bahá, quoted in *Star of the West*, Vol. II, 7–8, p .13.

They were not willing to have the body of Jesus Christ put in the Jews' cemetery. The Apostles went and bought a piece of land and interred him. Then the Jews took their refuse there. Later men came and built a great church over it. This was built by the mother of one of the Caesars, after three hundred years. Even up to this time in certain parts it is known as the Church of Refuse. This is really the Tomb of Christ.

'Abdu'l-Bahá, quoted in *Star of the West*, June 24, 1914, Vol. V, p. 85.

"Regarding your question relative to Surih 4, 156 of the 'Qur'án' in which Muḥammad says that the Jews did not crucify Jesus, the Christ but one like Him; what is meant by this passage is that although the Jews succeeded in destroying the physical body of Jesus, yet they were impotent to destroy the Divine reality in Him."

On behalf of Shoghi Effendi, quoted in *Lights of Guidance*, no. 1669.

18

Jesus, the Son of God

In many verses, the Bible refers to Jesus as the "Son of God" or the "Son of man." In the Bahá'í writings, He is titled the "Spirit of God," the "Son of God," the "Son of man," and the "Essence of the Spirit."

The title *Son of God* does not mean that God, the All-Glorious, impregnated Mary and produced a physical son—God is not a physical being and is far exalted above any human attribute. Rather, the term *Son of God* has a spiritual meaning. Similarly, other appellations have been given to other Manifestations of God: Moses was known as the Interlocutor, He Who spoke with God; Muḥammad was known as the Friend of God, or the Apostle of God; Bahá'u'lláh took the title "the Glory of God."

The verse in the Holy Qur'án appearing to deny the "Sonship" of Jesus regrettably became one of the causes of disputations and accusations between Christians and Muslims about the authenticity of each other's holy book. The Qur'án did not really deny that Jesus was the Son of God but was instead referring to the sayings and interpretation of most Christians who take the relationship between God and Jesus as a physical relationship instead of a spiritual one. Shoghi Effendi, Guardian of the Bahá'í Faith, explains this by saying: "... *when the Qur'án denies Christ is the Son of God it is not refuting His words but the false interpretation of them by the Christians who read into* *them a relationship of an almost corporeal nature, whereas Almighty God has no parents or offspring.*"*

Furthermore, Jesus conferred the title of "sons of God" on all those who believe in Him.† All true believers are sons of God in a metaphorical sense. Jesus Christ also explained that He and God were one in a figurative sense. For He was given the authority of God, and whoever accepted Him accepted God, whoever rejected Him rejected God.

---

* On behalf of Shoghi Effendi, in *Lights of Guidance,* no. 1652.
† John 1:12–13.

Some of the verses from the Holy Bible concerning Jesus, the Son of God:

Matthew 16:15–17 – He saith unto them, But whom say ye that I am? And Simon Peter answered and said, Thou art the Christ, the Son of the living God. And Jesus answered and said unto him, Blessed art thou, Simon Bar-jona: for flesh and blood hath not revealed it unto thee, but my Father which is in heaven.

John 1:12–13 – But as many as received him, to them gave he power to become the sons of God, even to them that believe on his name: Which were born, not of blood, nor of the will of the flesh, nor of the will of man, but of God.

John 10:27–30 – My sheep hear my voice, and I know them, and they follow me; and I give them eternal life, and they shall never perish, and no one shall snatch them out of my hand. My Father, who has given them to me, is greater than all, and no one is able to snatch them out of the Father's hand. I and the Father are one.

John 17:20–23 – I do not pray for these only, but also for those who believe in me through their word, that they may all be one; even as thou, Father, art in me, and I in thee, that they also may be in us, so that the world may believe that thou hast sent me. The glory which thou hast given me I have given to them, that they may be one even as we are one, I in them and thou in me, that they may become perfectly one. . . .

John 10:33–36 – The Jews answered him, "It is not for a good work that we stone you but for blasphemy; because you, being a man, make yourself God." Jesus answered them, "Is it not written in your law, 'I said, you are gods'? If he called them gods to whom the word of God came (and scripture cannot be broken) do you say of him whom the Father consecrated and sent into the world, 'You are blaspheming,' because I said, 'I am the Son of God'?"

John 5:19 – Jesus said to them, "Truly, truly, I say to you, the Son can do nothing of his own accord, but only what he sees the Father doing . . ."

John 5:23 – He who does not honor the Son does not honor the Father who sent him.

Some of the verses from the Holy Qur'án concerning the Son of God:

Sura 9:30 – Al-Tawbah – The Jews say, "Ezra (Ozair) is a son of God"; and the Christians say, "The Messiah is a son of God." Such are the sayings in their mouths! God do battle with them! How are they misguided!

Sura 25:2 – Al-Furqán – His the Kingdom of the Heavens and of the Earth! No son hath He begotten! No partner hath He in his Empire! All things hath He created, and decreeing hath decreed their destinies.

Sura 72:3 – Al-Jinn – And He—may the majesty of our Lord be exalted!— hath taken no spouse neither hath he any offspring.

Sura 39:6 – Al-Zumar – Had God desired to have had a son, he had surely chosen what he pleased out of his own creation. But praise be to Him! He is God, the One, the Almighty.

Sura 17:111 – Al-Isrá' – Say: Praise be to God who hath not begotten a son, who hath no partner in the Kingdom, nor any protector on account of weakness. And magnify him by proclaiming His greatness.

Sura 23:93 – Al-Mu'minún – God hath not begotten offspring; neither is there any other God with Him: else had each god assuredly taken away that which he had created, and some had assuredly uplifted themselves above others! Far from the glory of God, be what they affirm of Him!

Sura 10:69–70 – Yúnis – They say: "God hath begotten children." No! By his glory! He is the self-sufficient. All that is in the Heavens and all that is in the

225

Earth is His! Have ye warranty for that assertion? What! speak ye of God that which ye know not?

Say: Verily, they who devise this lie concerning God shall fare ill.

Sura 5:76–77 – Al-Má'idah – Infidels now are they who say, "God is the Messiah, Son of Mary;" for the Messiah said, "O children of Israel! Worship God, my Lord and your Lord." Whoever shall join other gods with God, God shall forbid him the Garden, and his abode shall be the Fire; and the wicked shall have no helpers.

They surely are Infidels who say, "God is the third of three:" for there is no God but one God: and if they refrain not from what they say, a grievous chastisement shall light on such of them as are Infidels.

Sura 5:79 – Al-Má'idah – The Messiah, Son of Mary, is but an Apostle; other Apostles have flourished before him; and his mother was a just person: they both ate food. Behold! How we make clear to them the signs! Then behold how they turn aside!

Sura 2:254 – Al-Baqarah – Some of the apostles we have endowed more highly than others: Those to whom God hath spoken, He hath raised to the loftiest grade, and to Jesus the Son of Mary we gave manifest signs, and we strengthened him with the Holy Spirit.

Sura 4:169–170 – Al-Nisá' – O ye people of the Book! Overstep not bounds in your religion; and of God, speak only truth. The Messiah, Jesus, son of Mary, is only an apostle of God, and his Word which he conveyed into Mary, and a Spirit proceeding from himself. Believe there in God and his apostles, and say not, "Three:" (there is a Trinity)—Forbear—it will be better for you. God is only one God! Far be it from His glory that He should have a son! His, whatever is in the Heavens, and whatever is in the Earth! And God is a sufficient Guardian.

The Messiah disdaineth not to be a servant of God, nor do the angels who are nigh unto Him.

Sura 18:3–4 – Al-Kahf – And that it may warn those who say, "God hath begotten a Son."

No knowledge of this have either they or their fathers! A grievous saying to come out of their mouths! They speak no other than a lie!

Some of the passages from the Bahá'í sacred texts concerning Jesus, the Son of God:

". . . each Manifestation of God hath a distinct individuality, a definitely pre-scribed mission, and predestined revelation, and specially designated limita-tions. Each one of them is known by a different name, is characterized by a special attribute, fulfils a definite mission, and is entrusted with a particular Revelation. Even as He saith: "Some of the Apostles We have caused to excel the others. To some God hath spoken, some He hath raised and exalted. And to Jesus, Son of Mary, We gave manifest signs, and We strengthened Him with the Holy Spirit.""

Bahá'u'lláh, Gleanings from the Writings of Bahá'u'lláh, no. 22.4.

After the departure of Christ many appeared who were instrumental in creat-ing factions, schisms and discussions. It became difficult to know which one was following the right path. One of these disturbers was Nestorius, a Syrian, who proclaimed that Christ was not a Prophet of God. This created a divi-sion and sect called the Nestorians. The Catholics declared Jesus Christ to be the Son of God, even pronouncing Him to be Deity itself. The Protestants announced the doctrine that Christ embodied two elements: the human and the divine. In brief, divisions were created in the religion of God. . . .

'Abdu'l-Bahá, The Promulgation of Universal Peace, p. 538.

Afterward Christ came, saying, "I am born of the Holy Spirit." Though it is now easy for the Christians to believe this assertion, at that time it was very difficult. According to the text of the Gospel the Pharisees said, "Is not this the son of Joseph of Nazareth Whom we know? How can He say, therefore, I came down from heaven?" [Cf. John 6:42]

'Abdu'l-Bahá, Some Answered Questions, p. 16.

Such were the words uttered by Christ. On account of these words they cav-
iled at and assailed Him when He said unto them, "Verily the Son is in the
Father, and the Father is in the Son" [John 14:10]. Be thou informed of this,
and learn thou the secrets of thy Lord. As for the deniers, they are veiled from
God: they see not, they hear not, neither do they understand.

'Abdu'l-Bahá, Selections from the Writings of 'Abdu'l-Bahá, no. 19.12.

As to the position of Christianity, let it be stated without any hesitation or
equivocation that its divine origin is unconditionally acknowledged, that the
Sonship and Divinity of Jesus Christ are fearlessly asserted, that the divine
inspiration of the Gospel is fully recognized, that the reality of the mystery of the Immaculacy of the Virgin Mary is confessed, and the primacy
of Peter, the Prince of the Apostles, is upheld and defended. The Founder
of the Christian Faith is designated by Bahá'u'lláh as the *"Spirit of God,"* is
proclaimed as the One Who *"appeared out of the breath of the Holy Ghost,"*
and is even extolled as the *"Essence of the Spirit."*

Shoghi Effendi, The Promised Day is Come, p. 179.

. . . when the Qur'án denies Christ is the Son of God it is not refuting His
words but the false interpretation of them by the Christians who read into
them a relationship of an almost corporeal nature, whereas Almighty God
has no parents or offspring. What is meant by Christ, is His spirit's relation to
the Infinite Spirit, and this the Qur'án does not deny. It is in a sense attributable—this kind of Sonship—to all the Prophets.

On behalf of Shoghi Effendi to an individual, in Lights of Guidance, no. 1652.

19

Was Jesus the Only One Who Had No Father?

Bahá'ís believe that Jesus was born into this world without a father. Both Bahá'u'lláh and 'Abdu'l-Bahá have stated that Jesus came into this world through the direct intervention of the Holy Spirit. Hence, His birth was miraculous.* Arguments over this issue are futile, and the greatness of Jesus Christ rests on His life and His teachings. He was a Manifestation of God Who, like all other Divine Teachers, demonstrated complete perfections and glory.

If we believe that the foundation of the greatness of Jesus Christ was His lack of an earthly father, then according to the Bible, it could be argued that there were others who were greater than He. The Book of Hebrews says that "Melchisedek, king of Salem" was without father or mother.† Also, Adam and Eve—according to the Bible—had neither a father nor a mother.‡

---

* On behalf of Shoghi Effendi, in *Lights of Guidance,* no. 1637.
† Hebrews 7:1–4.
‡ Genesis 1:27 and 2:7, 21–22.

The Qur'án describes the creation of Jesus by saying, "Verily, Jesus is as Adam in the sight of God. He created him of dust: He then said to him, 'Be'—and he was."*

From another perspective, the book of John describes the disciples of Jesus Christ as the "sons of God": "Which were born, not of blood, nor of the will of the flesh, nor of the will of man, but of God."† It is evident in this case that the spiritual reality of some great souls comes from God.

---

* Sura 3:52.
† John 1:13.

Some of the verses from the Holy Bible concerning the birth of Christ:

Matthew 1:18–25 – Now the birth of Jesus Christ took place in this way. When his mother Mary had been betrothed to Joseph, before they came together she was found to be with child of the Holy Spirit; and her husband Joseph, being a just man and unwilling to put her to shame, resolved to divorce her quietly. But as he considered this, behold, an angel of the Lord appeared to him in a dream, saying, "Joseph, son of David, do not fear to take Mary your wife, for that which is conceived in her is of the Holy Spirit; she will bear a son, and you shall call his name Jesus, for he will save his people from their sins." All this took place to fulfill what the Lord had spoken by the prophet:

"Behold, a virgin shall conceive and bear a son, and his name shall be called Emman'-u-el" (which means, God with us). When Joseph woke from sleep, he did as the angel of the Lord commanded him; he took his wife, but knew her not until she had borne a son; and he called his name Jesus.

Romans 1:2–4 – This gospel God announced beforehand in sacred scriptures through his prophets. It is about his Son: on the human level he was born of David's stock, but on the level of the spirit—the Holy Spirit—he was declared Son of God.

John 6:41–42 – The Jews then murmured at him, because he said, "I am the bread which came down from heaven." They said, "Is not this Jesus, the son of Joseph, whose father and mother we know? How does he now say, 'I have come down from heaven'?"

Mark 6:3 – Is not this the carpenter, the son of Mary, the brother of James, and Joses, and of Juda, and Simon? And are not his sisters here with us?

Hebrews 7:1–4 – For this Melchisedec, king of Salem, priest of the most high God, who met Abraham returning from the slaughter of the kings, and blessed him; To whom also Abraham gave a tenth part of all; first being by interpretation King of righteousness, and after that also King of Salem, which is, King of peace; Without father, without mother, without descent, having neither beginning of days, nor end of life; but made like unto the Son of God; abideth a priest continually. Now consider how great this man was, unto whom even the patriarch Abraham gave the tenth of the spoils.

John 1:12–13 – But as many as received him, to them gave he power to become the sons of God, even to them that believe on his name: Which were born, not of blood, nor of the will of the flesh, nor of the will of man, but of God.

Some of the verses from the Holy Qur'án concerning the birth of Christ:

Sura 19:17–23 – Maryam – . . . we sent our spirit to her, and he took before her the form of a perfect man.

She said: "I fly for refuge from thee to the God of Mercy! If thou fearest Him, begone from me."

He said: "I am only a messenger of thy Lord, that I may bestow on thee a holy son."

She said: "How shall I have a son, when man hath never touched me? And I am not unchaste."

He said: "So shall it be. Thy Lord hath said: 'Easy is this with me;' and we will make him a sign to mankind, and a mercy from us. For it is a thing decreed."

And she conceived him, and retired with him to a far-off place.

And the throes came upon her by the trunk of a palm. She said: "Oh, would that I had died ere this, and been a thing forgotten, forgotten quite!"

Sura 19:28–29 – Maryam – Then came she with the babe to her people, bearing him. They said, "O Mary! now hast thou done a strange thing!

O sister of Aaron! Thy father was not a man of wickedness, nor unchaste thy mother."

Sura 3:40–42 – Ál'Imrán – Remember when the angel said, "O Mary! Verily God announceth to thee the Word from Him: His name shall be, Messiah Jesus the son of Mary, illustrious in this world, and in the next, and one of those who have near access to God;

And He shall speak to men alike when in the cradle and when grown up; And he shall be one of the just."

She said, "How, O my Lord! Shall I have a son, when man hath not touched me?" He said, "Thus: God will create what He will; When He decreeth a thing, He only saith, 'Be,' and it is."

Sura 3:52 – Ál'Imrán – Verily, Jesus is as Adam in the sight of God. He created him of dust: He then said to him, "Be"—and he was.

Some of the passages from the Bahá'í sacred texts concerning the birth of Christ:

Likewise, reflect upon the state and condition of Mary. So deep was the perplexity of that most beauteous countenance, so grievous her case, that she bitterly regretted she had ever been born. To this beareth witness the text of the sacred verse wherein it is mentioned that after Mary had given birth to Jesus, she bemoaned her plight and cried out: "O would that I had died ere this, and been a thing forgotten, forgotten quite!" [Qur'án 19:22] I swear by God! Such lamenting consumeth the heart and shaketh the being. Such consternation of the soul, such despondency, could have been caused by no other than the censure of the enemy and the cavilings of the infidel and perverse. Reflect, what answer could Mary have given to the people around her? How could she claim that a Babe Whose father was unknown had been conceived of the Holy Ghost? Therefore did Mary, that veiled and immortal Countenance, take up her Child and return unto her home. No sooner had the eyes of the people fallen upon her than they raised their voice saying: "O sister of Aaron! Thy father was not a man of wickedness, nor unchaste thy mother" [Qur'án 19:28].

Bahá'u'lláh, The Book of Certitude, ¶59.

And now, meditate upon this most great convulsion, this grievous test. Notwithstanding all these things, God conferred upon that essence of the Spirit, Who was known amongst the people as fatherless, the glory of Prophethood, and made Him His testimony unto all that are in heaven and on earth.

Bahá'u'lláh, The Book of Certitude, ¶60.

The honor and greatness of Christ is not due to the fact that He did not have a human father, but to His perfections, bounties and divine glory. If the greatness of Christ is His being fatherless, then Adam is greater than Christ, for He had neither father nor mother. It is said in the Old Testament, "And the Lord God formed man of the dust of the ground, and breathed into his nostrils the breath of life; and man became a living soul" [Gen. 2:7]. Observe that it is said that Adam came into existence from the Spirit of life. Moreover, the expression which John uses in regard to the disciples proves that they also are from the Heavenly Father. Hence it is evident that the holy reality, meaning the real existence of every great man, comes from God and owes its being to the breath of the Holy Spirit.

The purport is that, if to be without a father is the greatest human glory, then Adam is greater than all, for He had neither father nor mother.

'Abdu'l-Bahá, *Some Answered Questions*, pp. 89–90.

With regard to your question concerning the Virgin Birth of Jesus; on this point, as on several others, the Bahá'í Teachings are in full agreement with the doctrines of the Catholic Church. In the "Kitáb-i-Íqán" [The Book of Certitude] and in a few other Tablets still unpublished, Bahá'u'lláh confirms, however indirectly, the Catholic conception of the Virgin Birth. Also 'Abdu'l-Bahá in the "Some Answered Questions," Chap. XII, p. 73, explicitly states that "Christ found existence through the Spirit of God" which statement necessarily implies, when viewed in the light of the text, that Jesus was not the son of Joseph."

On behalf of Shoghi Effendi to an individual, in *Lights of Guidance*, no. 1639.

20

The Meaning of Antichrist

What is meant by the term *antiChrist?* According to the Bible, anyone who does not believe in Jesus Christ, does not glorify Him, and does not follow His teachings, is an antiChrist.

The scriptures read, ". . . every spirit which confesses that Jesus Christ has come in the flesh is of God, and every spirit which does not confess Jesus is not of God. This is the spirit of antichrist, of which you heard that it was coming, and now it is in the world already."* The last part of the verse states clearly that the antiChrist was "in the world already"—that is, those who did not believe in Jesus Christ at that time were antiChrist; those who did not follow His teachings and opposed Him were also antiChrist. The scriptures do not state that the antiChrist would appear only at a certain time or at a certain place. Instead, they state that *any* person or "spirit" who denies or opposes Christ is an antiChrist.

All the Prophets and Manifestations of God suffered at the hands of those who denied and opposed Them. In this Dispensation, not only did Bahá'u'lláh Himself suffer at the hands of those who opposed Him, but He also suffered

---

* 1ˢᵗ John 4:2–3.

at the hands of Covenant-breakers—those who became His followers and then turned against Him. Mírzá Siyyid Muḥammad-i-Iṣfahání was one such Covenant-breaker who was described by Shoghi Effendi, Guardian of the Bahá'í Faith, as the "Antichrist of the Bahá'í Revelation."*

Furthermore, the Bible did not only say that there would be false prophets, but also false teachers and preachers, who would appear and spread heresies. They will be teaching and preaching in Christ's name and even do wonders; however, the Bible describes them by saying, "Many will say to me in that day, Lord, Lord, have we not prophesied in thy name? and in thy name have cast out devils? and in thy name done many wonderful works? And then will I profess unto them, I never knew you: depart from me, ye that work iniquity."† Even those who taught and preached in Christ's name could be called "antiChrist" because of their iniquity.

The Bible sets the standard by which a person can know the "truth" from "falsehood" by saying, "Ye shall know them by their fruits."‡

The Bahá'í sacred writings acknowledge the divinity of Jesus Christ and glorify Him.

---

* Shoghi Effendi, *God Passes By*, p. 164.
† Matthew 7:22–23.
‡ Matthew 7:16.

Some of the verses from the Holy Bible concerning the Antichrist:

1ˢᵗ John 2:22 – Who is the liar but he who denieth that Jesus is the Christ? He is anti-christ, that denieth the Father and the Son.

1ˢᵗ John 4:1–3 – Beloved, do not believe every spirit, but test the spirits to see whether they are of God; for many false prophets have gone out into the world. By this you know the Spirit of God: every spirit which confesses that Jesus Christ has come in the flesh is of God, and every spirit which does not confess Jesus is not of God. This is the spirit of antichrist, of which you heard that it was coming, and now it is in the world already.

2ⁿᵈ Epistle, Peter 2:1–3 – But there were false prophets also among the people, even as there shall be false teachers among you, who privily shall bring in damnable heresies, even denying the Lord that bought them, and bring upon themselves swift destruction. And many shall follow their pernicious ways; by reason of whom the way of truth shall be evil spoken of. And through covetousness shall they with feigned words make merchandise of you . . .

Matthew 23:13 – But woe to you, scribes and Pharisees, hypocrites! for ye shut up the kingdom of heaven against men; for ye neither go in yourselves, neither suffer ye them that are entering to go in.

Matthew 7:15–18 – Beware of false prophets, which come to you in sheep's clothing, but inwardly they are ravening wolves.

Ye shall know them by their fruits. Do men gather grapes of thorns, or figs of thistles? Even so every good tree bringeth forth good fruit; but a corrupt tree bringeth forth evil fruit.

A good tree cannot bring forth evil fruit, neither can a corrupt tree bring forth good fruit.

Matthew 7:20–23 – Wherefore by their fruits ye shall know them.

Not every one that saith unto me, Lord, Lord, shall enter into the kingdom of heaven; but he that doeth the will of my Father which is in heaven.

Many will say to me in that day, Lord, Lord, have we not prophesied in thy name? and in thy name have cast out devils? and in thy name done many wonderful works? And then will I profess unto them, I never knew you: depart from me, ye that work iniquity.

Matthew 24:23–24 – Then if any one says to you, Lo, here is the Christ, or there; believe it not. For there shall arise false Christs, and false prophets, and shall shew great signs and wonders; insomuch that, if it were possible, they shall deceive the very elect.

Some of the passages from the Bahá'í sacred text
concerning the meaning of the Antichrist:

192. God hath laid hold on him who led thee astray. ¶184
A reference to Siyyid Muḥammad-i-Isfahání, who is described by Shoghi Effendi as the "Antichrist of the Bahá'í Revelation." He was a man of corrupt character and great personal ambition who induced Mírzá Yaḥyá to oppose Bahá'u'lláh and to claim prophethood for himself.

Bahá'u'lláh, The Kitáb-í-Aqdas, note 192.

The Jews said, Christ was not Messiah but Antichrist, because one of the signs of the Messiah's coming was the dancing of Mount Zion, which had not yet come to pass. In reality, when His Holiness appeared, not only Mount Zion but all Palestine danced and rejoiced. Again in the scriptures it is said, "The trees of the field shall clap their hands." This is symbolical. There are terms and expressions of usage in every language which cannot be taken literally.

'Abdu'l-Bahá, *The Promulgation of Universal Peace*, pp. 344–45.

Consider the sad picture of Italy carrying war into Tripoli. If you should announce that Italy was a barbarous nation and not Christian, this would be vehemently denied. But would Christ sanction what they are doing in Tripoli? Is this destruction of human life obedience to His laws and teachings? Where does He command it? Where does He consent to it? He was killed by His enemies; He did not kill. He even loved and prayed for those who hung Him on the cross. Therefore, these wars and cruelties, this bloodshed and sorrow are Antichrist, not Christ.

'Abdu'l-Bahá, *The Promulgation of Universal Peace*, p. 7.

No less bitter is the conflict between sects and denominations. Christ was a divine Center of unity and love. Whenever discord prevails instead of unity, whenever hatred and antagonism take the place of love and spiritual fellowship, Antichrist reigns instead of Christ. Who is right in these controversies and hatreds between sects? . . . . to be a Christian is not merely to bear the name of Christ and say, "I belong to a Christian government." To be a real Christian is to be a servant in His Cause and Kingdom, to go forth under His banner of peace and love toward all mankind. . . .

'Abdu'l-Bahá, The Promulgation of Universal Peace, pp. 7–8.

We do not believe in Anti-Christ in the sense the Christians do. Anyone who violently and determinedly sought to oppose the Manifestation could be called an "anti-Christ," such as the Vazír in the Báb's day, Ḥájí Mírzá Áqásí.

On behalf of Shoghi Effendi to an individual,
in High Endeavours: Messages to Alaska, p. 69.

PART 3

SOME
ISLAMIC TOPICS

21

"The true religion with God is Islam"

If we examine the meaning of the word *Islam*, we find that *Islam* comes from the Arabic verb "aslam," which literally means "to submit oneself" or "to willingly surrender oneself" to the will of God; hence, a "Muslim" is one who willingly surrenders his will to the will of God. In one of His prayers, Bahá'u'lláh explains the concept of surrendering one's will to the will of God by saying, *"I implore Thee . . . to enable me so to surrender my will to what Thou hast decreed in Thy Tablets, that I may cease to discover within me any desire except what Thou didst desire through the power of Thy sovereignty, and any will save what Thou didst destine for me by Thy will."**

The Qur'án refers to the followers of any true religion from God as "Muslims." The Qur'án states that Abraham, Ishmael, Jacob, Moses, and the disciples of Christ were all Muslims—even though the Qur'án had not been revealed at the time they were living. The Qur'án does not differentiate between any of the Messengers or Manifestations of God and regards them all as one and the same, as it states, "we make no distinction between any

---

* Bahá'u'lláh, in *Bahá'í Prayers,* p. 161.

of His Apostles."* It further states that the One who revealed the Qur'án to Muḥammad is the same One who revealed the scriptures of old. The Qur'án reads, "We believe in it, for it is the truth from our Lord. We were Muslims before it came."† Thus, in broader terms, the meaning intended by the word *Islam* is submission to the will of God and to His teachings. The meaning, therefore, of the sacred verse in the Qur'án that states, "The true religion with God is Islam" is that the verbal confession of Faith or "Sh̲ahāda" is not enough, and nothing short of submission of one's will to the will of God and abiding by His Teachings is acceptable. The meaning is precisely the same as what Christ said in the Bible: "Not everyone who says to me 'Lord, Lord,' shall enter the kingdom of heaven, but he who does the will of my Father who is in heaven."‡ In the same way, Islam is submission to "the will of my Father"—abiding by the will of God, which is embodied in His teachings.

In this new Cycle, the revealed will of God is defined not merely by doing good deeds. Instead, we are encouraged to perform "deeds of stainless purity" supported by "the purest motive." The Báb says, *"The days when idle worship was deemed sufficient are ended. The time is come when naught but the purest motive, supported by deeds of stainless purity, can ascend to the throne of the Most High and be acceptable unto Him."*§

Hypothetically, if we accept that the words *Muslim* or *Islam* refer only to the followers of Muḥammad and that Muslims are the only ones who possess the "true" religion from God (which contradicts the Qur'án itself), we would also find that all previous revelations had the same concepts and that they were referred to as special and the only ones acceptable unto God at their time. For example, the Jews were referred to in the Old Testament as the

* Sura 2:285.
† Sura 28:53 ("It" here refers to the Qur'án).
‡ Matthew 7:21.
§ The Báb, quoted in Nabíl-i-A'ẓam, *The Dawn-breakers*, p. 93.

"chosen people" and "above all the nations that are upon the earth."* Christ said to His followers, "I am the way, I am the truth and I am life; no one comes to the Father except by me,"† meaning of course that it is only through the teachings of Christ that we find the way, the truth, and life eternal. As this is the case with all past revelations and as stated in the Qur'án that each age has its book,‡ it is evident that the real meaning of Islam is submission in words and in deeds to "any revealed religion irrespective of its Messenger."§

Bahá'u'lláh, the Manifestation of God for this glorious Day, reaffirms the concept of the Oneness of the Manifestations of God by saying: *"This is the changeless Faith of God, eternal in the past, eternal in the future."* **

* Deuteronomy 14:2.
† John 14:6.
‡ See chapter on "The Word of God."
§ Nakhjavání, 'Alí, "Notes on Bahá'í Proofs Based on the Holy Qur'án," p. 5.
** Bahá'u'lláh, The Kitáb-i-Aqdas, ¶182.

Some of the verses from the Holy Qur'án concerning the "True Religion":

Sura 3:17–19 – Ál-'Imrán – The true religion with God is Islam: and they to whom the Scriptures had been given, differed not till after "the knowledge" had come to them, and through mutual jealousy. But as for him who shall not believe in the signs of God—God will be prompt to reckon with him!

If they shall dispute with thee, then say: I have surrendered myself to God, as have they who follow me.

SAY to those who have received the Book, and to the common folk, Do ye surrender yourselves unto God? If they become Muslims, then are they guided aright: but if they turn away—thy duty is only preaching; and God's eye is on His servants.

Sura 3:78–79 – Ál-'Imrán – SAY: We believe in God, and in what hath been sent down to us, and what hath been sent down to Abraham, and Ismael, and Isaac, and Jacob, and the tribes, and in what was given to Moses, and Jesus, and the Prophets, from their Lord. We make no difference between them. And to Him are we resigned (Muslims).

Whoso desireth any other religion than Islam, that religion shall never be accepted from him, and in the next world he shall be among the lost.

Sura 3:60 – Ál-'Imrán – Abraham was neither Jew nor Christian; but he was sound in faith, a Muslim, and not of those who add gods to God.

Sura 5:72 – Al-Má'dah – Say: "People of the Book, you shall not be guided until you observe the Torah and the Gospel and that which is revealed to you from your Lord."

Sura 5:111 – Al-Má'dah – And when I revealed unto the Apostles, "Believe on me and on my Sent One," they said, "We believe; and bear thou witness that we are Muslims."

Sura 10:72–73 – Yúnis – Recite to them the history of Noah, when he said to his people, — If, O my people! My abode with you, and my reminding you of the signs of God, be grievous to you, yet in God is my trust: Muster, therefore, your designs and your false gods, and let not your design be carried on by you in the dark: then come to some decision about me, and delay not.

And if ye turn your backs on me, yet ask I no reward from you: my reward is with God alone, and I am commanded to be of the Muslims.

Sura 10:84 – Yúnis – And Moses said: "O my people! if ye believe in God, then put your trust in Him—if ye be Muslims."

Sura 12:102 – Yúsuf – "O my Lord, thou hast given me dominion, and hast taught me to expound dark sayings. Maker of the Heavens and of the Earth! My guardian art thou in this world and in the next! Cause thou me to die a Muslim, and join me with the just."

Sura 3:45 – Ál-'Imrán – And when Jesus perceived unbelief on their part, He said, "Who will be my helpers with God?" The apostles said, "We will be God's helpers! We believe in God, and bear thou witness that we are Muslims."

Sura 2:121–22 – Al-Baqarah – And when Abraham, with Ishmael, raised the foundations of the House, they said, "O Our Lord! accept it from us; for thou art the Hearer, the Knower.

O our Lord! Make us also Muslims, and our posterity a Muslim people; and teach us holy rites, and be turned towards us, for thou art He who turneth, the Merciful."

Sura 2:125–27 – Al-Baqarah – When his Lord said to him, "Resign thyself to me," he said, "I resign myself to the Lord of the Worlds."

And this to his children did Abraham bequeath, and Jacob also, saying, "O my children! Truly God hath chosen a religion for you; so die not unless ye be also Muslims."

Were ye present when Jacob was at the point of death? When he said to his sons, "Whom will ye worship when I am gone?" They said, "We will worship thy God and the God of thy fathers Abraham and Ismael and Isaac, one God, and to Him are we surrendered (Muslims)."

Sura 2:130 – Al-Baqarah – Say ye: "We believe in God, and that which hath been sent down to us, and that which hath been sent down to Abraham and Ismael and Isaac and Jacob and the tribes: and that which hath been given to Moses and to Jesus, and that which was given to the prophets from their Lord. No difference do we make between any of them: and to God are we resigned (Muslims)."

Sura 22:77 – Al-Haj – And do valiantly in the cause of God as it behoveth you to do for Him. He hath elected you, and hath not laid on you any hardship in religion, the Faith of your father Abraham. He hath named you the Muslims.

Sura 7:120–23 – Al-A'ráf – Said Pharaoh, "Have ye believed on him, ere I have given you leave? This truly is a plot . . ." They said, "Verily, to our Lord do we return;

And thou takest vengeance on us only because we have believed on the signs of our Lord when they came to us. Lord! Pour out constancy upon us, and cause us to die Muslims."

Sura 28: 52–53 – Al-Qasas – They to whom we gave the Scriptures before IT, do in IT believe.

And when it is recited to them they say, "We believe in it, for it is the truth from our Lord. We were Muslims before it came."*

---

* "It" in the above verse refers to the Qur'án. Notice the following verse, "We were Muslims before it came."

Some of the passages from the Bahá'í sacred texts concerning the "True Religion":

Even as He hath revealed: "No distinction do We make between any of His Messengers." For they, one and all, summon the people of the earth to acknowledge the unity of God. . . . Thus hath Muḥammad, the Point of the Qur'án, revealed: "I am all the Prophets." Likewise, He saith: "I am the first Adam, Noah, Moses, and Jesus.". . . This Revelation is exalted above the veils of plurality and the exigencies of number. Thus He saith: "Our Cause is but One." Inasmuch as the Cause is one and the same, the Exponents thereof also must needs be one and the same. Likewise, the Imáms of the Muḥammadan Faith, those lamps of certitude, have said: "Muḥammad is our first, Muḥammad is our last, Muḥammad our all."

Bahá'u'lláh, Gleanings from the Writings of Bahá'u'lláh, no. 22.2.

O Jews! If ye be intent on crucifying once again Jesus, the Spirit of God, put Me to death, for He hath once more, in My person, been made manifest unto you. Deal with Me as ye wish, for I have vowed to lay down My life in the path of God. I will fear no one, though the powers of earth and heaven be leagued against Me. Followers of the Gospel! If ye cherish the desire to slay Muḥammad, the Apostle of God, seize Me and put an end to My life, for I am He, and My Self is His Self. Do unto me as ye like, for the deepest longing of Mine heart is to attain the presence of My Best-Beloved in His Kingdom of Glory. Such is the Divine decree, if ye know it. Followers of Muḥammad! If it be your wish to riddle with your shafts the breast of Him Who hath caused His Book the Bayán to be sent down unto you, lay hands on Me and persecute Me, for I am His Well-Beloved, the revelation of His own Self, though My name be not His name.

Bahá'u'lláh, Gleanings from the Writings of Bahá'u'lláh, no. 47.1.

Every discerning observer will recognize that in the Dispensation of the Qur'án both the Book and the Cause of Jesus were confirmed. As to the matter of names, Muḥammad, Himself, declared: "I am Jesus." He recognized the truth of the signs, prophecies, and words of Jesus, and testified that they were all of God. In this sense, neither the person of Jesus nor His writings hath differed from that of Muḥammad and of His holy Book, inasmuch as both have championed the Cause of God, uttered His praise, and revealed His commandments. Thus it is that Jesus, Himself, declared: "I go away and come again unto you." Consider the sun. Were it to say now, "I am the sun of yesterday," it would speak the truth.

Bahá'u'lláh, *Gleanings from the Writings of Bahá'u'lláh*, no. 13.6.

Praise be to Thee, O Lord My God, for the wondrous revelations of Thy inscrutable decree and the manifold woes and trials Thou hast destined for Myself. At one time Thou didst deliver Me into the hands of Nimrod; at another Thou hast allowed Pharaoh's rod to persecute Me. Thou, alone, canst estimate, through Thine all-encompassing knowledge and the operation of Thy Will, the incalculable afflictions I have suffered at their hands. Again Thou didst cast Me into the prison-cell of the ungodly, for no reason except that I was moved to whisper into the ears of the well-favored denizens of Thy Kingdom an intimation of the vision with which Thou hadst, through Thy knowledge, inspired Me, and revealed to Me its meaning through the potency of Thy might. And again Thou didst decree that I be beheaded by the sword of the infidel. Again I was crucified for having unveiled to men's eyes the hidden gems of Thy glorious unity, for having revealed to them the wondrous signs of Thy sovereign and everlasting power. How bitter the humiliations heaped upon Me, in a subsequent age, on the plain of Karbilá! How lonely did I feel amidst Thy people! To what a state of helplessness I was reduced in that land! Unsatisfied with such indignities, My persecutors

255

decapitated Me, and, carrying aloft My head from land to land paraded it before the gaze of the unbelieving multitude, and deposited it on the seats of the perverse and faithless. In a later age, I was suspended, and My breast was made a target to the darts of the malicious cruelty of My foes. My limbs were riddled with bullets, and My body was torn asunder. Finally, behold how, in this Day, My treacherous enemies have leagued themselves against Me, and are continually plotting to instill the venom of hate and malice into the souls of Thy servants.

Bahá'u'lláh, Gleanings from the Writings of Bahá'u'lláh, no. 39.1.

The days when idle worship was deemed sufficient are ended. The time is come when naught but the purest motive, supported by deeds of stainless purity, can ascend to the throne of the Most High and be acceptable unto Him. 'The good word riseth up unto Him, and the righteous deed will cause it to be exalted before Him.'

The Báb, quoted in Nabíl-i-A'ẓam, The Dawn-breakers, p. 93.

22

"This day have I perfected your religion"

The teachings of Islam were perfect and complete during the Islamic cycle. Similarly, the teachings of the other religions of God were perfect during the age for which they were intended. The Qur'án affirms this concept by saying that other religions were complete during their time: "Then gave we the Book to Moses—complete for him who should do right, and a decision for all matters, and a guidance. . . ."* This is further explained by yet another verse: "To each age its Book. What He pleaseth will God abrogate or confirm: for with Him is the source of revelation."†

If by "perfect" and "complete" the Qur'án meant that there will be no more Revelations from God, it would not have referred in numerous passages to the coming of new Messengers or Manifestations from God, nor would it state, ". . . but of knowledge, only a little to you is given."‡ All divine religions come from God, and God does not reveal anything that is not perfect or

---

* Sura 6:155.
† Sura 13:38–39.
‡ Sura 17:87.

complete for the age in which His religion was intended. He is the source of all perfection and gives mankind what suits His evolutionary requirements of the time, as preordained by His will and purpose. The Qur'án also states that the words of God are endless: "Say: Should the sea become ink, to write the words of my Lord, the sea would surely fail ere the words of my Lord would fail, though we brought its like in aid."*

Furthermore, it is important to note that the Qur'án was revealed in stages during a twenty-three-year period and that the verse stating "this day have I perfected your religion" was revealed only eighty-one days before the passing of the Prophet of Allah.†

In this Day, Bahá'u'lláh has added a wealth of newly revealed teachings suited to the requirements of the age in which we live, and if we are to live in peace and harmony, we have to accept and abide by the teachings of the new Revelation from God.

---

* Sura 18:109.
† Al-Tibyán wal Burhán, Vol. I, p. 7, (Translated from Arabic).

Some of the verses from the Holy Qur'án concerning the "Perfection of Religion":

Sura 5:5 – Al-Ma'dah – This day have I perfected your religion for you, and have filled up the measure of my favors upon you: and it is my pleasure that Islam be your religion; . . . .

Sura 7:50–51 – Al-A'ráf – And now have we brought them the Book: with knowledge have we explained it; a guidance and a mercy to them that believe.

What have they to wait for now but its interpretation? When its interpretation shall come, they who aforetime were oblivious of it shall say, "The Prophets of our Lord did indeed bring the truth; shall we have any intercessor to intercede for us? Or could we not be sent back? Then would we act otherwise than we have acted." But they have ruined themselves; and the deities of their own devising have fled from them!

Sura 75:16–19 – Al-Qiyámah – Move not thy tongue in haste to follow and master this revelation:

For we will see to the collecting and the recital of it;

But when we have recited it, then follow thou the recital,

And, verily, afterwards it shall be ours to make it clear to thee.

Sura 6:155 – Al-An'ám – Then gave we the Book to Moses – complete for him who should do right, and a decision for all matters, and a guidance, and a mercy, that they might believe in the meeting with their Lord.

Blessed, too, this Book which we have sent down. Wherefore follow it and fear God, that ye may find mercy:

Sura 12:111 – Yúsuf – This is no new tale of fiction, but a confirmation of previous scriptures, and an explanation of all things, and guidance and mercy to those who believe.

Sura 16:66 – Al-Nahl – And we have sent down the Book to thee only, that thou mightest clear up to them the subject of their wranglings, and as a guidance and a mercy to those who believe.

Some of the passages from the Bahá'í sacred text concerning the "Perfection of Religion":

Say: By the righteousness of the Almighty! The measure of the favors of God hath been filled up, His Word hath been perfected, the light of His countenance hath been revealed, His sovereignty hath encompassed the whole of creation, the glory of His Revelation hath been made manifest, and His bounties have rained upon all mankind.

Bahá'u'lláh, Gleanings from the Writings of Bahá'u'lláh, no. 121.10.

Thus it is related in the "Biḥáru'l-Anvár," the "'Aválim," and the "Yanbú'" of Ṣádiq, son of Muḥammad, that he spoke these words: "Knowledge is twenty and seven letters. All that the Prophets have revealed are two letters thereof. No man thus far hath known more than these two letters. But when the Qá'im shall arise, He will cause the remaining twenty and five letters to be made manifest." Consider, He hath declared Knowledge to consist of twenty and seven letters, and regarded all the Prophets, from Adam even unto the "Seal," as Expounders of only two letters thereof and of having been sent down with these two letters. He also saith that the Qá'ím will reveal the remaining twenty and five letters.

Bahá'u'lláh, The Book of Certitude, ¶272.

This age is indeed as a hundred other ages: should ye gather the yield of a hundred ages, and set that against the accumulated product of our times, the yield of this one era will prove greater than that of a hundred gone before. Take ye, for an example, the sum total of all the books that were ever written in ages past, and compare that with the books and treatises that our era hath produced: these books, written in our day alone, far and away exceed the total number of volumes that have been written down the ages. See how powerful is the influence exerted by the Daystar of the world upon the inner essence of all created things!

'Abdu'l-Bahá, *Selections from the Writings of 'Abdu'l-Bahá*, no. 73.6.

23

"You are the noblest Nation that has ever been raised up for mankind"

In its time, the Islamic civilization was "the noblest Nation that has ever been raised up for mankind"* and was the envy of the whole world. It brought a great nation into being by uniting large numbers of people, and formed a society for the common good under one government. Islam created a civilization that benefited all nations; however, the Qur'án states, "Every nation hath its set time. And when their time is come, they shall not retard it an hour; and they shall not advance it."†

Being the "noblest nation" does not mean that there were no other noble or great civilizations that preceded Islam, nor does it mean that there would not be far greater civilizations to proceed the Islamic dispensation. The Qur'án itself mentions the greatness of the Jewish and Christian civilizations by saying, "O children of Israel! remember my favour wherewith I have favoured you, and that high above all mankind have I raised you."‡ Similarly it states, "Remember when God said, 'O Jesus! verily I will cause thee to die, and will

---

* Sura 3:100.
† Sura 7:32.
‡ Sura 2:47.

take thee up to myself and deliver thee from those who believe not; and I will place those who follow thee above those who believe not, until the day of resurrection.'"*

Furthermore, there are many references in the Qur'án regarding future Manifestations of God. The Qur'án states, "there shall come to you Apostles from among yourselves, rehearsing my signs to you."† He clearly indicates, "there shall come to you Apostles" and with the coming of new Messengers or Manifestations of God, new civilizations would come about in a process that had no beginning and will have no end.

With the coming of Bahá'u'lláh, the time of nationhood ended and a new civilization is emerging. Bahá'u'lláh brought about a whole New World Order for this Promised Day of God, based on the oneness and nobility of the human race and unity of all nations. This New World Order is envisioned to establish a civilization the likes of which humanity has never experienced and the old order will be "rolled up." The Qur'án itself predicted this Day and says, *"The Day that we roll up the heavens like a scroll rolled up for books (completed)—even as We produced the first Creation, so shall We produce a new one: a promise We have undertaken: truly shall We fulfill it."*‡ Similarly Bahá'u'lláh said, *"By My Self! The day is approaching when We will have rolled up the world and all that is therein, and spread out a new order in its stead. He, verily, is powerful over all things."*§

---

* Sura 3:48.
† Sura 7:33.
‡ Sura 21:104.
§ Bahá'u'lláh, *Gleanings from the Writings of Bahá'u'lláh*, no. 143.3.

"You are the noblest Nation that has ever been raised up for mankind"

The verse in the Holy Qur'án concerning "the noblest nation":

Sura 3:100–111 – Ál-'Imrán – You are the noblest nation that has ever been raised up for mankind. You enjoin justice and forbid evil you believe in Alláh. Had the People of the Book accepted Islam, it would have surely been better for them.

Some of the passages in the Bahá'í sacred text concerning "the noblest nation":

Reflect for a while upon the behavior of the companions of the Muḥammadan Dispensation. Consider how, through the reviving breath of Muḥammad, they were cleansed from the defilements of earthly vanities, were delivered from selfish desires, and were detached from all else but Him. Behold how they preceded all the peoples of the earth in attaining unto His holy Presence—the Presence of God Himself—how they renounced the world and all that is therein, and sacrificed freely and joyously their lives at the feet of the Manifestation of the All-Glorious.

Bahá'u'lláh, The Book of Certitude, ¶170.

When the light of Muḥammad dawned, the darkness of ignorance was dispelled from the deserts of Arabia. In a short period of time those barbarous peoples attained a superlative degree of civilization which, with Baghdád as its center, extended as far westward as Spain and afterward influenced the greater part of Europe.

'Abdu'l-Bahá, The Promulgation of Universal Peace,

p. 520.

During the Middle Ages, while Europe was in the lowest depths of barbarism, the Arab peoples were superior to the other nations of the earth in learning, in the arts, mathematics, civilization, government and other sciences.

'Abdu'l-Bahá, *Some Answered Questions*, p. 24.

A careful and thorough investigation of the historical record will establish the fact that the major part of the civilization of Europe is derived from Islám; for all the writings of Muslim scholars and divines and philosophers were gradually collected in Europe and were with the most painstaking care weighed and debated at academic gatherings and in the centers of learning, after which their valued contents were put to use.

'Abdu'l-Bahá, *The Secret of Divine Civilization*, p. 89.

Those European intellectuals who are well-informed as to the facts of Europe's past, and are characterized by truthfulness and a sense of justice, unanimously acknowledge that in every particular the basic elements of their civilization are derived from Islám. For example Draper, the well-known French authority, a writer whose accuracy, ability and learning are attested by all European scholars, in one of his best-known works, *The Intellectual Development of Europe,* has written a detailed account in this connection, that is, with reference to the derivation by the peoples of Europe of the fundamentals of civilization and the bases of progress and well-being from Islám.

'Abdu'l-Bahá, *The Secret of Divine Civilization*, pp. 92–93.

The Faith of Islám, the succeeding link in the chain of Divine Revelation, introduced, as Bahá'u'lláh Himself testifies, the conception of the nation as a unit and a vital stage in the organization of human society, and embodied it in its teachings. This indeed is what is meant by this brief yet highly significant and illuminating pronouncement of Bahá'u'lláh: *"Of old* [Islamic Dispensation] *it hath been revealed: 'Love of one's country is an element of the Faith of God.'"* This principle was established and stressed by the Apostle of God, inasmuch as the evolution of human society required it at that time. Nor could any stage above and beyond it have been envisaged, as world conditions preliminary to the establishment of a superior form of organization were as yet unobtainable. The conception of nationality, the attainment to the state of nationhood, may, therefore, be said to be the distinguishing characteristics of the Muḥammadan Dispensation, in the course of which the nations and races of the world, and particularly in Europe and America, were unified and achieved political independence.

Shoghi Effendi, *The Promised Day is Come*, ¶294.

24

"The Seal of the Prophets"

God, the Creator of heaven and earth, Who has neither beginning nor end, Whose worlds and creatures no mind can reckon or perceive, Whose Prophets and Messengers have no beginning or end, Whose bounties were never withheld from the world of being, can in no wise close the doors of His divine mercy or seal the dayspring of His ancient glory with any particular Messenger or religion. His creation, bestowals, and bounty will continue to the end that has no end.

The Prophet Muḥammad was indeed the Apostle of God and the seal of the Prophets and Messengers of the Adamic cycle—a cycle that began with Adam and ended with Muḥammad. Mankind, however, has now entered a new age and a new cycle, and Bahá'u'lláh describes the uniqueness of this new cycle by saying, *"This Day, however, is unique, and is to be distinguished from those that have preceded it. The designation 'Seal of the Prophets' fully revealeth its high station. The Prophetic Cycle hath, verily, ended. The Eternal Truth is now come."** So stupendous is the station of this Dispensation that all the Prophets and Messengers of bygone ages had yearned to attain it. Bahá'u'lláh states, *"Had Muḥammad, the Apostle of God, attained this Day, He would have*

---

* Bahá'u'lláh, *Gleanings from the Writings of Bahá'u'lláh*, no. 25.1.

269

*exclaimed: 'I have truly recognized Thee, O Thou the Desire of the Divine Mes-
sengers!' Had Abraham attained it, He too, falling prostrate upon the ground, and
in the utmost lowliness before the Lord thy God, would have cried: 'Mine heart
is filled with peace, O Thou Lord of all that is in heaven and on earth! I testify
that Thou hast unveiled before mine eyes all the glory of Thy power and the full
majesty of Thy law!'"** The station mankind can reach in this Dispensation
has never been witnessed, and Bahá'u'lláh further states, *"The heights which,
through the most gracious favor of God, mortal man can attain, in this Day,
are as yet unrevealed to his sight . . . The day, however, is approaching when the
potentialities of so great a favor will, by virtue of His behest, be manifested unto
men."*†

Concerning the culmination of the Adamic Cycle that ended with
Muḥammad, the Seal of the Prophets, Shoghi Effendi, Guardian of the Bahá'í
Faith, writes, ". . . posterity will recognize as standing at the confluence of
two universal prophetic cycles, the Adamic Cycle stretching back as far as
the first dawnings of the world's recorded religious history and the Bahá'í
Cycle destined to propel itself across the unborn reaches of time for a period
of no less than five thousand centuries."‡ Referring to the revealed verses of
Bahá'u'lláh, Shoghi Effendi further emphasizes the uniqueness of this new
Cycle and writes: *"'In this most mighty Revelation,' He moreover, states, 'all the
Dispensations of the past have attained their highest, their final consummation.'*
And again: *'None among the Manifestations of old, except to a prescribed degree,
hath ever completely apprehended the nature of this Revelation.' Referring to His
own station He declares: 'But for Him no Divine Messenger would have been*

---

* Bahá'u'lláh, quoted in Shoghi Effendi, *The World Order of Bahá'u'lláh*, p. 105.
† Bahá'u'lláh, *Gleanings from the Writings of Bahá'u'lláh*, no. 109.1.
‡ Shoghi Effendi, *God Passes By*, pp. 54–55.

invested with the Robe of Prophethood, nor would any of the sacred Scriptures have been revealed.'"*

It is important to understand that the phrase "Seal of the Prophets" (khá-tam an-Nabiyyín) has numerous meanings and that in the history of all religions, there were always such mysterious words that, when taken literally, veiled man from recognizing the new Revelation from God. Bahá'u'lláh says, *". . . how many are those who, through failure to understand its meaning, have allowed the term 'Seal of the Prophets' to obscure their understanding, and deprive them of the grace of all His manifold bounties! "*† He also states, *"Even as in the 'Beginning that hath no beginnings' the term 'last' is truly applicable unto Him who is the Educator of the visible and the Invisible, in like manner, are the terms 'first' and 'last' applicable unto His Manifestations. They are at the same time Exponents of both the 'first' and the 'last.' Whilst established upon the seat of the 'first,' they occupy the throne of the 'last.'"*‡ 'Abdu'l-Bahá further elucidates this point by saying, *"The past, the present, the future, all, in relation to God, are equal. Yesterday, today, tomorrow do not exist in the sun."*§

The "Words of God" are endless, and His Manifestations have neither beginning nor end. There are numerous verses in the Qur'án about the coming of the Promised One** and the endlessness of the "Words of God." The Qur'án says, "Should the sea become ink, to write the words of my Lord, the sea would surely fail ere the words of my Lord would fail, though we brought its like in aid."†† The Qur'án also states, "If all the trees that are upon the

* Shoghi Effendi, *God Passes By*, p. 99.
† Bahá'u'lláh, The Book of Certitude, ¶172.
‡ Bahá'u'lláh, The Book of Certitude, ¶174.
§ 'Abdu'l-Bahá, *Some Answered Questions*, p. 116.
** See the chapter in this book on "He Who was Promised."
†† Sura 18:109.

earth were to become pens, and if God should after that swell the sea into seven seas of ink, His words would not be exhausted: for God is Mighty, Wise."* It is obvious from these figurative verses, then, that the "Words of God" are endless, and His Divine Revelations have no beginning and will have no end.

It would be inconceivable to imagine that God, the everlasting Sovereign, Who has no beginning or end, would end His Revelations by one particular religion or another! Shoghi Effendi writes, "To contend that any particular religion is final, that *'all Revelation is ended, that the portals of Divine mercy are closed, that from the daysprings of eternal holiness no sun shall rise again, that the ocean of everlasting bounty is forever stilled, and that out of the Tabernacle of ancient glory the Messengers of God have ceased to be made manifest'* would indeed be nothing less than sheer blasphemy."†

The "Prophetic Cycle" has indeed ended with Muḥammad, the Seal of the Prophets, and the promised "Day of God" has been inaugurated with the coming of Bahá'u'lláh. A "new cycle" of Divine Revelations has begun, in a process that has no beginning and will have no end.

---

* Sura 31:27.
† Shoghi Effendi, *The World Order of Bahá'u'lláh,* p. 58.

The verse from the Holy Qur'án concerning the "Seal of the Prophets":

Sura 33:40 – Al-Ahzáb – Muhammad is not the father of any man among you, but he is the Apostle of God, and the seal of the prophets: and God knoweth all things.

References from the Bahá'í sacred texts concerning the "Seal of the Prophets":

In truth I say: On this day the blessed words "But He is the Apostle of God, and the Seal of the Prophets" have found their consummation in the verse "The day when mankind shall stand before the Lord of the worlds." Render thou thanksgiving unto God for so great a bounty.

Bahá'u'lláh, Epistle to the Son of the Wolf, p. 114.

It is evident that every age in which a Manifestation of God hath lived is divinely ordained, and may, in a sense, be characterized as God's appointed Day. This Day, however, is unique, and is to be distinguished from those that have preceded it. The designation "Seal of the Prophets" fully revealeth its high station. The Prophetic Cycle hath, verily, ended. The Eternal Truth is now come. He hath lifted up the Ensign of Power, and is now shedding upon the world the unclouded splendor of His Revelation.

Bahá'u'lláh, *Gleanings from the Writings of Bahá'u'lláh*, no. 25.1.

Know then that the paradise that appeareth in the day of God surpasseth every other paradise and excelleth the realities of Heaven. For when God—

blessed and glorified is He—sealed the station of prophethood in the person of Him Who was His Friend, His Chosen One, and His Treasure amongst His creatures, as hath been revealed from the Kingdom of glory: "but He is the Apostle of God and the Seal of the Prophets," He promised all men that they shall attain unto His own presence in the Day of Resurrection. In this He meant to emphasize the greatness of the Revelation to come, as it hath indeed been manifested through the power of truth. And there is of a certainty no paradise greater than this, nor station higher, should ye reflect upon the verses of the Qur'án. Blessed be he who knoweth of a certainty that he shall attain unto the presence of God on that day when His Beauty shall be made manifest.

Bahá'u'lláh, *The Pen of Glory,* no. 1.58.

Were any of the all-embracing Manifestations of God to declare: "I am God!" He verily speaketh the truth, and no doubt attacheth thereto. For it hath been repeatedly demonstrated that through their Revelation, their attributes and names, the Revelation of God, His name and His attributes, are made manifest in the world. Thus, He hath revealed: "Those shafts were God's, not Thine!" And also He saith: "In truth, they who plighted fealty unto thee, really plighted that fealty unto God." And were any of them to voice the utterance: "I am the Messenger of God," He also speaketh the truth, the indubitable truth. Even as He saith: "Muḥammad is not the father of any man among you, but He is the Messenger of God." Viewed in this light, they were all but Messengers of that ideal King, that unchangeable Essence. And were they all to proclaim: "I am the Seal of the Prophets," they verily utter but the truth, beyond the faintest shadow of doubt. For they are all but one person, one soul, one spirit, one being, one revelation. They are all the manifestation of the "Beginning" and the "End," the "First" and the "Last," the "Seen" and "Hidden"—all of which pertain to Him Who is the innermost Spirit of Spirits and eternal Essence of Essences.

Bahá'u'lláh, *The Book of Certitude,* ¶196.

Even as in the "Beginning that hath no beginnings" the term "last" is truly applicable unto Him who is the Educator of the visible and of the invisible, in like manner, are the terms "first" and "last" applicable unto His Manifestations. They are at the same time Exponents of both the "first" and the "last." Whilst established upon the seat of the "first," they occupy the throne of the "last." Were a discerning eye to be found, it will readily perceive that the exponents of the "first" and the "last," of the "manifest" and the "hidden," of the "beginning" and the "seal" are none other than these holy Beings, these Essences of Detachment, these divine Souls. And wert thou to soar in the holy realm of "God was alone, there was none else besides Him," thou wilt find in that Court all these names utterly nonexistent and completely forgotten. Then will thine eyes no longer be obscured by these veils, these terms, and allusions.

Bahá'u'lláh, *The Book of Certitude,* ¶174.

. . . yet how many are those who, through failure to understand its meaning, have allowed the term "Seal of the Prophets" to obscure their understanding, and deprive them of the grace of all His manifold bounties! Hath not Muḥammad, Himself, declared: "I am all the Prophets?" Hath He not said as We have already mentioned: "I am Adam, Noah, Moses, and Jesus?" Why should Muḥammad, that immortal Beauty, Who hath said: "I am the first Adam" be incapable of saying also: "I am the last Adam?" For even as He regarded Himself to be the "First of the Prophets"—that is Adam—in like manner, the "Seal of the Prophets" is also applicable unto that Divine Beauty.

275

It is admittedly obvious that being the "First of the Prophets," He likewise is their "Seal."

Bahá'u'lláh, The Book of Certitude, ¶172.

Furthermore, among the "veils of glory" are such terms as the "Seal of the Prophets" and the like, the removal of which is a supreme achievement in the sight of these baseborn and erring souls. All, by reason of these mysterious sayings, these grievous "veils of glory," have been hindered from beholding the light of truth. Have they not heard the melody of that bird of Heaven [Imám 'Alí], uttering this mystery: "A thousand Fáṭimihs I have espoused, all of whom were the daughters of Muḥammad, Son of 'Abdu'lláh, the 'Seal of the Prophets'"? Behold, how many are the mysteries that lie as yet unravelled within the tabernacle of the knowledge of God, and how numerous the gems of His wisdom that are still concealed in His inviolable treasuries! Shouldest thou ponder this in thine heart, thou wouldst realize that His handiwork knoweth neither beginning nor end. The domain of His decree is too vast for the tongue of mortals to describe, or for the bird of the human mind to traverse; and the dispensations of His providence are too mysterious for the mind of man to comprehend. His creation no end hath overtaken, and it hath ever existed from the "Beginning that hath no beginning"; and the Manifestations of His Beauty no beginning hath beheld, and they will continue to the "End that knoweth no end." Ponder this utterance in thine heart, and reflect how it is applicable unto all these holy Souls.

Bahá'u'lláh, The Book of Certitude, ¶178.

Likewise, strive thou to comprehend the meaning of the melody of that eternal beauty, Ḥusayn, son of 'Alí, who, addressing Salmán, spoke words such as these: "I was with a thousand Adams, the interval between each and the next Adam was fifty thousand years, and to each one of these I declared the Successorship conferred upon my father." He then recounteth certain details, until he saith: "I have fought one thousand battles in the path of God, the least and most insignificant of which was like the battle of K͟haybar, in which battle my father fought and contended against the infidels." Endeavor now to apprehend from these two traditions the mysteries of "end," "return," and "creation without beginning or end."

O my beloved! Immeasurably exalted is the celestial Melody above the strivings of human ear to hear or mind to grasp its mystery! How can the helpless ant step into the court of the All-Glorious? And yet, feeble souls, through lack of understanding, reject these abstruse utterances, and question the truth of such traditions. Nay, none can comprehend them save those that are possessed of an understanding heart. Say, He is that End for Whom no end in all the universe can be imagined, and for Whom no beginning in the world of creation can be conceived. Behold, O concourse of the earth, the splendors of the End, revealed in the Manifestations of the Beginning!

Bahá'u'lláh, *The Book of Certitude,* ¶179–80.

Even as the Lord of being hath in His unerring Book, after speaking of the "Seal" in His exalted utterance: "Muḥammad is the Apostle of God and the Seal of the Prophets," hath revealed unto all people the promise of "attainment unto the divine Presence." To this attainment to the presence of the immortal King testify the verses of the Book, some of which We have already mentioned. The one true God is My witness! Nothing more exalted or more explicit than "attainment unto the divine Presence" hath been revealed in the Qur'án. Well is it with him that hath attained thereunto, in the day wherein most of the people, even as ye witness, have turned away therefrom.

Bahá'u'lláh, *The Book of Certitude,* ¶181.

For over a thousand years they have been reciting this verse, and unwittingly pronouncing their censure against the Jews, utterly unaware that they themselves, openly and privily, are voicing the sentiments and belief of the Jewish people! Thou art surely aware of their idle contention, that all Revelation is ended, that the portals of Divine mercy are closed, that from the daysprings of eternal holiness no sun shall rise again, that the Ocean of everlasting bounty is forever stilled, and that out of the Tabernacle of ancient glory the Messengers of God have ceased to be made manifest. Such is the measure of the understanding of these small-minded, contemptible people. These people have imagined that the flow of God's all encompassing grace and plenteous mercies, the cessation of which no mind can contemplate, has been halted.

Bahá'u'lláh, The Book of Certitude, ¶148.

After the denials and denunciations which they uttered, and unto which We have referred, they protested saying: "No independent Prophet, according to our Scriptures, should arise after Moses and Jesus to abolish the Law of divine Revelation. Nay, he that is to be made manifest must needs fulfill the Law." Thereupon this verse, indicative of all the divine themes, and testifying to the truth that the flow of the grace of the All-Merciful can never cease, was revealed: "And Joseph came to you aforetime with clear tokens, but ye ceased not to doubt of the message with which He came to you, until, when He died, ye said, 'God will by no means raise up a Messenger after Him.' Thus God misleadeth him who is the transgressor, the doubter" [Qur'án 40:34]. Therefore, understand from this verse and know of a certainty that the people in every age, clinging to a verse of the Book, have uttered such vain and absurd sayings, contending that no Prophet should again be made manifest to the world. Even as the Christian divines who, holding fast to the verse of the Gospel to which We have already referred, have sought to

278

explain that the law of the Gospel shall at no time be annulled, and that no independent Prophet shall again be made manifest, unless He confirmeth the law of the Gospel.

Bahá'u'lláh, The Book of Certitude, ¶237.

Thus it is related in the "Biḥáru'l-Anvár," the "'Aválim," and the "Yanbú'" of Ṣádiq, son of Muḥammad, that he spoke these words: "Knowledge is twenty and seven letters. All that the Prophets have revealed are two letters thereof. No man thus far hath known more than these two letters. But when the Qá'im shall arise, He will cause the remaining twenty and five letters to be made manifest." Consider, He hath declared Knowledge to consist of twenty and seven letters, and regarded all the Prophets, from Adam even unto the "Seal," as Expounders of only two letters thereof and having been sent down with these two letters. He also saith that the Qá'im will reveal the remaining twenty and five letters.

Bahá'u'lláh, The Book of Certitude, ¶272.

Even as thou dost witness how the people of the Qur'án, like unto the people of old, have allowed the words "Seal of the Prophets" to veil their eyes. And yet, they themselves testify to this verse: "None knoweth the interpretation thereof but God and they that are well-grounded in knowledge" [Qur'án 3:7]. And when He Who is well-grounded in all knowledge, He who is the Mother, the Soul, the Secret, and the Essence thereof, revealeth that which is the least contrary to their desire, they bitterly oppose Him and shamelessly deny Him.

Bahá'u'lláh, The Book of Certitude, ¶237.

Thy vision is obscured by the belief that divine revelation ended with the coming of Muḥammad, and unto this We have borne witness in Our First

Epistle. Indeed, He who hath revealed verses unto Muḥammad, the Apostle of God, hath likewise revealed verses unto 'Alí-Muḥammad.

The Báb, *Selections from the Writings of the Báb*, p. 31.

When God sent forth His Prophet Muḥammad, on that day the termination of the prophetic cycle was foreordained in the knowledge of God. Yea, that promise hath indeed come true and the decree of God hath been accomplished as He hath ordained. Assuredly we are today living in the Days of God. These are the glorious days on the like of which the sun hath never risen in the past. These are the days which the people in bygone time eagerly expected. What hath then befallen you that ye are fast asleep? These are the days wherein God hath caused the Daystar of Truth to shine resplendent. What hath then caused you to keep your silence? These are the appointed days which ye have been yearningly awaiting in the past—the days of the advent of divine justice. Render ye thanks unto God, O ye concourse of believers.

The Báb, *Selections from the Writings of the Báb*, 6:11:5.

The purpose underlying this Revelation, as well as those that preceded it, has, in like manner, been to announce the advent of the Faith of Him Whom God will make manifest. And this Faith—the Faith of Him Whom God will make manifest—in its turn, together with all the Revelations gone before it, have as their object the Manifestation destined to succeed it. And the latter, no less than all the Revelations preceding it, prepare the way for the Revelation which is yet to follow. The process of the rise and setting of the Sun of Truth will thus indefinitely continue—a process that hath had no beginning and will have no end.

The Báb, quoted in Shoghi Effendi, *The World Order of Bahá'u'lláh*, p. 117.

This age is indeed as a hundred other ages: should ye gather the yield of a hundred ages, and set that against the accumulated product of our times, the yield of this one era will prove greater than that of a hundred gone before. Take ye, for an example, the sum total of all the books that were ever written in ages past, and compare that with the books and treatises that our era hath produced: these books, written in our day alone, far and away exceed the total number of volumes that have been written down the ages. See how powerful is the influence exerted by the Daystar of the world upon the inner essence of all created things!

'Abdu'l-Bahá, *Selections from the Writings of 'Abdu'l-Bahá*, no. 73.6.

As a further testimony to the greatness of the Revelation identified with Bahá'u'lláh may be cited the following extracts from a Tablet addressed by 'Abdu'l-Bahá to an eminent Zoroastrian follower of the Faith: *"Thou hadst written that in the sacred books of the followers of Zoroaster it is written that in the latter days, in three separate Dispensations, the sun must needs be brought to a standstill. In the first Dispensation, it is predicted, the sun will remain motionless for ten days; in the second for twice that time; in the third for no less than one whole month. The interpretation of this prophecy is this: the first Dispensation to which it refers is the Muḥammadan Dispensation during which the Sun of Truth stood still for ten days. Each day is reckoned as one century. The Muḥammadan Dispensation must have, therefore, lasted no less than one thousand years, which is precisely the period that has elapsed from the setting of the Star of the Imamate to the advent of the Dispensation proclaimed by the Báb. The second Dispensation referred to in this prophecy is the one inaugurated by the Báb Himself, which began in the year 1260 A.H. and was brought to a close in the year 1280 A.H. As to the third Dispensation—the Revelation proclaimed by Bahá'u'lláh—inasmuch as the Sun of Truth when attaining that station shineth in the plenitude of its meridian splendor its duration hath been fixed for a period of one whole month, which is the maximum time taken by the sun to pass through a sign of the Zodiac. From this thou canst imagine the magnitude of the Bahá'í cycle—a cycle that must extend over a period of at least five hundred thousand years."*

Shoghi Effendi, *The World Order of Bahá'u'lláh*, pp.101–2.

. . . a life which posterity will recognize as standing at the confluence of two universal prophetic cycles, the Adamic Cycle stretching back as far as the first dawnings of the world's recorded religious history and the Bahá'í Cycle destined to propel itself across the unborn reaches of time for a period of no less than five thousand centuries.

Shoghi Effendi, *God Passes By*, pp. 54–55.

A Revelation, hailed as the promise and crowning glory of past ages and centuries, as the consummation of all the Dispensations within the Adamic Cycle, inaugurating an era of at least a thousand years' duration, and a cycle destined to last no less than five thousand centuries, signalizing the end of the Prophetic Era and the beginning of the Era of Fulfillment.

Shoghi Effendi, *God Passes By*, p. 100.

"He around Whom the Point of the Bayán (Báb) hath revolved is come" is Bahá'u'lláh's confirmatory testimony to the inconceivable greatness and preeminent character of His own Revelation. *"If all who are in heaven and on earth,"* He moreover affirms, *"be invested in this day with the powers and attributes destined for the Letters of the Bayán, whose station is ten thousand times more glorious than that of the Letters of the Qur'ánic Dispensation, and if they one and all should, swift as the twinkling of an eye, hesitate to recognize My Revelation, they shall be accounted, in the sight of God, of those that have gone astray, and regarded as 'Letters of Negation.'" "Powerful is He, the King*

of Divine might," He, alluding to Himself in the Kitáb-i-Íqán, asserts, *"to extinguish with one letter of His wondrous words, the breath of life in the whole of the Bayán and the people thereof, and with one letter bestow upon them a new and everlasting life, and cause them to arise and speed out of the sepulchers of their vain and selfish desires." "This,"* He furthermore declares, *"is the king of days,"* the *"Day of God Himself,"* the *"Day which shall never be followed by night,"* the *"Springtime which autumn will never overtake," "the eye to past ages and centuries,"* for which *"the soul of every Prophet of God, of every Divine Messenger, hath thirsted,"* for which *"all the divers kindreds of the earth have yearned,"* through which *"God hath proved the hearts of the entire company of His Messengers and Prophets, and beyond them those that stand guard over His sacred and inviolable Sanctuary, the inmates of the Celestial Pavilion and dwellers of the Tabernacle of Glory." "In this most mighty Revelation,"* He moreover, states, *"all the Dispensations of the past have attained their highest, their final consummation."* And again: *"None among the Manifestations of old, except to a prescribed degree, hath ever completely apprehended the nature of this Revelation."* Referring to His own station He declares: *"But for Him no Divine Messenger would have been invested with the Robe of Prophethood, nor would any of the sacred Scriptures have been revealed."*

Shoghi Effendi, *God Passes By*, pp. 98–99.

"All the Prophets of God," asserts Bahá'u'lláh in the Kitáb-i-Iqán, *"abide in the same tabernacle, soar in the same heaven, are seated upon the same throne, utter the same speech, and proclaim the same Faith."* From the *"beginning that hath no beginning,"* these Exponents of the Unity of God and Channels of His incessant utterance have shed the light of the invisible Beauty upon mankind, and will continue, to the *"end that hath no end,"* to vouchsafe fresh revelations of His might and additional experiences of His inconceivable glory. To contend that any particular religion is final, that *"all Revelation is ended, that the portals*

of Divine mercy are closed, that from the daysprings of eternal holiness no sun shall rise again, that the ocean of everlasting bounty is forever stilled, and that out of the Tabernacle of ancient glory the Messengers of God have ceased to be made manifest" would indeed be nothing less than sheer blasphemy.

Shoghi Effendi, *The World Order of Bahá'u'lláh*, p. 58.

"Be fair, ye peoples of the world;" He thus appeals to mankind, *"is it meet and seemly for you to question the authority of one Whose presence 'He Who conversed with God"* (Moses) *hath longed to attain, the beauty of Whose countenance 'God's Well-beloved'* (Muḥammad) *had yearned to behold, through the potency of Whose love the 'Spirit of God'* (Jesus) *ascended to heaven, for Whose sake the 'Primal Point'* (the Báb) *offered up His life?"* *"Seize your chance,"* He admonishes His followers, *"inasmuch as a fleeting moment in this Day excelleth centuries of a bygone age . . . Neither sun nor moon hath witnessed a day such as this . . . It is evident that every age in which a Manifestation of God hath lived is divinely ordained and may, in a sense, be characterized as God's appointed Day. This Day however, is unique and is to be distinguished from those that have preceded it. The designation 'Seal of the Prophets' fully reveals and demonstrates its high station."*

Shoghi Effendi, *The World Order of Bahá'u'lláh*, pp. 106–7.

It should also be borne in mind that, great as is the power manifested by this Revelation and however vast the range of the Dispensation its Author has inaugurated, it emphatically repudiates the claim to be regarded as the final revelation of God's will and purpose for mankind. To hold such a conception of its character and functions would be tantamount to a betrayal of its cause and a denial of its truth. It must necessarily conflict with the fundamental principle which constitutes the bedrock of Bahá'í belief, the principle that religious truth is not absolute but relative, that Divine Revelation is orderly, continuous and progressive and not spasmodic or final. Indeed, the categorical rejection by the followers of the Faith of Bahá'u'lláh of the claim to finality which any religious system inaugurated by the Prophets of the past may advance is as clear and emphatic as their own refusal to claim that same finality for the Revelation with which they stand identified.

Shoghi Effendi, *The World Order of Bahá'u'lláh*, p. 115.

Nor does the Bahá'í Revelation, claiming as it does to be the culmination of a prophetic cycle and the fulfillment of the promise of all ages, attempt, under any circumstances, to invalidate those first and everlasting principles that animate and underlie the religions that have preceded it. The God-given authority, vested in each one of them, it admits and establishes as its firmest and ultimate basis. It regards them in no other light except as different stages in the eternal history and constant evolution of one religion, Divine and indivisible, of which it itself forms but an integral part.

Shoghi Effendi, *The World Order of Bahá'u'lláh*, p. 114.

— PART 4 —

MISCELLANEOUS TOPICS

25

Resurrection and Judgment Day

All of the prophetic religions speak of a day of resurrection and judgment. Although the scriptures speak extensively about this topic, it continues to be one of the most misunderstood topics in every religion, even though many clues have been given. For example, Jesus says, "I am the resurrection and the life."* One of the meanings of this verse is that those who recognized Him as the Son or Manifestation of God, believed in the new Revelation from God, and followed His teachings, have been resurrected from death to life; in other words, they have become spiritually alive. Otherwise, Jesus would not have said, "Let the dead bury their dead."† The meaning of this, of course, is that those who are spiritually dead should be left to bury their physically dead. Similarly, the Qur'án reads, "Make answer to the appeal of God and his apostle when he calleth you to that which giveth you life."‡ It is the acceptance or recognition of the new Manifestation of God that resurrects a person from spiritual death to spiritual life.

---

* John 11:25.
† Luke 9:60.
‡ Sura 8:24.

As for the meaning of judgment, Jesus says, "And this is the judgment, that the light has come into the world, and men loved darkness rather than light, because their deeds were evil."* Here again, Jesus describes His coming to the world as "the light," while those who recognized the "light" have been saved, and those who "loved darkness rather than light" have brought themselves to judgment and were deprived of everlasting life.

Similarly, the Qur'án refers to the coming of the Prophet Muḥammad as the day of resurrection and says, "for this is the day of the Resurrection—but ye knew it not."† In other words, the majority of people did not recognize the "light" or the new Manifestation from God. In an Islamic tradition, the Prophet Muḥammad said, "When the Qá'im [the Promised One] riseth, that day is the Day of Resurrection."‡ It is the coming of a new Manifestation of God and His Revelation that brings about spiritual revival to the souls of men and rescues them from the upheaval of such a time.

The Day of Resurrection is not a physical phenomenon; it is a spiritual occurrence, and nothing noticeable will happen to the material world. The Báb says, *"The Day of Resurrection is a day on which the sun riseth and setteth like unto any other day."* § He also says, *". . . the Day of Resurrection is said to be the greatest of all days, yet it is like unto any other day."** The Qur'án also compares the Day of Resurrection to the coming of spring, a new life cycle that resurrects the previous spring. It says, "It is God who sendeth forth winds which raise the clouds aloft: then drive we them on to some land dead from drought, and give life thereby to the earth after its death. So shall be the resurrection."††

---

* John 3:19.
† Sura 30:56.
‡ Hadíth, quoted in The Book of Certitude, ¶152.
§ The Báb, *Selections from the Writings of the Báb*, 3:3:1.
** The Báb, *Selections from the Writings of the Báb*, 3:3:2.
†† Sura 35:10.

Yet many Christians and Muslims understand the Day of Resurrection and Judgment to be "the end of times" rather than the beginning of a new spiritual life cycle. We can ask ourselves, was it "the end of times" when Christ said, "I am the resurrection . . ." or when Muḥammad said, "this is the day of Resurrection—but ye knew it not"? The Qur'án says, "no change canst thou find in God's mode of dealing."* So if it was not the end of times when Christ or Muḥammad came, why would it be the end of times this time, and why would people expect grand apocalyptic scenes in which bodies rise up from their graves to a physical judgment day, and angels fly down from the sky, and people are sent to a physical heaven or a physical hell? It is the rational soul of man that is rewarded or punished and not the body, as Christ says, "the flesh profiteth nothing."†

For Bahá'ís, every Age in which a divine Manifestation of God proclaims His Cause is a Day of "Resurrection" by which people are "judged." Those who recognize and accept the new Manifestation of God and live by His teachings have been "resurrected" from death to life. Those who did not recognize the Manifestation of God have been judged and deprived themselves from acquiring the spirit of faith or experiencing spiritual rebirth.

---

* Sura 48:23.
† John 6:63.

Some of the verses from the Holy Bible concerning "Resurrection" and "Judgment Day":

John 11:25–26 – Jesus said to her, "I am the resurrection and the life; he who believes in me, though he die, yet shall he live, and whoever lives and believes in me shall never die. Do you believe this?"

John 9:39–41 – Jesus said, "For judgment I came into this world, that those who do not see may see, and that those who see may become blind." Some of the Pharisees near him heard this, and they said to him, 'Are we also blind?' Jesus said to them, "If you were blind, you would have no guilt; but now that you say, 'We see,' your guilt remains."

John 3:18–19 – He who believes in him is not condemned; he who does not believe is condemned already, because he has not believed in the name of the only Son of God. And this is the judgment, that the light has come into the world, and men loved darkness rather than light, because their deeds were evil.

John 5:22–27 – For the Father judgeth no man, but hath committed all judgment unto the Son: That all men should honour the Son, even as they honour the Father. He that honoureth not the Son honoureth not the Father which hath sent him. Verily, verily, I say unto you, He that heareth my word, and believeth on him that sent me, hath everlasting life, and shall not come into condemnation; but is passed from death unto life. Verily, verily, I say unto you, The hour is coming, and now is, when the dead shall hear the voice of the Son of God: and they that hear shall live. For as the Father hath life in himself; so hath he given to the Son to have life in himself; And hath given him authority to execute judgment also, because he is the Son of man.

John 12:30–31 – Jesus answered, "This voice has come for your sake, not for mine. Now is the judgment of this world, now shall the ruler of this world be cast out. . . ."

Isaiah 65:17 – For, behold, I create new heavens and a new earth: and the former shall not be remembered, nor come into mind.

Some of the verses from the Holy Qur'án and Hadíth concerning "Resurrection" and "Judgment Day":

Sura 35:10 – Al-Fátir – It is God who sendeth forth winds which raise the clouds aloft: then drive we them on to some land dead from drought, and give life thereby to the earth after its death. So shall be the resurrection.

Sura 17:14 – Al-Isrá' – . . . and on the day of resurrection will we bring forth to him a book which shall be proffered to him wide open.

Sura 50:40–41 – Qáf – And listen for the day where on the crier shall cry from a place near to every one alike:

The day on which men shall in truth hear that shout will be the day of their coming forth from the grave.

Sura 8:24 – Al-Anfál – O ye faithful! – Make answer to the appeal of God and his apostle when he calleth you to that which giveth you life.

Sura 83:4–20 – Al-Mutaffifín – What! Have they no thought that they shall be raised again
For the great day?
The day when mankind shall stand before the Lord of the worlds.
Yes! The register of the wicked is in Sidjin.
And who shall make thee understand what Sidjin is?
It is a book distinctly written.
Woe, on that day, to those who treated our signs as lies,
Who treated the day of judgment as a lie!

None treat it as a lie, save the transgressor, the criminal,
Who, when our signs are rehearsed to him, saith, 'Tales of the Ancients!'
Yes; but their own works have got the mastery over their hearts.
Yes; they shall be shut out as by a veil from their Lord on that day;
Then shall they be burned in Hell-fire:
Then shall it be said to them, 'This is what ye deemed a lie.'
Even so. But the register of the righteous is in Illiyoun.
And who shall make thee understand what Illiyoun is?
A book distinctly written;

Sura 29:25 – Al-'Ankabút – But on the day of resurrection some of you shall deny the others, and some of you shall curse the others; and your abode shall be the fire, and ye shall have none to help.

Sura 7:32–33 – Al-A'ráf – Every nation hath its set time. And when their time is come, they shall not retard it an hour; and they shall not advance it.

O Children of Adam! There shall come to you Apostles from among yourselves, rehearsing my signs to you; and whoso shall fear God and do good works, no fear shall be upon them, neither shall they be put to grief.

Sura 32:4 – Al-Sajdah – From the Heaven to the Earth He governeth all things: hereafter shall they come up to him on a day whose length shall be a thousand of such years as ye reckon.

Sura 22:46 – Al-Haj – And they will bid thee to hasten the chastisement. But God cannot fail His threat. And verily, a day with thy Lord is as a thousand years, as ye reckon them!

Sura 22:1–2 – Al-Haj – O Men of Mecca, fear your Lord. Verily, the earth-quake of the last Hour will be a tremendous thing!

On the day when ye shall behold it, every suckling woman shall forsake her sucking babe; and every woman that hath a burden in her womb shall cast her burden; and thou shalt see men drunken, yet are they not drunken: but it is the mighty chastisement of God!

Sura 19:40 – Maryam – Warn them of the day of sighing when the decree shall be accomplished, while they are sunk in heedlessness and while they believe not.

Sura 79:6–8 – Al-Názi'át – One day, the disturbing trumpet-blast shall dis-turb it,

Which the second blast shall follow:

Men's hearts on that day shall quake.

Sura 27:89–90 – Al-Namlah – On that day there shall be a blast on the trumpet, and all that are in the heavens, and all that are on the earth shall be terror-stricken, save him whom God pleaseth to deliver; and all shall come to him in humble guise.

And thou shalt see the mountains, which thou thinkest so firm, pass away with the passing of a cloud! 'Tis the work of God, who ordereth all things! of all that ye do is He well aware.

Sura 69:13–16 – Al-Háqqah – But when one blast shall be blown on the trumpet,

And the earth and the mountains shall be upheaved, and shall both be crushed into dust at a single crushing,

On that day the woe that must come suddenly shall suddenly come,

And the heaven shall cleave asunder, for on that day it shall be fragile;

Sura 7:50–51— Al-A'ráf – And now have we brought them the Book: with knowledge have we explained it; a guidance and a mercy to them that believe.

What have they to wait for now but its interpretation? When its interpretation shall come, they who aforetime were oblivious of it shall say, 'The Prophets of our Lord did indeed bring the truth; shall we have any intercessor to intercede for us? Or could we not be sent back? Then would we act otherwise than we have acted.' But they have ruined themselves; and the deities of their own devising have fled from them!

Sura 14:1 – Ibráhím – This Book have we sent down to thee that by their Lord's permission thou mayest bring men out of darkness into light, into the path of the Mighty, the Glorious.

Sura 30:54–56 – Al-Rúm – And on the day whereon the Hour shall arrive, the wicked will swear,

That not above an hour have they waited: Even so did they utter lies on earth:

But they to whom knowledge and faith have been given will say, "Ye have waited, in accordance with the book of God, till the day of Resurrection: for this is the day of the Resurrection—but ye knew it not."

Sura 30:29 – Al-Rúm – Set thou thy face then, as a true convert, towards the Faith which God hath made, and for which He hath made man. No change is there in the creation of God. This is the right Faith, but the greater part of men know it not.

Sura 14:49 – Ibráhím – On the day when the Earth shall be changed into another Earth, and the Heavens also, men shall come forth unto God, the Only, the Victorious.

Sura 39:67 – Al-Zumar – . . . for on the resurrection day the whole Earth shall be but his handful, and in his right hand shall the Heavens be folded together. Praise be to Him! and high be He uplifted above the partners they join with Him!

And there shall be a blast on the trumpet, and all who are in the Heavens and all who are in the Earth shall expire, save those whom God shall vouchsafe to live. Then shall there be another blast on it, and lo! Arising they shall gaze around them:

And the earth shall shine with the light of her lord . . .

Sura 13:2 – Al-Ra'd – He maketh his signs clear, that ye may have firm faith in a meeting with your Lord.

Hadíth, quoted in The Book of Certitude, ¶152 – "When the Qá'im riseth, that day is the Day of Resurrection."

Some of the passages from the Bahá'í sacred texts concerning "Resurrection" and "Judgment Day":

. . . by "Resurrection" is meant the rise of the Manifestation of God to proclaim His Cause, and by "attainment unto the divine Presence" is meant attainment unto the presence of His Beauty in the person of His Manifestation.

Bahá'u'lláh, The Book of Certitude,
¶182.

Have they not heard the well-known tradition: "When the Qá'im riseth, that day is the Day of Resurrection?" In like manner, the Imams, those unquenchable lights of divine guidance, have interpreted the verse: "What can such expect but that God should come down to them overshadowed with clouds," [Qur'án 2:210]—a sign which they have unquestionably regarded as one of the features of the Day of Resurrection—as referring to Qá'im and His manifestation.

Bahá'u'lláh, The Book of Certitude,
¶152.

Therefore, whosoever, and in whatever Dispensation, hath recognized and attained unto the presence of these glorious, these resplendent and most excellent Luminaries, hath verily attained unto the "Presence of God" Himself, and entered the city of eternal and immortal life. Attainment unto such presence is possible only in the Day of Resurrection, which is the Day of the rise of God Himself through His all-embracing Revelation.

This is the meaning of the "Day of Resurrection," spoken of in all of the scriptures, and announced unto all people.

Bahá'u'lláh, The Book of Certitude, ¶151–52.

Strive, therefore, O my brother, to grasp the meaning of "Resurrection," and cleanse thine ears from the idle sayings of these rejected people. Shouldst thou step into the realm of complete detachment, thou wilt readily testify that no day is mightier than this Day, and that no resurrection more awful than this Resurrection can ever be conceived.

Bahá'u'lláh, The Book of Certitude, ¶153.

Verily We have sounded the Trumpet which is none other than My Pen of Glory, and lo, mankind hath swooned away before it, save them whom God pleaseth to deliver as a token of His grace. He is the Lord of bounty, the Ancient of Days.

Bahá'u'lláh, *Tablets of Bahá'u'lláh*, p. 61.

"The Hour" hath come upon them, while they are disporting themselves. They have been seized by their forelock, and yet know it not.

The thing that must come hath come suddenly; behold how they flee from it! The inevitable hath come to pass; witness how they have cast it behind their backs! This is the Day whereon every man will fly from himself, how much more from his kindred, could ye but perceive it. Say: By God! The blast hath been blown on the trumpet, and lo, mankind hath swooned away before us! The Herald hath cried out, and the Summoner raised His voice saying: "The Kingdom is God's, the Most Powerful, the Help in Peril, the Self-Subsisting."

Bahá'u'lláh, *Gleanings from the Writings of Bahá'u'lláh*, no. 18.1–2.

That the term "sun" hath been applied to the leaders of religion is due to their lofty position, their fame, and renown. Such are the universally recognized divines of every age, who speak with authority, and whose fame is securely established. If they be in the likeness of the Sun of Truth, they will surely be accounted as the most exalted of all luminaries; otherwise, they are to be recognized as the focal centers of hellish fire. Even as He saith: "Verily, the sun and the moon are both condemned to the torment of infernal fire."[Qur'án 55:5] You are no doubt familiar with the interpretation of the term "sun" and "moon" mentioned in this verse; no need therefore to refer unto it. And whosoever is of the element of this "sun" and "moon," that is, followeth the example of these leaders in setting his face towards falsehood and in turning away from the truth he undoubtedly cometh out of infernal gloom and returneth thereunto.

Bahá'u'lláh, The Book of Certitude, ¶36.

The Day of Resurrection is a Day on which the sun riseth and setteth like unto any other day. How oft hath the Day of Resurrection dawned, and the people of the land where it occurred did not learn of the event. Had they heard, they would not have believed, and thus they were not told!

The Báb, *Selections from the Writings of the Báb*, 3:3:1.

It is for this reason that the Day of Resurrection is said to be the greatest of all days, yet it is like unto any other day.

The Báb, *Selections from the Writings of the Báb*, 3:3:2.

. . . what is meant by the Day of Resurrection is this, that from the time of the appearance of Him Who is the Tree of divine Reality, at whatever period and under whatever name, until the moment of His disappearance, is the Day of Resurrection.

For example, from the inception of the mission of Jesus—may peace be upon Him—till the day of His ascension was the Resurrection of Moses. For during that period the Revelation of God shone forth through the appearance of that divine Reality, Who rewarded by His Word everyone who believed in

Moses, and punished by His Word everyone who did not believe; inasmuch as God's Testimony for that Day was that which He had solemnly affirmed in the Gospel.

The Báb, *Selections from the Writings of the Báb*, 3:35:1–2.

When the Apostle of God (Muḥammad) appeared, He did not announce unto the unbelievers that the Resurrection had come, for they could not bear the news. That Day is indeed an infinitely mighty Day, for in it the Divine Tree proclaimeth from eternity unto eternity, "Verily, I am God. No God is there but Me." Yet those who are veiled believe that He is one like unto them. . . .

The Báb, *Selections from the Writings of the Báb*, 3:3:2.

And from the inception of the Revelation of the Apostle of God—may the blessings of God be upon Him—till the day of His ascension was the Resurrection of Jesus . . . And from the moment when the Tree of the Bayán appeared until it disappeareth is the Resurrection of the Apostle of God, as is divinely foretold in the Qur'án; the beginning of which was when two hours and eleven minutes had passed on the eve of the fifth of Jamád'íyu'l-Avval, 1260 A.H. [22 May 1844], which is the year 1270 of the Declaration of the Mission of Muḥammad. This was the beginning of the Day of Resurrection of the Qur'án, and until the disappearance of the Tree of divine Reality is the Resurrection of the Qur'án.

The Báb, *Selections from the Writings of the Báb*, 3:35:2.

26

Opposition to the Manifestations of God

Opposition to the Manifestations of God can be found in the history of all religions. There has never been a time when the majority of people accepted a new Revelation from any Messenger or Manifestation of God with open arms. All the Manifestations of God suffered from the ignorance, arrogance, corruption, and opposition from the majority of the people They were teaching. The Bible says, "I send unto you prophets, and wise men, and scribes: and some of them ye shall kill and crucify; and some of them shall ye scourge in your synagogues, and persecute them from city to city."* Similarly, the Qur'án states, "Oh! The misery that rests upon my servants! No apostle cometh to them but they laugh him to scorn."†

In every age, the nature of the opposition to God's Manifestations has always been the same, and mankind has always had the free will to accept or reject the new Revelation from God. Without exception, it was the religious leaders—as well as the rulers, the wealthy, and some leaders of thought—

---

* Matthew 23:34.
† Sura 36:29.

who led the people away from the Manifestations of God. Jesus described the religious leaders of His time, the Pharisees, as "serpents," a "generation of vipers," and "hypocrites." The Pharisees rejected Jesus Christ because, according to their understanding, Christ did not meet the conditions or signs foretold in their scriptures. For example, they expected that the Messiah would come from an unknown place and that Elijah would come before Him; that Christ would have a Kingdom, sit on the throne of David and rule the world with a rod of iron; that He would promulgate the Law of Moses and establish justice and righteousness to such an extent that it would extend to the animals, with even the wolf and the lamb feeding together. Literally, none of these things took place, and the Pharisees and their followers failed to apprehend the intrinsic truth behind the signs they were expecting.

In the same way, Muḥammad, the Prophet of God, suffered so greatly from the opposition and cruelty of the people that He had to flee to Medina for His safety. All that the people saw in Him was His being a man like them, and only the most obscure of people followed Him. He revealed a verse in the Qur'án that reads, "Then said the chiefs of his people who believed not, 'We see in thee but a man like ourselves; and we see not who have followed thee except our meanest ones of hasty judgment, nor see we any excellence in you above ourselves: nay, we deem you liars.'"* The people were so sure of themselves that they said, "God! if this be the very truth from before thee, rain down stones upon us from Heaven, or lay on us some grievous chastisement."†

Just as in the past, many people opposed and persecuted the Manifestations of God, in recent history many people opposed and persecuted the Báb and

---

* Sura 11:29.
† Sura 8:32.

Bahá'u'lláh. The majority of religious leaders led the way and were responsible for the execution of the Báb and the imprisonment of Bahá'u'lláh for forty years under the most deplorable conditions. A glimpse of Bahá'u'lláh's suffering can be felt from the following account: "The Síyáh-<u>Ch</u>ál, into which Bahá'u'lláh was thrown, originally a reservoir of water for one of the public baths of Ṭihrán, was a subterranean dungeon in which criminals of the worst type were wont to be confined. The darkness, the filth, and the character of the prisoners, combined to make of that pestilential dungeon the most abominable place to which human beings could be condemned. His feet were placed in stocks, and around His neck were fastened the Qará-Guhar chains, infamous throughout Persia for their galling weight. For three days and three nights, no manner of food or drink was given to Bahá'u'lláh. Rest and sleep were both impossible to Him. The place was infested with vermin, and the stench of that gloomy abode was enough to crush the very spirits of those who were condemned to suffer its horrors."* Bahá'u'lláh, addressing the people of the Qur'án, affirms, *"O people of the Qur'án, Verily, the Prophet of God, Muḥammad, sheddeth tears at the sight of your cruelty. Ye have assuredly followed your evil and corrupt desires, and turned away your face from the light of guidance. Erelong will ye witness the result of your deeds; for the Lord, My God, lieth in wait and is watchful of your behavior. . . . O concourse of Muslim divines! By your deeds the exalted station of the people hath been abased, the standard of Islám hath been reversed, and its mighty throne hath fallen."†*

Another reason for opposition to the Manifestations of God, beside the lack of understanding of the scriptures, is the willful misleading of the people by their religious leaders, whether due to arrogance or the fear of losing their

---

* Nabíl-i-Aʻẓam, *The Dawn-breakers*, p. 608.
† Bahá'u'lláh, quoted in Shoghi Effendi, *The World Order of Bahá'u'lláh*, p. 179

influence or positions. Addressing the religious leaders of His time, Jesus says, "But woe to you, scribes and Pharisees, hypocrites! for ye shut up the kingdom of heaven against men; for ye neither go in yourselves, neither suffer ye them that are entering to go in."* Similarly, the Qur'án states: "Say: O people of the Book! Why repel believers from the way of God?"† Also it says, "O people of the Book! Why disbelieve the signs of God, of which yourselves have been witnesses? O people of the Book! Why clothe ye the truth with falsehood? Why wittingly hide the truth?"‡ The Qur'án even describes what the people would say to God because of their waywardness: "Oh our Lord! Indeed we obeyed our chiefs and our great ones, and they misled us from the way of God."§

However, notwithstanding the opposition and persecutions the Manifestations of God encounter in this world, no power has ever frustrated God's will or purpose. In fact, the spread and propagation of any religion has always been the result of these very attacks and opposition against the new Revelation from God.

Concerning the opposition to this promised Day of God—the Revelation proclaimed by the Báb in 1844 and inaugurated by Bahá'u'lláh in 1863—'Abdu'l-Bahá says: "Indeed, the attacks and the obstructiveness of the ignorant but cause the Word of God to be exalted, and spread His signs and tokens far and wide. Were it not for this opposition by the disdainful, this obduracy of the slanderers, this shouting from the pulpits, this crying and wailing of great and small alike, these accusations of unbelief leveled by the ignorant, this uproar from the foolish—how could news of the advent

---

* Matthew 23:13.
† Sura 3:94.
‡ Sura 3:63–64.
§ Sura 33:67.

of the Primal Point and the bright dawning of the Daystar of Bahá ever
have reached to east and west?"* 'Abdu'l-Bahá further states, "Wherefore we
should never grieve over the blindness of the unwitting, the attacks of the
foolish, the hostility of the low and base, the heedlessness of the divines, the
charges of infidelity brought against us by the empty of mind. Such too was
their way in ages past, nor would it be thus if they were of those who know;
but they are benighted, and they come not close to understanding what is
told them.†

The events now taking place are nothing other than what is written in the
Qur'án when it says, "The Day that we roll up the heavens like a scroll rolled
up for books (completed)—even as We produced the first Creation, so shall
We produce a new one: a promise We have undertaken: truly shall We fulfill
it."‡ Similarly Bahá'u'lláh says, *"Soon will the present-day order be rolled up,
and a new one spread out in its stead. Verily, thy Lord speaketh the truth, and is
the Knower of things unseen."*§

Bahá'u'lláh, describing what the Mahdi or the Promised One will do in this
promised Day of God, affirms an Islamic Hadíth saying: "'Abu-'Abdi'lláh,
questioned concerning the character of the Mihdí, answered saying: 'He will
perform that which Muhammad, the Messenger of God, hath performed,
and will demolish whatever hath been before Him even as the Messenger of
God hath demolished the ways of those that preceded Him.'"**

Opposition to the Manifestations of God never frustrated the Divine Will
but was always used as a means to propagate it. In this glorious Day of God,

---

* 'Abdu'l-Bahá, *Selections from the Writings of 'Abdu'l-Bahá*, no. 195.2.
† 'Abdu'l-Bahá, *Selections from the Writings of 'Abdu'l-Bahá*, no. 195.3.
‡ Sura 21:104.
§ Bahá'u'lláh, *Gleanings from the Writings of Bahá'u'lláh*, no. 4.2.
** Bahá'u'lláh, The Book of Certitude, ¶269.

Bahá'u'lláh reassures mankind by saying, *"Grieve thou not at men's failure to apprehend the Truth. Ere long thou shalt find them turning towards God, the Lord of all mankind. We have indeed, through the potency of the Most Sublime Word, encompassed the whole world, and the time is approaching when God will have subdued the hearts of all that dwell on earth. He is in truth the Omnipotent, the All-Powerful."**

* Bahá'u'lláh, *Tablets of Bahá'u'lláh*, pp. 263–64.

Some biblical verses concerning the opposition to the Manifestations of God:

Matthew 23:37 – O Jerusalem, Jerusalem, killing the prophets and stoning those who are sent to you! How often would I have gathered your children together as a hen gathers her brood under her wings, and you would not!

Matthew 23:13 – But woe to you, scribes and Pharisees, hypocrites! for ye shut up the kingdom of heaven against men; for ye neither go in yourselves, neither suffer ye them that are entering to go in.

Matthew 23:27–34 – Woe unto you, scribes and Pharisees, hypocrites! because ye build the tombs of the prophets, and garnish the sepulchres of the righteous, And say, If we had been in the days of our fathers, we would not have been partakers with them in the blood of the prophets.

Wherefore ye be witnesses unto yourselves, that ye are the children of them which killed the prophets.

Fill ye up then the measure of your fathers.

Ye serpents, ye generation of vipers, how can ye escape the damnation of hell? Wherefore, behold, I send unto you prophets, and wise men, and scribes: and some of them ye shall kill and crucify; and some of them shall ye scourge in your synagogues, and persecute them from city to city.

Mark 7:6–8 – Well did Isaiah prophesy of you hypocrites, as it is written, 'This people honors me with their lips, but their heart is far from me; in vain do they worship me, teaching as doctrines the precepts of men.' You leave the commandment of God, and hold fast the tradition of men.

Some Islamic verses concerning the opposition to the Messengers or Manifestations of God:

Sura 36:29 – Yá Sín – Oh! The misery that rests upon my servants! No apostle cometh to them but they laugh him to scorn.

Sura 38:67–68 – Sád – SAY: this is a weighty message, From which ye turn aside!

Sura 2:81 – Al-Baqarah – So oft then as an apostle cometh to you with that which your souls desire not, swell ye with pride, and treat some as impostors, and slay others?

Sura 23:46 – Al-Mu'minún – Then sent We our apostles one after another. Oft as their apostle presented himself to a nation, they treated him as a liar; and we caused one nation to follow another; and we made them the burden of a tale. Away then with the people who believe not!

Sura 33:67 – Al-Ahzáb – And they shall say: "Oh our Lord! Indeed we obeyed our chiefs and our great ones, and they misled us from the way of God."

Sura 6:116 – Al-An'ám – But if thou obey most men in this land, from the path of God will they mislead thee: they follow but a conceit, and they are only liars.

Sura 43:21–24 – Al-Zukhruf – But say they: "Verily we found our fathers of that persuasion, and verily, by their footsteps do we guide ourselves."

And thus never before thy time did we send a warner to any city but its wealthy ones said: "Verily we found our fathers with a religion, and in their tracks we tread."

SAY,—such was our command to that apostle—"What! Even if I bring you a religion more right than that ye found your fathers following?" And they said, "Verily we believe not in your message."

Sura 11:29 – Húd – Then said the chiefs of his people who believed not, "We see in thee but a man like ourselves; and we see not who have followed thee except our meanest ones of hasty judgment, nor see we any excellence in you above ourselves: nay, we deem you liars."

Sura 6:35 – Al-An'ám – But if their estrangement be grievous to thee, and if thou art able to seek out an opening into the earth or a ladder into Heaven, that thou mightest bring them a sign. . . . But if God pleased, He would surely bring them, one and all, to the guidance!

Sura 17:16–18 – Al-Isrá' – For his own good shall the guided yield to guidance, and to his own loss only shall the erring err; and the heavy laden shall not be laden with another's load. We never punished until we had first sent an apostle.

And when we willed to destroy a city, to its affluent ones did we address our bidding; but when they acted criminally therein, just was its doom, and we destroyed it with an utter destruction.

And since Noah, how many nations have we exterminated! And of the sins of his servants thy Lord is sufficiently informed, observant.

Sura 6:133–34 – Al-An'ám – And thy Lord is the Rich one, full of compassion! He can destroy you if He please, and cause whom He will to succeed you, as he raised you up from the offspring of other people:

Verily, that which is threatened you shall surely come to pass, neither shall ye weaken its might.

Sura 37:35–37 – Al-Saffát – Because when it was said to them, There is no God but God, they swelled with pride,

And said, 'Shall we then abandon our gods for a crazed poet?'

Nay, he cometh with truth and confirmeth the Sent Ones of old.

Sura 40:31–35 – Ghafir – Then said he who believed, 'O my people! Truly I fear for you the like of the day of the allies,

The like of the state of the people of Noah and Ad and Themoud,

And of those who came after them; yet God willeth not injustice to his servants.

And, O my people! I indeed fear for you the day of mutual outcry –

The day when ye shall be turned back from the Judgment into hell. No protector shall ye have then against God. And he whom God shall mislead no guide shall there be for him.

'Aválim, quoted in The Book of Certitude, ¶270 – A Youth from Baní-Háshim shall be made manifest, Who will reveal a new Book and promulgate a new law. . . . Most of His enemies will be the divines.

Sura 3:62–64 – Ál-'Imrán – A party among the people of the Book would fain mislead you: but they only mislead themselves, and perceive it not.

O people of the Book! Why disbelieve the signs of God, of which yourselves have been witnesses?

O people of the Book! Why clothe ye the truth with falsehood? Why wittingly hide the truth?

Sura 3:94–95 – Ál-'Imrán – Say: O people of the Book! Why repel believers from the way of God? Ye fain would make it crooked, and yet ye are its witnesses! But God is not regardless of what ye do.

O believers! If ye obey some amongst those who have received the Scripture, after your very Faith will they make you infidels!

Sura 7:34 – Al-A'ráf – But they who charge our signs with falsehood, and turn away from them in their pride, shall be inmates of the fire: for ever shall they abide therein.

Sura 8:32–33 – Al-Anfál – And oft as our signs were rehearsed to them, they said, "Now have we heard: if we pleased we could certainly utter its like! Yes, it is mere tales of the ancients."

And when they said, "God! If this be the very truth from before thee, rain down stones upon us from Heaven, or lay on us some grievous chastisements."

Sura 16:38 – Al-Nahl – And to every people have we sent an apostle saying: Worship God and turn away from Taghout. Some of them there were whom God guided, and there were others decreed to err. But go through the land and see what hath been the end of those who treated my apostles as liars!

Sura 20:122–123 – Tá' Há' – And whoso followeth my guidance shall not err, and shall not be wretched: But whoso turneth away from my monition, his truly shall be a life of misery.

Sura 11:11 – Húd – And if we defer their chastisement to some definite time, they will exclaim, 'What keepeth it back?' What! Will it not come upon them on a day when there shall be none to avert it from them? And that at which they scoffed shall enclose them in on every side.

Sura 14:44–46 – Ibráhím – Warn men therefore of the day when the punishment shall overtake them,

And when the evil doers shall say, "O our Lord! respite us yet a little while: To thy call will we make answer; thine Apostles will we follow."

Sura 44:9–13 – Al-Dukhán – But mark them on the day when the Heaven shall give out a palpable SMOKE,

Which shall enshroud mankind: this will be an afflictive torment.

They will cry, "Our Lord! Relieve us from this torment: see! We are believers."

But how did warning avail them, when an undoubted apostle had come to them; And they turned their backs on him.

Some passages from the Bahá'í sacred texts concerning the opposition to the Manifestations from God:

Open the doors of your hearts. He Who is the Spirit verily standeth before them. Wherefore keep ye Him Who hath purposed to draw you nigh unto a Resplendent Spot? Say: We, in truth, have opened unto you the gates of the Kingdom. Will ye bar the doors of your houses in My face? This indeed is naught but a grievous error. He, verily, hath again come down from heaven, even as He came down from it the first time. Beware lest ye dispute that which He proclaimeth, even as the people before you disputed His utterances. Thus instructeth you the True One, could ye but perceive it.

Bahá'u'lláh, Tablets of Bahá'u'lláh, p. 11.

. . . in every age and Dispensation, whenever the invisible Essence was revealed in the person of His Manifestation, certain souls, obscure and detached from all worldly entanglements, would seek illumination from the Sun of Prophethood and Moon of Divine guidance, and would attain unto the Divine Presence. For this reason, the divines of the age and those possessed of wealth, would scorn and scoff at these people.

Bahá'u'lláh, Gleanings from the Writings of Bahá'u'lláh, no. 91.1.

Judge thou fairly, I adjure thee by God. What proof did the Jewish doctors adduce wherewith to condemn Him Who was the Spirit of God (Jesus Christ), when He came unto them with truth? What could have been the evidence produced by the Pharisees and the idolatrous priests to justify their denial of Muḥammad, the Apostle of God when He came unto them with a Book that judged between truth and falsehood with a justice which turned into light the darkness of the earth, and enraptured the hearts of such as had known Him? Indeed thou hast produced, in this day, the same proofs which the foolish divines advanced in that age. Unto this testifieth He Who is the King of the realm of grace in this great Prison. Thou hast, truly, walked in their ways, nay, hast surpassed them in their cruelty, and hast deemed thyself to be helping the Faith and defending the Law of God, the All-Knowing, the All-Wise. By Him Who is the Truth! Thine iniquity hath made Gabriel to groan, and hath drawn tears from the Law of God, through which the breezes of justice have been wafted over all who are in heaven and on earth. Hast thou fondly imagined that the judgment thou didst pronounce hath profited thee? Unto thy loss testifieth He with Whom is the knowledge of all things as recorded in the preserved Tablet.

Bahá'u'lláh, Epistle to the Son of the Wolf, pp. 81–82.

Behold how the people, as a result of the verdict pronounced by the divines of His age, have cast Abraham, the Friend of God, into fire; how Moses, He Who held converse with the Almighty, was denounced as liar and slanderer. Reflect how Jesus, the Spirit of God, was, notwithstanding His extreme meekness and perfect tender-heartedness, treated by His enemies. So fierce was the opposition which He, the Essence of Being and Lord of the visible and invisible, had to face, that He had nowhere to lay His head. He wandered continually from place to place, deprived of a permanent abode. Ponder that which befell Muḥammad, the Seal of the Prophets, may the life of all else be a sacrifice unto Him. How severe the afflictions which the leaders of the Jewish people and of the idol-worshipers caused to rain upon Him, Who is the sovereign Lord of all, in consequence of His proclamation of the unity of God and of the truth of His Message! By the righteousness of My Cause! My Pen groaneth, and all created things weep with a great weeping, as a result of the woes He suffered at the hands of them that have broken the Covenant of God, violated His Testament, rejected His proofs, and disputed His signs. Thus recount We unto thee the tale of that which happened in days past, haply thou mayest comprehend.

Bahá'u'lláh, *Gleanings from the Writings of Bahá'u'lláh*, no. 23.2.

O Ye that are Foolish, yet have a Name to be Wise! Wherefore do ye wear the guise of shepherds, when inwardly ye have become wolves, intent upon My flock? Ye are even as the star, which riseth ere the dawn, and which, though it seem radiant and luminous, leadeth the wayfarers of My city astray into the paths of perdition.

Bahá'u'lláh, *The Hidden Words*, Persian no. 24.

Among them is the tradition, "And when the Standard of Truth is made manifest, the people of both the East and the West curse it."

Bahá'u'lláh, The Book of Certitude, ¶267.

. . . in all sacred books mention hath been made of the divines of every age. Thus He saith: "O people of the Book! Why disbelieve the signs of God to which ye yourselves have been witnesses?" [Qur'án 3:70] And also He saith: "O people of the Book! Why clothe ye the truth with falsehood? Why wittingly hide the truth?" [Qur'án 3:71] Again, He saith: "Say, O people of the Book! Why repel believers from the way of God?" [Qur'án 3:99] It is evident that by the "people of the Book," who have repelled their fellowmen from the straight path of God, is meant none other than the divines of that age, whose names and character have been revealed in the sacred books, and alluded to in the verses and traditions recorded therein, were you to observe with the eye of God.

Bahá'u'lláh, The Book of Certitude, ¶15.

The people of the Qur'án have risen up against Us without any clear proof or evidence, tormenting Us at every moment with a fresh torment. They idly imagine that tribulations can frustrate Our Purpose. Vain indeed is that which they have imagined. Verily, thy Lord is the One Who ordaineth whatsoever He pleaseth.

Bahá'u'lláh, Tablets of Bahá'u'lláh, p. 15.

Leaders of religion, in every age, have hindered their people from attaining the shores of eternal salvation, inasmuch as they held the reins of authority in their mighty grasp. Some for the lust of leadership, others through want of knowledge and understanding, have been the cause of the deprivation of the people. By their sanction and authority, every Prophet of God hath drunk from the chalice of sacrifice, and winged His flight unto the heights of glory. What unspeakable cruelties they that have occupied the seats of authority and learning have inflicted upon the true Monarchs of the world, those Gems of divine virtue! Content with a transitory dominion, they have deprived themselves of an everlasting sovereignty.

Bahá'u'lláh, The Book of Certitude, ¶15.

Let it be known, however, that none of these doctors and divines to whom we have referred was invested with the rank and dignity of leadership. For well-known and influential leaders of religion, who occupy the seats of authority and exercise the functions of leadership, can in no wise bear allegiance to the Revealer of truth, except whomsoever thy Lord willeth. But for a few, such things have never come to pass. "And few of My servants are the thankful"[Qur'án 34:13]. Even as in this Dispensation, not one amongst the renowned divines, in the grasp of whose authority were held the reins of the people, hath embraced the Faith. Nay, they have striven against it with such animosity and determination that no ear hath heard and no eye hath seen the like.

Bahá'u'lláh, The Book of Certitude, ¶255.

For what reason do they refuse to embrace the Truth, and allow certain traditions, the significance of which they have failed to grasp, to withhold them from the recognition of the Revelation of God and His Beauty, and to cause them to dwell in the infernal abyss? Such things are to be attributed to naught but the faithlessness of the divines and doctors of the age. Of these, Ṣádiq, son of Muḥammad, hath said: "The religious doctors of that age shall be the most wicked of the divines beneath the shadow of heaven. Out of them hath mischief proceeded, and unto them it shall return."

Bahá'u'lláh, The Book of Certitude, ¶275.

Consider those who rejected the Spirit [Jesus] when He came unto them with manifest dominion. How numerous the Pharisees who had secluded themselves in synagogues in His name, lamenting over their separation from Him, and yet when the portals of reunion were flung open and the divine Luminary shone resplendent from the Dayspring of Beauty, they disbelieved in God, the Exalted, the Mighty. They failed to attain His presence, notwithstanding that His advent had been promised them in the Book of Isaiah as well as in the Books of the Prophets and the Messengers. No one from among them turned his face towards the Dayspring of divine bounty except such as were destitute of any power amongst men. And yet, today, every man endowed with power and invested with sovereignty prideth himself on His Name. Moreover, call thou to mind the one who sentenced Jesus to death. He was the most learned of His age in His own country, whilst he who was only a fisherman believed in Him. Take good heed and be of them that observe the warning.

Bahá'u'lláh, *Tablets of Bahá'u'lláh*, pp. 9–10.

Consider the Dispensation of Jesus Christ. Behold, how all the learned men of that generation, though eagerly anticipating the coming of the Promised One, have nevertheless denied Him. Both Annas, the most learned among the divines of His day, and Caiaphas, the high priest, denounced Him and pronounced the sentence of His death.

Bahá'u'lláh, *Gleanings from the Writings of Bahá'u'lláh*, no. 35.3.

In like manner, when Muḥammad, the Prophet of God—may all men be a sacrifice unto Him—appeared, the learned men of Mecca and Medina arose, in the early days of His Revelation, against Him and rejected His Message, while they who were destitute of all learning recognized and embraced His Faith. Ponder a while. Consider how Balál, the Ethiopian, unlettered though he was, ascended into the heaven of faith and certitude, whilst 'Abdu'lláh Ubayy, a leader among the learned, maliciously strove to oppose Him. Behold, how a mere shepherd was so carried away by the ecstasy of the words of God that he was able to gain admittance into the habitation of his Best-Beloved, and was united to Him Who is the Lord of Mankind, whilst they who prided themselves on their knowledge and wisdom strayed far from His path and remained deprived of His grace. For this reason He hath written: "He that is exalted among you shall be abased, and he that is abased shall be exalted." References to this theme are to be found in most of the heavenly Books, as well as in the sayings of the Prophets and Messengers of God.

Bahá'u'lláh, *Gleanings from the Writings of Bahá'u'lláh*, no. 35.4.

Consider the past. How many, both high and low, have, at all times, yearningly awaited the advent of the Manifestations of God in the sanctified persons of His chosen Ones. How often have they expected His coming, how frequently have they prayed that the breeze of divine mercy might blow, and the promised Beauty step forth from behind the veil of concealment, and be made manifest to all the world. And whensoever the portals of grace did open, and the clouds of divine bounty did rain upon mankind, and the light of the Unseen did shine above the horizon of celestial might, they all denied Him, and turned away from His face—the face of God Himself. Refer ye, to verify this truth, to that which hath been recorded in every sacred Book.

Bahá'u'lláh, The Book of Certitude, ¶3.

These leaders, owing to their immersion in selfish desires, and their pursuit of transitory and sordid things, have regarded these divine Luminaries as being opposed to the standards of their knowledge and understanding, and the opponents of their ways and judgments. As they have literally interpreted the Word of God, and the sayings and traditions of the Letters of Unity, and expounded them according to their own deficient understanding, they have therefore deprived themselves and all their people of the bountiful showers of the grace and mercies of God.

Bahá'u'lláh, The Book of Certitude, ¶89.

. . . the sovereignty of Muḥammad, the Messenger of God, is today apparent and manifest amongst the people. You are well aware of what befell His Faith in the early days of His dispensation. What woeful sufferings did the hand of the infidel and erring, the divines of that age and their associates, inflict upon that spiritual Essence, that most pure and holy Being! How abundant the thorns and briars which they have strewn over His path! It is evident that wretched generation, in their wicked and satanic fancy, regarded every injury to that immortal Being as a means to the attainment of an abiding felicity; inasmuch as the recognized divines of that age, such as 'Abdu'lláh-i-Ubayy, 'Abú-'Ámir, the hermit, Ka'b-Ibn-i-Aṣhraf, and Naḍr-Ibn-i-Ḥáriṯh, all treated Him as an impostor, and pronounced Him a lunatic and a calumniator. Such sore accusations they brought against Him that in recounting them

God forbiddeth the ink to flow, Our pen to move, or the page to bear them. These malicious imputations provoked the people to arise and torment Him. And how fierce that torment if the divines of the age be its chief instigators, if they denounce Him to their followers, cast Him out from their midst, and declare Him a miscreant! Hath not the same befallen this Servant, and been witnessed by all?

Bahá'u'lláh, The Book of Certitude, ¶114.

Notwithstanding the divinely inspired admonitions of all the Prophets, the Saints, and Chosen ones of God, enjoining the people to see with their own eyes and hear with their own ears, they have disdainfully rejected their counsels and have blindly followed, and will continue to follow, the leaders of their Faith. Should a poor and obscure person, destitute of the attire of men of learning, address them saying: "Follow ye, O people! the Messengers of God" [Qur'án 36:20], they would, greatly surprised at such a statement, reply: "What! Meanest thou that all these divines, all these exponents of learning, with all their authority, their pomp and pageantry, have erred, and failed to distinguish truth from falsehood? Dost thou, and people like thyself, pretend to have comprehended that which they have not understood?" If numbers and excellence of apparel be regarded as the criterions of learning and truth, the peoples of a bygone age, whom those of today have never surpassed in numbers, magnificence and power, should certainly be accounted a superior and worthier people.

Bahá'u'lláh, The Book of Certitude, ¶176.

Not one Prophet of God was made manifest Who did not fall victim to the relentless hate, to the denunciation, denial, and execration of the clerics of His day!

Bahá'u'lláh, The Book of Certitude, ¶177.

"O heedless one! Rely not on thy glory, and thy power. Thou art even as the last trace of sunlight upon the mountain-top. Soon will it fade away as decreed by God, the All-Possessing, the Most High. . . . O foolish doubter! Because of you the Apostle (Muḥammad) lamented, and the Chaste One (Fáṭimih) cried out, and the countries were laid waste, and darkness fell upon all regions. O concourse of divines! Because of you the people were abased, and the banner of Islám was hauled down, and its mighty throne subverted. Every time a man of discernment hath sought to hold fast unto that which would exalt Islám, you raised a clamor, and thereby was he deterred from achieving his purposes, while the land remained fallen in clear ruin."

Bahá'u'lláh, Epistle to the Son of the Wolf, pp. 99–100.

"O heedless ones! Though the wonders of My mercy have encompassed all created things, both visible and invisible, and though the revelations of My grace and bounty have permeated every atom of the universe, yet the rod with which I can chastise the wicked is grievous, and the fierceness of Mine anger against them terrible. . . . The day is approaching when the wrathful anger of the Almighty will have taken hold of them. He, verily, is the Omnipotent, the All-Subduing, the Most Powerful. He shall cleanse the earth from the defilement of their corruption, and shall give it for an heritage unto such of His servants as are nigh unto Him."

Bahá'u'lláh, quoted in Shoghi Effendi, *The Advent of Divine Justice*, p. 81.

Thou seest, O my God, how the wrongs committed by such of Thy creatures as have turned their backs to Thee have come in between Him in Whom Thy Godhead is manifest and Thy servants. Send down upon them, O my Lord, what will cause them to be busied with each others' concerns. Let, then, their violence be confined to their own selves, that the land and they that dwell therein may find peace.

Bahá'u'lláh, *Prayers and Meditations*, p. 196.

Grieve thou not at men's failure to apprehend the Truth. Ere long thou shalt find them turning towards God, the Lord of all mankind. We have indeed, through the potency of the Most Sublime Word, encompassed the whole world, and the time is approaching when God will have subdued the hearts of all that dwell on earth. He is in truth the Omnipotent, the All-Powerful.

Bahá'u'lláh, *Tablets of Bahá'u'lláh*, pp. 263–64.

Consider those who opposed the Son, when He came unto them with sovereignty and power. How many the Pharisees who were waiting to behold Him, and were lamenting over their separation from Him! And yet, when the fragrance of His coming was wafted over them, and His beauty was unveiled, they turned aside from Him and disputed with Him.

Bahá'u'lláh, "Súriy-i-Haykal," *The Summons of the Lord of Hosts*, ¶108.

They are even as the Pharisees who both prayed and fasted, and then did sentence Jesus Christ to death.

'Abdu'l-Bahá, *Selections from the Writings of 'Abdu'l-Bahá*, no. 146.7.

How else could the Tree of Anísá have been planted here, the flag of the Testament be flown, the intoxicating cup of the Covenant be lifted to these lips? All these blessings and bestowals, the very means of proclaiming the Faith, have come about through the scorn of the ignorant, the opposition of the foolish, the stubbornness of the dull-witted, the violence of the aggressor. Had it not been for these things, the news of the Báb's advent would not, to this day, have reached even into lands hard by. Wherefore we should never grieve over the blindness of the unwitting, the attacks of the foolish, the hostility of the low and base, the heedlessness of the divines, the charges of infidelity brought against us by the empty of mind.

'Abdu'l-Bahá, *Selections from the Writings of 'Abdu'l-Bahá*, no. 195.3.

When Christ appeared, twenty centuries ago, although the Jews were eagerly awaiting His Coming, and prayed every day, with tears, saying: "O God, hasten the Revelation of the Messiah," yet when the Sun of Truth dawned, they denied Him and rose against Him with the greatest enmity, and eventually crucified that divine Spirit, the Word of God, and named Him Beelzebub, the evil one, as is recorded in the Gospel. The reason for this was that they said: "The Revelation of Christ, according to the clear text of the Torah, will be attested by certain signs, and so long as these signs have not appeared, whoso layeth claim to be a Messiah is an impostor. Among these signs is this, that the Messiah should come from an unknown place, yet we all know this man's house in Nazareth, and can any good thing come out of Nazareth? The second sign is that He shall rule with a rod of iron, that is, He must act with the sword, but this Messiah has not even a wooden staff. Another of the conditions and signs is this: He must sit upon the throne of David and establish David's sovereignty. Now, far from being enthroned, this man has not even a mat to sit on. Another of the conditions is this: the promulgation of all the laws of the Torah; yet this man has abrogated these laws, and has even broken the sabbath day, although it is the clear text of the Torah that whosoever layeth claim to prophethood and revealeth miracles and breaketh the sabbath day, must be put to death. Another of the signs is this, that in His reign justice will be so advanced that righteousness and well-doing will extend from the human even to the animal world—the snake and the mouse will share one hole, and the eagle and the partridge one nest, the lion and the gazelle shall dwell in one pasture, and the wolf and the kid shall drink from one fountain. Yet now, injustice and tyranny have waxed so great in His time that they have crucified Him! Another of the conditions is this, that in the days of the Messiah the Jews will prosper and triumph over all the peoples of the world, but now they are living in the utmost abasement and servitude in the empire of the Romans. Then how can this be the Messiah promised in the Torah?"

'Abdu'l-Bahá, *Selections from the Writings of 'Abdu'l-Bahá*, no. 20.1.

Blessed are the just souls who seek the truth. But failing justice, the people attack, dispute and openly deny the evidence, like the Pharisees who, at the manifestation of Christ, denied with the greatest obstinacy the explanations of Christ and of His disciples. They obscured Christ's Cause before the ignorant people, saying, "These prophecies are not of Jesus, but of the Promised One Who shall come later, according to the conditions mentioned in the Bible." Some of these conditions were that He must have a kingdom, be seated on the throne of David, enforce the Law of the Bible, and manifest such justice that the wolf and lamb shall gather at the same spring.

And thus they prevented the people from knowing Christ.

'Abdu'l-Bahá, *Some Answered Questions*, pp. 71–72.

How great, how very great is the Cause! How very fierce the onslaught of all the peoples and kindreds of the earth. Ere long shall the clamor of the multitude throughout Africa, throughout America, the cry of the European and of the Turk, the groaning of India and China, be heard from far and near. One and all, they shall arise with all their power to resist His Cause. Then shall the knights of the Lord, assisted by His grace from on high, strengthened by faith, aided by the power of understanding, and reinforced by the legions of the Covenant, arise and make manifest the truth of the verse: "Behold the confusion that hath befallen the tribes of the defeated!"

'Abdu'l-Bahá, quoted in Shoghi Effendi, *The World Order of Bahá'u'lláh*, p. 17.

27

The Select Few

Despite the intense opposition to the Manifestations of God, there are always a select few who, by the bounty and grace of God, are aided to recognize the new Manifestation of God. These believers, who are in most cases the lowliest among His servants, always manage to withstand the trials, difficulties, and ordeals that assail them as a result of their acceptance of the new Manifestation of God. Those who attain this station, abide by His teachings, and remain firm and steadfast in His path, are enabled to acquire the Spirit of Faith, which is the true difference between spiritual life and death.

Bahá'u'lláh describes the station of these select few by saying, *"The soul that hath remained faithful to the Cause of God, and stood unwaveringly firm in His Path shall, after his ascension, be possessed of such power that all the worlds which the Almighty hath created can benefit through him."**

In the history of every religion, the "select few" who were chosen by the bounty of God, were mostly from the "meek" and "lowly." This demonstrates the power of the Manifestations of God who promulgates His Word by using the meek and lowly, despite the opposition of the influential majority. Christ

---

* Bahá'u'lláh, *Gleanings from the Writings of Bahá'u'lláh*, no. 82.7.

says, "Blessed are the meek: for they shall inherit the earth."* Similarly, the Qur'án reads, "And We desire to show favour to those who were brought low in the land, and to make them spiritual leaders among men, and to make of them Our heirs."†

---

* Matthew 5:5.
† Sura 28:5.

Some biblical verses concerning the "select few":

Matthew 22:14 – For many are called, but few are chosen.

Matthew 7:21 – Not every one who says to me, "Lord, Lord," shall enter the kingdom of heaven, but he who does the will of my Father who is in heaven.

Luke 6:22–23 – Blessed are ye when men shall hate you, and when they shall separate you from their company, and shall reproach you, and cast out your name as evil, for the Son of man's sake.

Rejoice ye in that day, and leap for joy: for, behold, your reward is great in heaven: for in the like manner did their fathers unto the prophets.

Matthew 5:3–16 – Blessed are the poor in spirit: for theirs is the kingdom of heaven.

Blessed are they that mourn: for they shall be comforted.

Blessed are the meek: for they shall inherit the earth.

Blessed are they which do hunger and thirst after righteousness: for they shall be filled.

Blessed are the merciful: for they shall obtain mercy.

Blessed are the pure in heart: for they shall see God.

Blessed are the peacemakers: for they shall be called the children of God.

Blessed are they which are persecuted for righteousness' sake: for theirs is the kingdom of heaven.

Blessed are ye, when men shall revile you, and persecute you, and shall say all manner of evil against you falsely, for my sake.

Rejoice, and be exceeding glad: for great is your reward in heaven: for so persecuted they the prophets which were before you.

Ye are the salt of the earth: but if the salt have lost his savour, wherewith shall it be salted? it is thenceforth good for nothing, but to be cast out, and to be trodden under foot of men.

Ye are the light of the world. A city that is set on an hill cannot be hid.

Neither do men light a candle, and put it under a bushel, but on a candlestick; and it giveth light unto all that are in the house.

Let your light so shine before men, that they may see your good works, and glorify your Father which is in heaven.

Some Qur'ánic verses concerning the "select few":

Sura 29:69 – Al-ʿAnkabút – And whoso maketh efforts for us, in our ways will we guide them: for God is assuredly with those who do righteous deeds.

Sura 89:27–30 – Al-Fajr – Oh, thou soul which art at rest, Return to thy Lord, Pleased, and pleasing him: Enter thou among my servants, And enter thou my Paradise.

Sura 7:33 – Al-Aʿráf – O children of Adam! There shall come to you Apostles from among yourselves, rehearsing my signs to you; and whoso shall fear God and do good works, no fear shall be upon them, neither shall they be put to grief.

Sura 53:32 – Al-Najm – And whatever is in the Heavens and in the Earth is God's, that he may reward those who do evil according to their deeds: and those who do good will He reward with good things.

Sura 2:105–6 – Al-Baqarah – And they say, "None but Jews or Christians shall enter Paradise:" This is their wish. SAY: Give your proofs if ye speak the truth.

But they who set their face with resignation Godward, and do what is right,—their reward is with their Lord; no fear shall come on them, neither shall they be grieved.

Sura 11:116–17 – Húd – And observe prayer at early morning, at the close of the day, and at the approach of night; for the good deeds drive away the evil deeds. This is a warning for those who reflect:

And persevere steadfastly, for verily God will not suffer the reward of the righteous to perish.

Sura 16:128 – Al-Nahl – Endure then with patience. But thy patient endurance must be sought in none but God. And be not grieved about the infidels, and be not troubled at their devises; for God is with those who fear him and do good deeds.

Sura 28:5 – Al-Qasas – 'And We desire to show favour to those who were brought low in the land, and to make them spiritual leaders among men, and to make of them Our heirs.'

Sura 4:71 – Al-Nisa' – And whoever shall obey God and the Apostle, these shall be with those of the Prophets, and of the Sincere, and of the Martyrs, and of the Just, to whom God hath been gracious. These are a goodly band!

Some passages from the Bahá'í sacred text concerning the "select few":

The Book of God is wide open, and His Word is summoning mankind unto Him. No more than a mere handful, however, hath been found willing to cleave to His Cause, or to become the instruments for its promotion. These few have been endued with the Divine Elixir that can, alone, transmute into purest gold the dross of the world, and have been empowered to administer the infallible remedy for all the ills that afflict the children of men. No man can obtain everlasting life, unless he embraceth the truth of this inestimable, this wondrous, and sublime Revelation.

Bahá'u'lláh, Gleanings from the Writings of Bahá'u'lláh, no. 92.1.

The station which he who hath truly recognized this Revelation will attain is the same as the one ordained for such prophets of the house of Israel as are not regarded as Manifestations "endowed with constancy."
Bahá'u'lláh, quoted in Shoghi Effendi, The World Order of Bahá'u'lláh, p. 111.

By the sorrows which afflict the beauty of the All-Glorious! Such is the station ordained for the true believer that if to an extent smaller than a needle's eye the glory of that station were to be unveiled to mankind, every beholder would be consumed away in his longing to attain it. For this reason it hath been decreed that in this earthly life the full measure of the glory of his own station should remain concealed from the eyes of such a believer.
Bahá'u'lláh, quoted in Shoghi Effendi, The World Order of Bahá'u'lláh, p. 108.

Know thou, of a truth, that if the soul of man hath walked in the ways of God, it will, assuredly, return and be gathered to the glory of the Beloved. By the righteousness of God! It shall attain a station such as no pen can depict, or tongue describe. The soul that hath remained faithful to the Cause of God, and stood unwaveringly firm in His Path shall, after his ascension, be possessed of such power that all the worlds which the Almighty hath created can benefit through him. Such a soul provideth, at the bidding of the Ideal King and Divine Educator, the pure leaven that leaveneth the world of being, and furnisheth the power through which the arts and wonders of the world are made manifest. Consider how meal needeth leaven to be leavened with. Those souls that are the symbols of detachment are the leaven of the world. Meditate on this, and be of the thankful.

Bahá'u'lláh, *Gleanings from the Writings of Bahá'u'lláh*, no. 82.7.

Whoso hath, in this Day, refused to allow the doubts and fancies of men to turn him away from Him Who is the Eternal Truth, and hath not suffered the tumult provoked by the ecclesiastical and secular authorities to deter him from recognizing His Message, such a man will be regarded by God, the Lord of all men, as one of His mighty signs, and will be numbered among them whose names have been inscribed by the Pen of the Most High in His Book.

Bahá'u'lláh, *Gleanings from the Writings of Bahá'u'lláh*, no. 82.2.

O peoples of the world! Forsake all evil, hold fast that which is good. Strive to be shining examples unto all mankind, and true reminders of the virtues of God amidst men. He that riseth to serve My Cause should manifest My wisdom, and bend every effort to banish ignorance from the earth. Be united in counsel, be one in thought. Let each morn be better than its eve and each morrow richer than its yesterday. Man's merit lieth in service and virtue and not in the pageantry of wealth and riches. Take heed that your words be purged from idle fancies and worldly desires and your deeds be cleansed from craftiness and suspicion. Dissipate not the wealth of your precious lives in the pursuit of evil and corrupt affection, nor let your endeavours be spent in promoting your personal interest. Be generous in your days of plenty, and be patient in the hour of loss. Adversity is followed by success and rejoicings follow woe. Guard against idleness and sloth, and cling unto that which profiteth mankind, whether young or old, whether high or low. Beware lest ye sow tares of dissension among men or plant thorns of doubt in pure and radiant hearts.

Bahá'u'lláh, *Tablets of Bahá'u'lláh*, p. 138.

O COMRADES!

The gates that open on the Placeless stand wide and the habitation of the loved one is adorned with the lovers' blood, yet all but a few remain bereft of this celestial city, and even of these few, none but the smallest handful hath been found with a pure heart and sanctified spirit.

Bahá'u'lláh, The Hidden Words, Persian no. 17.

O ye beloved of the Lord! Commit not that which defileth the limpid stream of love or destroyeth the sweet fragrance of friendship. By the righteousness of the Lord! Ye were created to show love one to another and not perversity and rancour. Take pride not in love for yourselves but in love for your fellow-creatures. Glory not in love for your country, but in love for all mankind. Let your eye be chaste, your hand faithful, your tongue truthful and your heart enlightened. Abase not the station of the learned in Bahá and belittle not the rank of such rulers as administer justice amidst you. Set your reliance on the army of justice, put on the armour of wisdom, let your adorning be forgiveness and mercy and that which cheereth the hearts of the well-favoured of God.

Bahá'u'lláh, *Tablets of Bahá'u'lláh*, pp. 138–39.

Say: Beware, O people of Bahá, lest ye walk in the ways of them whose words differ from their deeds. Strive that ye may be enabled to manifest to

337

the peoples of the earth the signs of God, and to mirror forth His commandments. Let your acts be a guide unto all mankind, for the professions of most men, be they high or low, differ from their conduct. It is through your deeds that ye can distinguish yourselves from others. Through them the brightness of your light can be shed upon the whole earth. Happy is the man that heedeth My counsel, and keepeth the precepts prescribed by Him Who is the All-Knowing, the All-Wise.

Bahá'u'lláh, *Gleanings from the Writings of Bahá'u'lláh*, no. 139.8.

Indeed shouldst Thou desire to confer blessing upon a servant Thou wouldst blot out from the realm of his heart every mention or disposition except Thine Own mention; and shouldst Thou ordain evil for a servant by reason of that which his hands have unjustly wrought before Thy face, Thou wouldst test him with the benefits of this world and of the next that he might become preoccupied therewith and forget Thy remembrance.

The Báb, in *Bahá'í Prayers*, p. 174.

It is from the bounty of God that man is selected for the highest degree; and the differences which exist between men in regard to spiritual progress and heavenly perfections are also due to the choice of the Compassionate One. For faith, which is life eternal, is the sign of bounty, and not the result of justice. The flame of the fire of love, in this world of earth and water, comes through the power of attraction and not by effort and striving. Nevertheless, by effort and perseverance, knowledge, science and other perfections can be acquired; but only the light of the Divine Beauty can transport and move the spirits through the force of attraction. Therefore, it is said: "Many are called, but few are chosen" [Matthew 22:14].

'Abdu'l-Bahá, *Some Answered Questions*, p. 130.

28

Two Messengers to Appear

The holy scriptures foretell the coming of two Manifestations of God who are to appear one after the other. Often, the prophecies indicate that one will prepare the way for the other. In the Bible, that Day is described as the "Day of the Lord," when God's Kingdom will be established and "His Will" shall be done on earth as it is in heaven. It is also depicted as a day of "woe" because it is a day of reckoning and a day of suffering for unbelievers. The Qur'án describes that Day as the "Day of God," the "Last Day," the "Day of Judgment," or the "Day of Reckoning,"* and it is depicted by a "trumpet blast" because it is the Day of the "Great Announcement."

The book of Revelation states that the first woe has passed, that two woes would be coming, and that after the coming of the "second woe," the "third woe" would come quickly.† Similarly, the Qur'án states that there would be two "trumpet blasts"—one following the other—and that after the second "trumpet blast," the "earth shall shine with the *light of her Lord.*"‡ The Qur'án

---

* Shoghi Effendi, *God Passes By*, p. 96.
† Revelation 9:12 and 11:14.
‡ Sura 39:68–69.

describes these two trumpet blasts, proclaiming the "Great Announcement," as being in reality a single blast. In other words, it would be as one Revelation: "Verily, it will be but a single blast."*

Bahá'u'lláh explains the reason for sounding the second trumpet blast by saying: Upon Our arrival in 'Iráq We found the Cause of God [followers of the Báb] sunk in deep apathy and the breeze of divine revelation stilled. Most of the believers were faint and dispirited, nay utterly lost and dead. Hence there was a second blast on the Trumpet, whereupon the Tongue of Grandeur uttered these blessed words: 'We have sounded the Trumpet for the second time.' Thus the whole world was quickened through the vitalizing breaths of divine revelation and inspiration."†

'Abdu'l-Bahá explains that the descriptions in the Old Testament of the Lord of Hosts and the Messiah referred to the two Manifestations of God who were to appear one after the other. Likewise, similar references in the Gospel regarding the return of Christ and the return of Elijah also relate to the appearance of these twin Manifestations. In Islam, references were made to two who would appear—the Mahdí and the Messiah.‡ Shoghi Effendi, referencing Siyyid Kázim-i-Rashtí,§ predicts that after the Qá'ím is slain, the Qayyúm would be made manifest.**

---

* Sura 79:13.

† Bahá'u'lláh, *Tablets of Bahá'u'lláh,* p. 131.

‡ 'Abdu'l-Bahá, *Some Answered Questions,* p. 39.

§ Siyyid Kázim-i-Rashtí was the disciple and successor of Shaykh Aḥmad-i-Aḥsá'í, founder of the Shaykhí school that prepared its followers for the coming of the promised Day of God.

** Shoghi Effendi, *God Passes By,* p. 97.

Some of the verses from the Holy Bible concerning the two Manifestations of God prophesied to appear:

Malachi 3:1 – Behold, I send my messenger to prepare the way before me, and the Lord whom you seek will suddenly come to his temple; the messenger of the covenant in whom you delight, behold, he is coming, says the Lord of hosts.

Malachi 4:5 – Behold, I will send you Elijah the prophet before the great and terrible day of the Lord comes.

Zechariah 4:11–14 – Then I said to him, "What are these two olive trees on the right and the left of the lamp stand?" And a second time I said to him, "What are these two branches of the olive trees, which are beside the two golden pipes from which the oil is poured out?" He said to me, "Do you not know what these are?" I said, "No, my lord." Then he said, "These are the two anointed who stand by the Lord of the whole earth."

Ezekiel 30:1–3 – The word of the Lord came to me 'Son of man, prophesy and say: These are the words of the Lord God; Woe, woe for the day! For a day is near, a day of the Lord is near, a day of cloud, a day of reckoning for the nations.

Revelation 9:12 – The first woe has passed; behold, two woes are still to come.

Revelation 11:14–15 – The second woe is past; and, behold, the third woe cometh quickly. And the seventh angel sounded; and there were great voices in heaven, saying, the kingdoms of this world are become the kingdoms of our Lord, and of his Christ; and he shall reign for ever and ever.

Some of the verses from the Holy Qur'án concerning the two Manifestations of God prophesied to appear:

Sura 79:6–8 & 13 – Al-Názi'át – One day, the disturbing trumpet-blast shall disturb it,
Which the second blast shall follow:
Men's hearts on that day shall quake:-
Verily, it will be but a single blast.

Sura 39:68–69 – Al-Zumar – And there shall be a blast on the trumpet, and all who are in the Heavens and all who are in the Earth shall expire, save those whom God shall vouchsafe to live. Then shall there be another blast on it, and lo! they shall gaze around them:

And the earth shall shine with the light of her Lord.

Sura 55:46–47 – Al-Rahmán – But for those who dread the majesty of their Lord shall be two gardens:

Which then of the bounties of your Lord will ye twain deny?

Some of the verses from the Bahá'í sacred texts concerning the two Manifestations of God:

By Him Who is the Great Announcement! The All-Merciful is come invested with undoubted sovereignty. The Balance hath been appointed, and all them that dwell on earth have been gathered together. The Trumpet hath been blown, and lo, all eyes have stared up with terror, and the hearts of all who are in the heavens and on the earth have trembled, except them whom the breath of the verses of God hath quickened, and who have detached themselves from all things.

Bahá'u'lláh, *Gleanings from the Writings of Bahá'u'lláh*, no. 17.1.

O Ḥusayn! Consider the eagerness with which certain peoples and nations have anticipated the return of Imám-Ḥusayn, whose coming, after the appearance of the Qá'im, hath been prophesied, in days past, by the chosen ones of God, exalted be His glory. These holy ones have, moreover, announced that when He Who is the Dayspring of the manifold grace of God manifesteth Himself, all the Prophets and Messengers, including the Qá'im, will gather together beneath the shadow of the sacred Standard which the Promised One will raise. That hour is now come. The world is illumined with the effulgent glory of His countenance.

Bahá'u'lláh, *Gleanings from the Writings of Bahá'u'lláh*, no. 9.1.

The Hour which We had concealed from the knowledge of the peoples of the earth and of the favoured angels hath come to pass. Say, verily, He hath testified of Me, and I do testify of Him. Indeed, He hath purposed no one other than Me. Unto this beareth witness every fair-minded and understanding soul.

Bahá'u'lláh, *Tablets of Bahá'u'lláh*, p. 11.

I swear by the righteousness of God! The Blast hath been blown on the Trumpet of the Bayán as decreed by the Lord, the Merciful, and all that are in the heavens and on the earth have swooned away except such as have detached themselves from the world, cleaving fast unto the Cord of God, the Lord of mankind. This is the Day in which the earth shineth with the effulgent light of thy Lord, but the people are lost in error and have been shut out as by a veil.

Bahá'u'lláh, *Tablets of Bahá'u'lláh*, p. 244.

The blast hath been blown on the trumpet, and lo, mankind hath swooned away before us! The Herald hath cried out, and the Summoner raised His voice saying: "The Kingdom is God's, the Most Powerful, the Help in Peril, the Self-Subsisting."

Bahá'u'lláh, *Gleanings from the Writings of Bahá'u'lláh*, no. 18.2.

All the peoples of the world are awaiting two Manifestations, Who must be contemporaneous; all wait for the fulfillment of this promise. In the Bible the Jews have the promise of the Lord of Hosts and the Messiah; in the Gospel the return of Christ and Elijah is promised.

In the religion of Muḥammad there is the promise of the Mihdí and the Messiah, and it is the same with the Zoroastrian and the other religions, but if we relate these matters in detail, it would take too long. The essential fact is that all are promised two Manifestations, Who will come, one following on the other.

'Abdu'l-Bahá, *Some Answered Questions*, p. 39.

"The second woe is past; and, behold, the third woe cometh quickly." The first woe is the appearance of the Prophet, Muḥammad, the son of 'Abdu'lláh— peace be upon Him! The second woe is that of the Báb—to Him be glory and praise! The third woe is the great day of the manifestation of the Lord of Hosts and the radiance of the Beauty of the Promised One. The explanation of this subject, woe, is mentioned in the thirtieth chapter of Ezekiel, where it is said: "The word of the Lord came again unto me, saying, Son of man, prophesy and say, Thus saith the Lord God; Howl ye, Woe worth the day! For the day is near, even the day of the Lord is near."

Therefore, it is certain that the day of woe is the day of the Lord; for in that day woe is for the neglectful, woe is for the sinners, woe is for the ignorant. That is why it is said, "The second woe is past; behold the third woe cometh quickly!" This third woe is the day of the manifestation of Bahá'u'lláh, the day of God; and it is near to the day of the appearance of the Báb.

'Abdu'l-Bahá, *Some Answered Questions*, p. 56.

. . . regarding the rise of the Sun of Truth in this century, He ['Abdu'l-Bahá] sets forth, briefly but conclusively, what should remain for all time our true conception of the relationship between the two Manifestations associated with the Bahá'í Dispensation. "*In making such a statement,*" He explains, "*I had in mind no one else except the Báb and Bahá'u'lláh, the character of Whose Revelations it had been my purpose to elucidate. The Revelation of the Báb may be likened to the sun, its station corresponding to the first sign of the Zodiac— the sign of Aries—which the sun enters at the Vernal Equinox. The station of Bahá'u'lláh's Revelation, on the other hand, is represented by the sign Leo, the sun's mid-summer and highest station. By this is meant that this holy Dispensation is illumined with the light of the Sun of Truth shining from its most exalted station, and in the plenitude of its resplendency, its heat and glory.*"

"*The Báb, the Exalted One,*" 'Abdu'l-Bahá more specifically affirms in another Tablet, "*is the Morn of Truth, the splendor of Whose light shineth throughout all regions. He is also the Harbinger of the Most Great Light, the Abhá Luminary. The Blessed Beauty is the One promised by the sacred books of the past, the*

345

Miscellaneous Topics

revelation of the Source of light that shone upon Mount Sinai, Whose fire glowed in the midst of the Burning Bush. We are, one and all, servants of their threshold, and stand each as a lowly keeper at their door." "*Every proof and prophecy,*" is His still more emphatic warning, "*every manner of evidence, whether based on reason or on the text of the scriptures and traditions, are to be regarded as centred in the persons of Bahá'u'lláh and the Báb. In them is to be found their complete fulfillment.*"

Shoghi Effendi, The World Order of Bahá'u'lláh, pp. 127–28.

Siyyid Káẓim-i-Rashtí, Shaykh Aḥmad's disciple and successor, had likewise written: "The Qá'im must needs be put to death. After He has been slain the world will have attained the age of eighteen." In his Sharḥ-i-Qaṣídiy-i-Lámíyyih he had even alluded to the name "Bahá." Furthermore, to his disciples, as his days drew to a close, he had significantly declared: "Verily, I say, after the Qá'im the Qayyúm will be made manifest. For when the star of the former has set the sun of the beauty of Ḥusayn will rise and illuminate the whole world."

Shoghi Effendi, God Passes By, p. 97.

St. John the Divine had himself, with reference to these two successive Revelations, clearly prophesied: "The second woe is past; and, behold the third woe cometh quickly." "*This third woe,*" 'Abdu'l-Bahá, commenting upon this verse, has explained, "*is the day of the Manifestation of Bahá'u'lláh, the Day of God, and it is near to the day of the appearance of the Báb.*" "*All the peoples of the world,*" He moreover has asserted, "*are awaiting two Manifestations, Who must be contemporaneous; all wait for the fulfillment of this promise.*" And again: "*The essential fact is that all are promised two Manifestations, Who will come one following on the other.*" Shaykh Aḥmad-i-Aḥsá'í, that luminous star of Divine guidance who had so clearly perceived, before the year sixty, the approaching glory of Bahá'u'lláh, and laid stress upon "the twin Revelations which are to follow each other in rapid succession," had, on his part, made this significant statement regarding the approaching hour of that supreme Revelation, in an epistle addressed in his own hand to Siyyid Kazim: "The mystery of this Cause must needs be made manifest, and the secret of this Message must needs be divulged. I can say no more. I can appoint no time. His Cause will be made known after Ḥín (68)."

Shoghi Effendi, *God Passes By*, pp. 92–93.

To Him Muḥammad, the Apostle of God, had alluded in His Book as the *"Great Announcement,"* and declared His Day to be the Day whereon *"God"* will *"come down" "overshadowed with clouds,"* the Day whereon *"thy Lord shall come and the angels rank on rank,"* and *"The Spirit shall arise and the angels shall be ranged in order."* . . . the Day whereon the second *"Trumpet blast"* will be sounded, the *"Day when mankind shall stand before the Lord of the world,"* and *"all shall come to Him in humble guise,"* the Day when *"thou shalt see the mountains, which thou thinkest so firm, pass away with the passing of a cloud."*

Shoghi Effendi, *God Passes By*, p. 96.

As a further testimony to the greatness of the Revelation identified with Bahá'u'lláh may be cited the following extracts from a Tablet addressed by 'Abdu'l-Bahá to an eminent Zoroastrian follower of the Faith: "*Thou hadst written that in the sacred books of the followers of Zoroaster it is written that in the latter days, in three separate Dispensations, the sun must needs be brought to a standstill. In the first Dispensation, it is predicted, the sun will remain motionless for ten days; in the second for twice that time; in the third for no less than one whole month. The interpretation of this prophecy is this: the first Dispensation to which it refers is the Muḥammadan Dispensation during which the Sun of Truth stood still for ten days. Each day is reckoned as one century. The Muḥammadan*

Dispensation must have, therefore, lasted no less than one thousand years, which is precisely the period that has elapsed from the setting of the Star of the Imamate to the advent of the Dispensation proclaimed by the Báb. The second Dispensation referred to in this prophecy is the one inaugurated by the Báb Himself, which began in the year 1260 A.H. and was brought to a close in the year 1280 A.H. As to the third Dispensation—the Revelation proclaimed by Bahá'u'lláh—inasmuch as the Sun of Truth when attaining that station shineth in the plenitude of its meridian splendor its duration hath been fixed for a period of one whole month, which is the maximum time taken by the sun to pass through a sign of the Zodiac. From this thou canst imagine the magnitude of the Bahá'í cycle—a cycle that must extend over a period of at least five hundred thousand years."

Shoghi Effendi, The World Order of Bahá'u'lláh, pp. 101–2.

In the works of the learned and far-famed Muḥyi'd-Dín-i-'Arabí, many references are to be found regarding both the year of the advent and the name of the promised Manifestation. Among them are the following: "The ministers and upholders of His Faith shall be of the people of Persia." "In His name, the name of the Guardian ['Alí] precedeth that of the Prophet [Muḥammad]." "The year of His Revelation is identical with half of that number which is divisible by nine [2520]." Mírzá Muḥammad-i-Akhbárí, in his poems relating to the year of the Manifestation, makes the following prediction: "In the year Ghars [the numerical value of the letters of which is 1260] the earth shall be illumined by His light, and in Gharasih [1265] the world shall be suffused with its glory. If thou livest until the year Gharasí [1270], thou shalt witness how the nations, the rulers, the peoples, and the Faith of God shall all have been renewed." In a tradition ascribed to the Imám 'Alí, the Commander of the Faithful, it is likewise recorded: "In Ghars the Tree of Divine guidance shall be planted."

Nabíl-i-A'ẓam, The Dawn-breakers, pp. 49–50.

29

Future Manifestations of God

Just as previous Messengers foretold the coming of the One who would appear after Them, so did Bahá'u'lláh foretell of Those who would come after Him, and He gave specific signs. However, He made it clear that no Manifestation of God will appear before the expiration of a full thousand years after His Revelation.

Bahá'u'lláh also admonished humanity not to deal with the One who would come after Him as they have dealt with Him and previous Manifestations of God. He also warned imposters who would claim a Revelation from God before the lapse of a thousand years and that God would deal with them mercilessly, as God is terrible in His punishment.

The Divine Revelations have continued and will always continue to the end that has no end, and mankind will always be subjected to tests, to measure its motives and the purity of hearts. Nothing, however, will frustrate God's plan or purpose.

Some of the passages from the Bahá'í sacred texts concerning future Manifestations of God:

"God hath sent down His Messengers to succeed to Moses and Jesus, and He will continue to do so till 'the end that hath no end'; so that His grace may, from the heaven of Divine bounty, be continually vouchsafed to mankind."

"I am not apprehensive for My own self," Bahá'u'lláh still more explicitly declares, *"My fears are for Him Who will be sent down unto you after Me—Him Who will be invested with great sovereignty and mighty dominion."* And again He writes in the Súratu'l-Haykal: *"By those words which I have revealed, Myself is not intended, but rather He Who will come after Me. To it is witness God, the All-Knowing." "Deal not with Him,"* He adds, *"as ye have dealt with Me."*

Bahá'u'lláh, quoted in Shoghi Effendi, *The World Order of Bahá'u'lláh*, pp. 116–17.

Whoso layeth claim to a Revelation direct from God, ere the expiration of a full thousand years, such a man is assuredly a lying imposter. We pray God that He may graciously assist him to retract and repudiate such claim. Should he repent, God will, no doubt, forgive him. If, however, he persisteth in his error, God will, assuredly, send down one who will deal mercilessly with him. Terrible, indeed, is God in punishing! Whosoever interpreteth this verse otherwise than its obvious meaning is deprived of the Spirit of God and of His mercy which encompasseth all created things. Fear God, and follow not your idle fancies. Nay, rather follow the bidding of your Lord, the Almighty, the All-Wise.

Bahá'u'lláh, *Gleanings from the Writings of Bahá'u'lláh*, no. 166.1.

Be ye assured, moreover, that the works and acts of each and every one of these Manifestations of God, nay whatever pertaineth unto them, and whatsoever they may manifest in the future, are all ordained by God, and are a reflection of His Will and Purpose.

Bahá'u'lláh, *Gleanings from the Writings of Bahá'u'lláh*, no. 24.

"It is clear and evident," He [the Báb] writes in the Persian Bayán, *"that the object of all preceding Dispensations hath been to pave the way for the advent of Muḥammad, the Apostle of God. These, including the Muḥammadan Dispensation, have had, in their turn, as their objective the Revelation proclaimed by the Qá'im. The purpose underlying this Revelation, as well as those that preceded it, has, in like manner, been to announce the advent of the Faith of Him Whom God will make manifest. And this Faith—the Faith of Him Whom God will make manifest—in its turn, together with all the Revelations gone before it, have as their object the Manifestation destined to succeed it. And the latter, no less than all the Revelations preceding it, prepare the way for the Revelation which is yet to follow. The process of the rise and setting of the Sun of Truth will thus indefinitely continue—a process that hath had no beginning and will have no end."*

The Báb, quoted in Shoghi Effendi, *The World Order of Bahá'u'lláh*, p. 117.

"Concerning the Manifestations that will come down in the future 'in the shadow of the clouds,' know verily that in so far as their relation to the source of their inspiration is concerned they are under the shadow of the Ancient Beauty. In their relation, however, to the age in which they appear, each and every one of them 'doeth whatsoever He willeth.'"

'Abdu'l-Bahá, quoted in Shoghi Effendi, *The World Order of Bahá'u'lláh*, p. 111.

The holy Manifestations Who have been the Sources or Founders of the various religious systems were united and agreed in purpose and teaching. Abraham, Moses, Zoroaster, Buddha, Jesus, Muḥammad, the Báb and Bahá'u'lláh are one in spirit and reality. Moreover, each Prophet fulfilled the promise of the One Who came before Him and, likewise, Each announced the One Who would follow.

'Abdu'l-Bahá, *The Promulgation of Universal Peace*, p. 276.

. . . great as is the power manifested by this Revelation and however vast the range of the Dispensation its Author has inaugurated, it emphatically repudiates the claim to be regarded as the final revelation of God's will and purpose for mankind. To hold such a conception of its character and functions would be tantamount to a betrayal of its cause and a denial of its truth. It must necessarily conflict with the fundamental principle which constitutes the bedrock of Bahá'í belief, the principle that religious truth is not absolute but relative, that Divine Revelation is orderly, continuous and progressive and not spasmodic or final. Indeed, the categorical rejection by the followers of the Faith of Bahá'u'lláh of the claim to finality which any religious system inaugurated by the Prophets of the past may advance is as clear and emphatic as their own refusal to claim that same finality for the Revelation with which they stand identified.

Shoghi Effendi, *The World Order of Bahá'u'lláh*, p. 115.

Bibliography

Selections from the Bible are from King James Version, published by Christian Heritage Publishing Co., SC 1986; the Revised Standard Version of the Old and New Testaments, published by The Delegates of the Oxford University Press and The Syndics of the Cambridge University Press, 1970; the Revised Standard Version, translated from the Original Tongues, published in New York by Thomas Nelson & Sons, 1946.

Selections from the Qur'án are from J. M. Rodwell's translation of the Qur'án, published by Phoenix, London, 1994, & N. J. Dawood's translation of the Qur'án, Penguin Books Ltd, Harmondsworth, Middlesex, England, 1985.

Selections from the Writings of Bahá'u'lláh

Epistle to the Son of the Wolf. Translated by Shoghi Effendi. 1ˢᵗ pocket-sized ed. Wilmette, IL: Bahá'í Publishing Trust, 1988.

Gleanings from the Writings of Bahá'u'lláh. Translated by Shoghi Effendi. New ed. Wilmette, IL: Bahá'í Publishing, 2005.

The Hidden Words of Bahá'u'lláh. Translated by Shoghi Effendi. New ed. Wilmette, IL: Bahá'í Publishing, 2005.

The Kitáb-i-Aqdas: The Most Holy Book. 1ˢᵗ pocket-sized ed. Wilmette, IL: Bahá'í Publishing Trust, 1993.

The Kitáb-i-Íqán: The Book of Certitude. Translated by Shoghi Effendi. Wilmette, IL: Bahá'í Publishing, 2003.

The Pen of Glory: Selected Works of Bahá'u'lláh. Wilmette, IL: Bahá'í Publishing, 2008.

Prayers and Meditations. Translated by Shoghi Effendi. 1ˢᵗ pocket-sized ed. Wilmette, IL: Bahá'í Publishing Trust, 1987.

Tablets of Bahá'u'lláh Revealed after the Kitáb-i-Aqdas. Wilmette, IL: Bahá'í Publishing Trust, 1988.

The Summons of the Lord of Hosts. Wilmette, IL: Bahá'í Publishing, 2006.

Selections from the Writings of the Báb

Selections from the Writings of the Báb. Compiled by the Research Department of the Universal House of Justice. Translated by Habib Taherzadeh et al. 1ˢᵗ pocket-sized ed. Wilmette, IL: Bahá'í Publishing Trust, 2006.

Selections from the Writings of 'Abdu'l-Bahá

'Abdu'l-Bahá in London: Addresses and Notes of Conversations. London: Bahá'í Publishing Trust, 1987.

Foundations of World Unity. Wilmette, IL: Bahá'í Publishing Trust, 1972.

Paris Talks: Addresses Given by 'Abdu'l-Bahá in Paris in 1911. Wilmette, IL: Bahá'í Publishing, 2006.

The Promulgation of Universal Peace: Talks Delivered by 'Abdu'l-Bahá during His Visit to the United States and Canada in 1912. Compiled by Howard MacNutt. Wilmette, IL: Bahá'í Publishing Trust, 2007.

The Secret of Divine Civilization. Translated by Marzieh Gail and Ali-Kuli Khan. 1st pocket-sized ed. Wilmette, IL: Bahá'í Publishing Trust, 1990.

Selections from the Writings of 'Abdu'l-Bahá. Compiled by the Research Department of the Universal House of Justice. Translated by a Committee at the Bahá'í World Center and by Marzieh Gail. Wilmette, IL: Bahá'í Publishing, 2010.

Some Answered Questions. Compiled and translated by Laura Clifford Barney. 1st pocket-sized ed. Wilmette, IL: Bahá'í Publishing Trust, 2004.

Selections from the Writings of Shoghi Effendi

The Advent of Divine Justice. New ed. Wilmette, IL: Bahá'í Publishing Trust, 2006.

God Passes By. Rev. ed. Wilmette, IL: Bahá'í Publishing Trust, 1974.

The Promised Day Is Come. Wilmette, IL: Bahá'í Publishing Trust, 1996.

The World Order of Bahá'u'lláh: Selected Letters. New ed. Wilmette, IL: Bahá'í Publishing Trust, 1991.

Compilations

Bahá'u'lláh, the Báb, and 'Abdu'l-Bahá. *Bahá'í Prayers: A Selection of Prayers Revealed by Bahá'u'lláh, the Báb, and 'Abdu'l-Bahá.* New ed. Wilmette, IL: Bahá'í Publishing Trust, 1991.

Hanna, Nabil, comp. *Bible Proofs: A Fireside Aid for Teaching Christians.* Los Angeles: Kalimát Press, 1988.

Hornby, Helen, comp. *Lights of Guidance: A Bahá'í Reference File.* 6th ed. New Delhi, India: Bahá'í Publishing Trust, 1999.

Paine, Mabel Hyde, comp. *The Divine Art of Living: Selections from the Writings of Bahá'u'lláh, the Báb, and 'Abdu'l-Bahá.* Revised edition. Wilmette, IL: Bahá'í Publishing, 2006.

Other Works

Aḥmad Ḥamdí Al-Muḥammad. *Al-Tibyán wal-Burhán.* Vol. I. Beirut, 1962.

Esslemont, J. E. *Bahá'u'lláh and the New Era: An Introduction to the Bahá'í Faith.* Wilmette, IL: Bahá'í Publishing, 2006.

Nabíl-i-A'ẓam (Muḥamman-i-Zarandí). *The Dawn-Breakers: Nabíl's Narrative of the Early Days of the Bahá'í Revelation.* Translated and edited by Shoghi Effendi. Wilmette, IL: Bahá'í Publishing Trust, 1999.

Nakhjavání, 'Alí. "Notes on Bahá'í Proofs Based on the Holy Qur'án." Unpublished notes. Approved by the National Spiritual Assembly of the Bahá'ís of Central and East Africa.

Rabbani, Rúḥíyyih. *Prescription for Living.* New Delhi: Bahá'í Publishing Trust, 1950.

Star of the West. Vol. II, V. Published from 1910 to 1933.

Taherzadeh, Adib. *The Covenant of Bahá'u'lláh.* Oxford: George Ronald, 1992.

———. *The Revelation of Bahá'u'lláh.* Vol. I. Oxford: George Ronald, 1974.

PUBLISHING

Bahá'í Publishing
and the Bahá'í Faith

Bahá'í Publishing produces books based on the teachings of the Bahá'í Faith. Founded over 160 years ago, the Bahá'í Faith has spread to some 235 nations and territories and is now accepted by more than five million people. The word "Bahá'í" means "follower of Bahá'u'lláh." Bahá'u'lláh, the founder of the Bahá'í Faith, asserted that He is the Messenger of God for all of humanity in this day. The cornerstone of His teachings is the establishment of the spiritual unity of humankind, which will be achieved by personal transformation and the application of clearly identified spiritual principles. Bahá'ís also believe that there is but one religion and that all the Messengers of God—among them Abraham, Zoroaster, Moses, Krishna, Buddha, Jesus, and Muḥammad—have progressively revealed its nature. Together, the world's great religions are expressions of a single, unfolding divine plan. Human beings, not God's Messengers, are the source of religious divisions, prejudices, and hatreds.

The Bahá'í Faith is not a sect or denomination of another religion, nor is it a cult or a social movement. Rather, it is a globally recognized independent world religion founded on new books of scripture revealed by Bahá'u'lláh.

Bahá'í Publishing is an imprint of the National Spiritual Assembly of the Bahá'ís of the United States.

For more information about the Bahá'í Faith,
or to contact Bahá'ís near you,
visit http://www.bahai.us/
or call
1-800-22-unite

Other Books Available from Bahá'í Publishing

AMERICA'S SACRED CALLING
Building A New Spiritual Reality
John Fitzgerald Medina
$14.00 U.S. / $16.00 CAN
Trade Paper
ISBN 978-1-931847-79-7

A call to action for America to embrace a new society that honors the spiritual reality of the human soul.

America's Sacred Calling describes a blueprint for creating a new society that uplifts and honors the spiritual reality of the human soul while fostering the conditions for humankind to transcend the existential fears, anxieties, and petty concerns of this temporal physical world. Author John Medina examines the Western-dominated worldview that pervades so much of the modern world as we know it, and perceives a rampant materialism that is detrimental to the psychological and spiritual development of humankind. At the same time, Medina explores the writings of the Bahá'í Faith and uncovers prophecies that foreshadow a glorious destiny for the United States and its peoples. Focusing on the activities of the American Bahá'í community and the mission given to its members, Medina finds a great source of hope for the future—a future in which the American nation "will lead all nations spiritually" and play a key role in the unification of the entire planet.

FOUNDERS OF FAITH

THE PARALLEL LIVES OF GOD'S MESSENGERS

Harold Rosen

$17.00 U.S. / $19.00 CAN

Trade Paper

ISBN 978-1-931847-78-0

An exploration of the lives of Moses, Zoroaster, Krishna, Buddha, Jesus Christ, Muḥammad, and Bahá'u'lláh that examines their backgrounds, missions, teachings, and legacies, and finds the patterns that link these Founders of the world's religions.

Founders of Faith explores the lives of the Founders of the world's major religions—including Judaism, Zoroastrianism, Hinduism, Buddhism, Christianity, Islam, and the Bahá'í Faith—and reveals that they are linked by sets of striking patterns. These patterns suggest that our world's religions share universal teachings and have a common divine source. Author Harold Rosen explains how the Founders of the major religions function as the teachers of humanity; how their station differs from that of seers, visionaries, and minor prophets; and how their teachings transformed not only the civilizations that embraced them, but also humanity as a whole. *Founders of Faith* provides an examination of the rise and fall of religious civilizations, an illustrative overview of six such civilizations, as well as the background and apparent shape of the emerging global civilization.

FOUNTAIN OF WISDOM

A Collection of the Writings from Bahá'u'lláh

Bahá'u'lláh

$14.00 U.S. / $16.00 CAN

Trade Paper

ISBN 978-1-931847-80-3

A timeless collection of writings penned by the Prophet-Founder of the Bahá'í Faith with a universal message that all humanity is one race, destined to live in peace and harmony.

Fountain of Wisdom is a collection of the writings of Bahá'u'lláh, the Prophet-Founder of the Bahá'í Faith, in which He explains some of the "precepts and principles that lie at the very core of His Faith." Revealed during the final years of His ministry, the sixteen tablets contained in this volume cover a wide range of topics and place emphasis on principles such as the oneness and wholeness of the human race, collective security, justice, trustworthiness, and moderation in all things.

SPIRIT OF FAITH

THE ONENESS OF GOD

Bahá'í Publishing

$12.00 U.S. / $14.00 CAN

Hardcover

ISBN 978-1-931847-76-6

The new Spirit of Faith *series presents a selection of uplifting prayers and writings that focus on the oneness and unity of God for spiritual seekers of all faiths.*

Spirit of Faith: The Oneness of God is a compilation of writings and prayers that offers hope for a better future—one filled with unity, understanding, and acceptance between all peoples and religions of the world. This collection of sacred scripture demonstrates that we are all part of a single, unfolding, divine creation. The *Spirit of Faith* series will explore important spiritual topics—such as the unity of humanity, the eternal covenant of God, the promise of world peace, and much more—by taking an in-depth look at how the writings of the Bahá'í Faiths view these issues. The series is designed to encourage readers of all faiths to think about spiritual issues, and to take time to pray and meditate on these important spiritual topics.

To view our complete catalog,
Please visit http://books.bahai.us